Co-Design and Social Innovation

Social innovation is an increasingly popular topic, perhaps even a buzz word. It is frequently associated with "design thinking", and particularly with co-design, which brings the beneficiaries of social innovation into the process of solving their own problems.

This book explores how design approaches in general, and thinking about co-design in particular, relate to the broader social innovation phe nomenon. Is "design" one of several ways to approach social innovation, or is it implicit in every social innovation process? Can social innovation be credible or effective if end-users are not fully engaged in the process? If end-users are to be fully engaged, what are the implications for the organization and delivery of social innovation? Can co-design deliver efficient solutions, on a scale that responds to the major challenges that social innovation seeks to address?

Drawing on and integrating several distinct theoretical streams, the book proposes a framework to address such questions. It challenges both practi-tioners and researchers to focus not only on social innovation as an exciting global phenomenon, but also on the micro-practices and local connections that actually produce change in people's lives.

Garth M. Britton is Adjunct Senior Research Fellow at the University of Queensland, Australia.

Routledge Studies in Social Enterprise and Social Innovation

Series Editors: Rocio Nogales, Lars Hulgård, and Jacques Defourny

A Social Enterprise seeks to achieve social, cultural, community, economic, or environmental outcomes; whilst remaining revenue generating business. A Social Innovation is said to be a new idea or initiative to a social problem that is more effective, efficient, sustainable, or just than the current process and which sees the Society it is operating in receive the primary value created rather than a private organization of firms.

Routledge Studies in Social Enterprise and Social Innovation looks to examine these increasingly important academic research themes as a central concept for social theories and policies. It looks to examine and explore the activities of social participation among civil society organizations, SMEs, governments, and research institutions, publishing the breakthrough books of the new frontiers of the field as well as the state of the nation defining books that help advance the field.

Co-Design and Social Innovation

Innovation

Connections, Tensions and
Opportunities

Garth M. Britton

Routledge
Taylor & Francis Group

LONDON AND NEW YORK

First published 2017 by Routledge

2 Park Square, Milton Park, Abingdon, OxfordshireX14 4RN

52 Vanderbilt Avenue, New York, NY 10017

Routledge is an imprint of the Taylor & Francis Group, an informa business

First issued in paperback 2019

Library of Congress Cataloging-in-Publication Data
A catalog record for this book has been requested

ISBN: 978-1-138-18846-4 (hbk)
ISBN: 978-0-367-24298-5 (pbk)

Typeset in Sabon
by Apex CoVantage, LLC

Contents

Preface

Social innovation is an increasingly popular topic, perhaps even a buzz word. Policy makers promote it; philanthropists seek to fund it in ever more effective ways; academics study it; not-for-profit organizations try to show they are able to deliver it, and that it has lasting effects. At the time of writing, a Google search on social innovation yields four million hits; Amazon.com lists 1,508 titles containing the term; a topic search on Web of Science for "social innovation" or various cognate terms[1] retrieves more than 2,200 results, seventy-three percent of them in the current or five prior years. Under the 44th Presidency, the White House established an Office of Social Innovation and Civic Participation (White House 2017), although the 45th Presidency has not announced any plans in this area at the time of writing. A sense of excitement pervades reports on what social innovation has achieved; the world's biggest problems are finally coming within reach of our ability to solve them. Novel ways of organizing, funding, and working are being generated constantly, and old distinctions between private, public and not-for-profit sectors are being rendered obsolete as distinctly modern forms of collaboration are developed and deployed.

The allure of social innovation seems to draw from two particularly heady sources. On the one hand, it deals with problems that are presented as either new to our times, such as climate change, or that were previously seen as being beyond our means or as requiring massive resources or authority to address, such as global hunger or poverty. Social innovation offers up another possibility; that, in fact, there are ways for individuals and organizations to act and bring about meaningful improvement on even the most complex problems we face. In addition to this message of empowerment, and in support of it, social innovation is presented as breaking down "old" ways of doing things, offering a platform for radical new techniques and a new breed of entrepreneur, who is no longer solely concerned with seeking material rewards. The social innovator is a new breed, a forerunner and instigator of a future that is both more human and more prosperous for all.

In this way, social innovation at times both departs from and reinforces modernist ideas about how society works. On the one hand, it seems to be preoccupied with identifying and propagating the techniques that allow social innovation to occur, in a celebration of human mastery; on the other, it seems to break down existing categorizations of the institutions of society and accepted views of how they should act to address problems. Old-fashioned notions of planning and organization are challenged by new concepts. Networks are seen as preferable to hierarchies; experimentation is encouraged, so failure is to be tolerated. Speed and agility are more important than efficiency or perfection. Problems, and their solutions, are increasingly understood in systemic terms, rather than the linear models of causation that are supposed to have prevailed in some earlier period. Many of these ideas are drawn from the world of the designer, and "design thinking" has become in some measure a frame for the way that social innovators are expected to approach their task. Design encapsulates both the novelty and unconventionality of the work of social innovation, but it also carries with it the promise that there are ways to enable a rational, even professional, approach to the problems that social innovators seek to address. Design thinking also specifically opens up the possibility of there being multiple ways to achieve a purpose, encouraging a view of innovation as a process of enquiry rather than the application of any pre-conceived models. In this way, the "end users" of social innovation are brought into the process of solving their own problems. They are no longer mute "consumers"; instead, they are actors with their own preferences and values that need to at least be considered in developing the solutions they will live with. Co-design appears as a particular recognition of this rehabilitation of the beneficiary[2] of social innovation, and the domains of design and innovation increasingly seem to converge and overlap (Manzini and Rizzo 2011, 201). We even see the term "social design" being used as a virtual synonym for social innovation (Armstrong *et al*. 2014, Yang and Sung 2016).

This book does not aim to add to the already voluminous stream of work describing, codifying, or promoting social innovation. Instead, it seeks to explore how design approaches in general, and thinking about co-design in particular, relate to the broader social innovation phenomenon. Although, in practice, the two traditions intersect and feed off each other, both are themselves founded on multiple and sometimes contradictory foundations. Social innovation, in its insatiable search for new techniques, has drawn extensively on design thinking, pragmatically taking over both terminology and processes where they seem to offer potential ways forward. Design has made a corresponding movement towards a focus on social arrangements and issues. However, several questions remain unanswered (or even unasked). Is "design" one of several ways to approach social innovation, or is it implicit in every social innovation process? Can social innovation be credible or effective if end-users are not fully engaged in developing the solutions it offers? But, if end-users are to be fully engaged, what are the implications for how we must organize, plan and deliver social innovation? How can "co-design" co-exist with efficient problem-solving and solution delivery? How can we reconcile engaging beneficiaries in social innovation with developing the large-scale solutions that seem necessary to deliver the ambition of social innovation? Such questions have significant conceptual aspects that make them difficult to approach empirically, and it is those aspects that this work explores, aiming to develop a framework that connects the two domains more explicitly, and that might serve to stimulate new approaches in both practice and research.

The book is organized in three parts. The first presents a review of the overlapping space where social innovation and co-design meet. The approach is to identify the tensions and commonalties that exist within and between both domains, and then to derive from these some central propositions about how they relate and what issues are raised by considering them together. The second part of the book integrates a number of theoretical perspectives, and explores how they might respond to these issues. In the third section, the existing state of the field is re-examined in the light of these suggestions, and implications for both practice and further research are developed.

Readers will note that the treatment of some claims for the benefits of co-design and social innovation may seem neutral or even slightly skeptical. Much of the primary material available on the practice of both social innovation and co-design does double duty as advocacy for programs or organizations that are active in the field. Such accounts, as worthy and inspiring as they often are, are necessarily prone to selectivity, if only because of a lack of resources to produce more exhaustive reports, and therefore need to be critically assessed. Social innovation and co-design appear attractive; however, there is a very real risk that the claims made on their behalf will run ahead of what they can deliver, or that the terms will become flavorless placebos, mere similes for collaboration. As we will see, there are examples of overclaim that amount to hubris, and actually stand in the way of achieving what are otherwise very laudable intentions. It is to be hoped that this research can assist in mitigating that risk, by presenting a view of the field that both treats it realistically and also identifies some promising directions for its further development.

Notes

1 Social innovation, social design, social entrepreneurship, or social enterprise
2 For the moment, we will use this term in preference to "end-user" or "consumer", or any of the several other possibilities, since it seems to have the most general and value-free implications.

References

Armstrong, Leah, Jocelyn Bailey, Guy Julier, and Lucy Kimbell. 2014. *Social Design Futures*. Brighton: University of Brighton. Retrieved from http://mappingsocial design.org/2014/10/09/social-design-futures-report

Manzini, Ezio, and Francesca Rizzo. 2011. "Small Projects/Large Changes: Participatory Design as an Open Participated Process." *CoDesign* 7 (3):199–215. doi: 10.1080/15710882.2011.630472.

White House. 2017. "Office of Social Innovation and Civic Participation." accessed 25/1/17. https://obamawhitehouse.archives.gov/administration/eop/sicp.

Yang, Chen-Fu, and Tung-Jung Sung. 2016. "Service Design for Social Innovation through Participatory Action Research." *International Journal of Design* 10 (1):21–36.

Part 1

Social Innovation and Co-Design—Mapping the Territory

1 Social Innovation as Context

Even a cursory examination of the literature that presents, promotes and evaluates social innovation reveals an overwhelming diversity, which extends not only to practical methods and fields of application, something that might reasonably be anticipated given the burgeoning case-book its practice has generated in recent years, but even to its purposes and modalities of operation. Social innovation has been described as ". . . a quasi-concept, one whose utility lies less in fabricating certainty than in fostering cohesion across a policy network, composed of researchers, analysts and decision-makers" (Jenson and Harrisson 2013, 14). This description seems equally applicable to the broader networks of practitioners and academics who are also engaged in social innovation in its many guises—social innovation is defined as much by the community of practitioners that it draws together as by the unified set of practices or purposes it represents, or that clearly distinguish it from other activity. The field is made harder to grasp because distinctions are also drawn between "social entrepreneurship", "social enterprise", and "social innovation" and the terms may be conflated (Grimm *et al.* 2013, 440). Phills *et al.* make a case for treating both social entrepreneurship and social enterprise as special cases of social innovation, which they see as a more flexible conceptualization that draws attention not only to the person or organization that brings about the innovation, but also to the mechanisms by which it is brought about (Phills, Deiglmeier, and Miller 2008). Although, for convenience, we will accept Phills *et al.*'s proposal that the terms are related, raise many of the same issues, and address many of the same concerns, it is important to note that this usage is not necessarily generalized: for instance, "social innovation" may also be used more restrictively than we intend here, to denote acts of "civic entrepreneurs" who create innovation in the public sector (Keohane 2013, 129).

There is much diversity in the type of "social" problem being addressed by social innovation, ranging from international development aid; to national or local health, poverty, or education; or to gender equity and sustainability, and much more. Some of this divergence reflects different perspectives on the levels at which innovation takes place. The Bureau of European Policy Advisors (BEPA) identifies three categories of social innovation. The first, playing out at a "social" level, is concerned with specific, and often immediate or pressing, social challenges that are associated with a locality, group or issue; the second, a "societal" level, is "directed towards society as a whole", establishing or reforming institutions that allow it to function in an improved fashion; the third, described as "systemic", addresses structural aspects of society, involving "fundamental changes in attitudes and values, strategies and policies, organisational structures and processes, delivery systems and services" (Hubert 2011, 10). The distinction between social and societal levels is one of scope, whereas the systemic category pays attention to changing parameters or values that cut across these levels, such as people's understanding of climate change (Hubert 2011, 10). BEPA sees each of the levels as being subsets of the others: achieving innovation at the social level potentially forms part of change at the societal level, and the fact of enabling these innovations may contribute to systemic change (43).

Murray, Caulier-Grice and Mulgan (2010) propose that social innovations need to address not only observable problems affecting people's day-to-day lives, but also to contribute to "higher-level" reform: they must "simultaneously meet social needs and create new social relationships and collaboration . . . they are both good for society and enhance society's capacity to act" (Murray, Caulier-Grice, and Mulgan 2010, 3). BEPA also distinguishes between a "process" and an "outcome" definition of social innovation: "the concept . . . stems from the need for change both in terms of the outcomes that innovation is expected to deliver and the process through which these outcomes are generated. . . . [I]t relates *not only to developing innovative solutions but also to new forms of organisation and interactions to tackle social issues*" (Hubert 2011, 36, emphasis in original). Both of these views link the creation of new social relationships to the longer-term capacity of society. Because their benefits are both immediate and carry future potential, social innovations must be seen not only with reference to the specific problems they are able to solve, but also in terms of the foundations they lay for future progress: "they leave behind compelling new social relationships between previously separate individuals and groups which matter greatly to the people involved, contribute to the diffusion and embedding of the innovation, and fuel a cumulative dynamic whereby each innovation opens up the possibility of further innovations" (Mulgan *et al.* 2007, 35).

Seen in this way, social innovation goes beyond being "social" merely because it is not solely for private benefit: it achieves both a specific social purpose and a general one of benefitting society by building its capacity to adapt and create. Hence, a social innovation process might be directed at achieving change at any of the levels defined, but in doing so have consequences that go well beyond the original intention. Caulier-Grice *et al.* draw on Schumpeter to propose a categorization of seven types of social innovation outcomes, noting that they may also be classed as incremental developments of something already existing; radical new ways of understanding or acting; or "generative" of further development (2012, 24–25). Even the most limited or specific outcomes may thus have far-reaching effects at the societal or systemic level: the provision of services that allow people to communicate by phone who are otherwise unable to do so because of hearing or other disabilities not only improves the individual's quality of life, but opens up possibilities for active economic and political participation that can have much broader impact. Similarly, the provision of a new service may lead to the development of new organizational forms and institutional frameworks: the emergence of on-line gambling services has impacted not only the way providers of gambling services organize themselves, but also the ways that sporting systems raise funds and communicate what is occurring during games; the way governments regulate the industry; and the way social services need to be organized to connect with and support problem gamblers.

The diversity of approaches to understanding and classifying social innovation, the levels at which it occurs, and the difficulties in establishing causal links between specific actions and outcomes are reflected in the wide variety of definitions applied to it (see for example Borzaga and Bodini 2012, Howaldt and Schwarz 2010, Hubert 2011, Mulgan *et al.* 2007, Nicholls, Simon, and Gabriel 2015, Phills, Deiglmeier, and Miller 2008, Pol and Ville 2009). Huybrechts and Nicholls take the position that ". . . the diversity of discourses that characterize the definitional debates around social entrepreneurship reflect the internal logics of a broad range of influential, resource holding actors who are actively involved in shaping the field, rather than any attempts at capturing the 'reality' of the field itself (Dart 2004, Dey and Steyaert 2010, Nicholls 2010)" (2012, 33), an observation that appears to apply equally to social innovation in the broad. This encourages us to move beyond taxonomic approaches to understanding social innovation, and to pay attention not only to conceptual and empirical distinctions within it, but also to the underlying purposes and strategies of those who are working in and promoting it. If social innovation is indeed being mobilized as a "quasi-concept", and effort is being expended to create an impression of coherence, it is of interest to examine the ways in which this "unity" is being constructed, and the dynamics of inclusion, exclusion, and legitimation that are entailed by those constructions. While the different proponents of social innovation all see their activity in some measure as "doing good", it cannot be taken for granted that they agree on what constitutes "good"; and while they are able to share their experiences in a lively exchange aimed at developing their practices, the place of any specific practice (and particularly co-design) within social innovation may differ quite markedly depending on who is invoking it: ". . . we are struck that social innovation, as it is currently conceived, could suggest myriad different and sometimes conflicting policy adjustments" (Grimm *et al.* 2013, 446). The different constructions of social innovation are suggestive of quite different values and assumptions about the nature of innovation and society itself, and therefore cannot be simply ignored. Hence, rather than attempting to (once again) reestablish definitional order by distilling some normative statement of what qualifies and what does not qualify as social innovation, this work will treat it as a "concept-in-use" and focus on the way it is presented and enacted.

The Stories of Social Innovation

Social innovators are extraordinarily diverse, the ways they approach social innovation and conceive of it having effect are equally divergent, and the types of problems on which it is brought to bear are legion. However, most social innovation activity is framed within specific narratives that explicitly or implicitly explain why it is necessary and justify the sort of approach being taken. These framing narratives place social innovation in history, and at the same time imply a broader diagnosis of society, presenting a sort of origin story or creation myth. They co-exist, sometimes overlap, and occasionally conflict, but present quite distinct perspectives on social innovation that reveal differences in both underlying value orientations and assumptions about the nature of and solutions to social problems. This chapter identifies and examines three broad narrative streams, with an emphasis on the diversity of interpretations and pre-occupations that they reveal. Along the way, a number of key players in social innovation will be mentioned, but it should be emphasized that a comprehensive survey of the plethora of organizations that are producing (or claim to be producing) social innovation is well beyond the scope of this book, and mention of any specific players in what follows is merely by way of example, rather than claiming to present any form of systematic, let alone exhaustive, survey of "social innovators". The chapter will conclude by summarizing some of the key tensions between the narratives, tensions that impact both on the way co-design is situated within the practice of social innovation and on the sorts of outcomes it is expected to produce.

The different stories of social innovation, although often emphasizing the recency and dramatic progress of the phenomenon, are all set against depictions of the past that significantly affect their current perspectives. Attempting to address the problems of humanity is not a recent pursuit, and modern approaches to social innovation both grow out of and sometimes reject aspects of past attempts to mitigate against the effects of poverty, disease or disadvantage. One approach is represented by the philanthropic foundations, many of which have existed around the globe for more than a century, making charitable donations and supporting a multitude of activities intended to alleviate suffering or tackle its root causes. Often founded based on endowments by successful business people, and reflecting a wide variety of priorities, preferences and beliefs about how best to assist people, these have complemented and sometimes replaced government programs with similar objectives. In the US, some 86,700 foundations were listed in 2014, with total assets of USD 865 billion, and making gifts of more than USD 60 billion (Foundation Center 2016). Although the foundations seldom directly engage in social innovation, more often acting as funders and suppliers of expertise and other resources for operating groups (often not-for-profits or charities), the sheer scale of financial influence wielded by these organizations means that they may exert significant influence on any area they choose to become engaged with.

A different approach is exemplified by the Young Foundation, which grew out of an urban studies think tank, the Institute for Community Studies, in the United Kingdom. This was founded by Michael Young, who had an important influence on the establishment of the post-war welfare state in Britain. Rather than playing a funding role, the Young Foundation and similar organizations more often research social innovation; train those wishing to engage in it; promote and advocate for it; and may become directly involved in its implementation. The Young Foundation itself is credited with establishing "more than 60 organisations, including the Open University, the Consumers' Association, the Economic and Social Research Council, and the School for Social Entrepreneurs" (Young Foundation 2016). Although this approach to social innovation also aims to address social issues, it tends to address this by emphasizing building social capacity or establishing new institutions that embody social change.

A third perspective points to precursors to social innovation in the work of Benjamin Franklin, Max Weber, Émile Durkheim and Joseph Schumpeter, which are seen to have reemerged in the French social movements of the 1970s (Nussbaumer and Moulaert 2006). Other contributing forces were protest and worker movements addressing a diverse range of social concerns, and the growth of "niche, alternative, self-standing experiments" (Moulaert 2005, 66) that explored new ways of living and relating. These more sociological perspectives present social innovation as paying attention to contextually situated relationships and their role in innovation more generally, redressing a tendency to depict it as a primarily economic or technological phenomenon. Rather than being seen as resulting from philanthropic flows of cash or the establishment of new organizations, institutions or policies, this narrative sees social innovation as an on-going process of adaptation, one that is inherently contested and political. The actors are not necessarily institutional or powerful in their own right, but may be transient expressions of broader social concerns or conflicts.

Against each of these historical frames, the recent burgeoning of social innovation is presented in quite distinct ways. From the sociological perspective, a reduction in the visibility of social innovation activity occurred during the prosperous 1980s and 1990s, although research centers, like the Centre de Recherche sur les Innovations Sociales (CRISES) in Canada, were established during this time. This period also saw the establishment of a new "post-fordist" neoliberal discourse that asserted the pre-eminence of market ideology as the normative model of social relationships. According to this tradition, during the first decade of the 21st century, and particularly after the financial crisis of 2008, this hegemony has been increasingly challenged, and social innovation has become more relevant than ever: "'the return of social innovation' is manifested by the utilization of the concept as an alternative to the logic of the market and to the generalized movement to privatize systems of economic allocation, and so is expressed in terms of solidarity and reciprocity (Nyssens 2000)" (Nussbaumer and Moulaert 2006, 73, own translation).[1]

"Philanthrocapitalism"

This reading of the last decade of the 20th and first decade of the 21st centuries is, not surprisingly, not universally accepted. In another narrative, this period is one of sweeping change for business and the global economy, where revolutionary new technologies, techniques, and ways of operating are developed, which can now be applied in the social sphere. It also sees the emergence of a new type of entrepreneur, who is concerned not only with making profits but also with making a positive impact on the world. "The common thread . . . is that of mutual advantage: the unprecedented alignment of financial and social incentives toward a greater public good" (Eggers and Macmillan 2013, 7). This is not merely a natural evolution of past practices: it represents a "tectonic shift" in "less than a generation" (Keohane 2013, 1). Although people have always turned their minds to intractable issues like poverty or famine, "[w]hat is different about this new activism is its momentum, sweep, and fundamental approach to problem solving" (Keohane 2013, 1). These new ways of thinking about business have been enabled by (and perhaps even arise from) the epochal advances of information and communications technology of recent decades. The private sector has learned to grapple with the massive change driven by these technologies, building entire markets that did not exist twenty years ago, as well as seeing whole business models wither and be replaced. Companies could not "'cost-cut their way' to growth and success, [so they] turned their focus to innovation as the way to organic growth" (Bates 2012, loc183). Their speed, agility and inventiveness is now available to revolutionize the social sphere. By using the same clever ways that corporations have discovered for generating clarity and precision about the problems they are trying to solve, social innovation can proceed along a disciplined and replicable path. Solutions take the form of "business models", which describe how they create value for the various participants in the solution, and so become "sustainable". Like all good business ideas, these models then need to be pushed out to the broadest possible market, and so are likely to have to overcome "not invented here" attitudes (loc 343) or other irrational objections that might deny their inherent practicality and self-evident value.

Three new orientations underpin these changes. Firstly, there is the search for new ways of doing things (or new things to do) that do not merely extend existing markets or strengthen existing positions, but that remake entire systems to create opportunities that were not visible before. This appears to draw on management ideas such as "Disruptive Innovation" (Christensen

2003, Christensen *et al.* 2006, Christensen and Hart 2002, Christensen, Raynor, and McDonald 2015, Mezue, Christensen, and van Bever 2015) or "Blue Ocean Strategy" (Kim and Mauborgne 2004). At their heart lies the idea that innovation now takes place at a systemic level (or should, if it is to enable survival), and so makes previous ways of doing things obsolete, rather than incrementally improving or progressively substituting for them. However, the "systemic level" that is evoked in this narrative is very much economic in its substance and dynamics: it is very hard to find a mention of political or social systems, except as impediments to the application of rational solutions.

Secondly, a fundamentally new orientation is claimed towards delivering real outcomes for consumers, meeting needs that they may not have been able to articulate for themselves, in ways that they may not yet have realized were possible (Ulwick 2005, Ulwick and Leonard 2002). This is contrasted with "traditional" approaches that are said to have asked consumers for solutions, leading to at best incremental development or even downright imitation. In addition, the consumer is now presented as being dramatically more empowered, and directly accessible to companies through channels that were simply not available in even the recent past, because of the internet and the profusion of devices we now use in our everyday lives, so that it is now possible (and desirable) to engage them directly in the design or delivery of the solutions to be offered (Prahalad and Ramaswamy 2000).

Thirdly, business is said to have moved towards a deliberate, systematic process of designing solutions, away from haphazard or incremental approaches that are supposed to have applied in the past. This design process usually consists of a number of phases (often overlapping or recursive) that lead from a deep engagement with the consumer in their real-world context (which may even be described as "ethnographic"); to an ideation phase, including prototyping; and thence to implementation.

All these changes are said to signal a fundamental shift away from reliance on government as the default provider of solutions in the social sphere, as ways are found to bring the workings of markets to sectors that were previously excluded from them, and that were also poorly served by the public sector, if they were served at all (Eggers and Macmillan 2013, 3–4). The fact that there are still significant social problems to solve suggests that the traditional means of resolving them have been in some way ineffective: "Government failure, both real and perceived, also shaped the early stages of the social entrepreneurship revolution. . . . It is neither surprising nor coincidental that the heightened embrace of entrepreneurship in the last generation in the nonprofit, private, and even public sectors has taken place in an era of ideological and political backlash against government" (Keohane 2013, 3). We will describe this narrative as "Philanthrocapitalistic", adopting the term coined by *The Economist* (2006).

A key role is reserved in this narrative for the "entrepreneur", who originally identifies an issue and galvanizes a response. Bringing the new ways of business thinking to bear on the social sphere demands a special set of entrepreneurial skills; moreover, it is not merely a technical challenge, but also calls for particular personal qualities and a desire to achieve something more meaningful and positive for the world than merely making a (private) profit (although this motivation is more or less explicitly reinforced as valid, just not exclusive of broader benefit). We are told that such entrepreneurs are "passionate, resourceful, system-changing, history-making innovators who could unbalance static social, political, and economic equations" (10). These special individuals are rare—it has been suggested that only "about 1 in 10 million people" (Iwanowski 2012) are likely to qualify as "Fellows" of Ashoka, a pivotal organization that "launched the field of social entrepreneurship" (Ashoka n. d.-a). These individuals are recognized as "the world's leading social entrepreneurs" (Ashoka n. d.-b).

This narrative also pays particular attention to the emergence of a wave of powerful new actors that have challenged the way the US philanthropic sector operates, portraying them as exemplars of the revolution that has occurred (although many of these actors do not necessarily themselves subscribe fully to the narrative). Ashoka, one of the first of these, was established in 1980. It supports the Fellows mentioned above by providing "start-up financing, professional support services, and connections to a global network across the business and social sectors, and a platform for people dedicated to changing the world". The network of Ashoka Fellows now numbers more than 3,000 people in eighty-nine countries (Ashoka n. d.-b). Another key player, the Skoll Foundation, was established in 1999 by Jeff Skoll, founding President of eBay. It "drives large-scale change by investing in, connecting, and celebrating social entrepreneurs and the innovators who help them solve the world's most pressing problems" (Skoll Foundation 2015b), in particular by making awards that assist existing social entrepreneurs to scale their work, and by supporting research and education in social entrepreneurship at the Skoll Centre for Social Entrepreneurship at the Saïd Business School, Oxford University. One of the largest organizations in the field, the Bill & Melinda Gates Foundation (the Gates Foundation), was established in 2000. With a trust endowment now at USD 39.6 billion, and having made grants of USD 36.7 billion up to the end of 2015 (Gates Foundation 2016a), it operates on a grand scale, making tightly focused grants to partners working in a few areas that are considered by the Gates Foundation to be "the biggest barriers that prevent people from making the most of their lives" (2016b). Other key players followed. Acumen, which identifies itself as a "venture capital fund for the poor" that "raises charitable donations to invest in companies, leaders, and ideas that are changing the way the world tackles poverty" (Acumen 2016a), was established in 2001 with seed capital from the Rockefeller Foundation, Cisco Systems Foundation and other philanthropists. The Omidyar Network, established in 2004 by Pierre Omidyar, the founder of eBay, "invests in entrepreneurs who share our commitment to advancing social good at the pace and scale the world needs today" (Omidyar Network 2016). In the Philanthrocapitalistic narrative, the newcomers are distinguished by being particularly "business-like" and "results-oriented". Although their methods and approaches vary widely, these organizations, and the many others like them, were all founded by successful entrepreneurs and reflect their founders' beliefs about how best to bring about change in the world, and the priority areas and ways of doing so. They are particularly associated with a more hard-nosed approach to evaluation and evidence. For instance, several of the newcomers have supported work to strengthen evaluation of international aid programs, which had been presented as allocating massive amounts of funding to programs without ever properly establishing whether they are effective or not (Picciotto 2012, 215). A significant movement to demand the application of randomized control (RCT) methodologies as the only credible form of evaluation has arisen which, although not universally supported by international philanthropic foundations, is indicative of a growing focus on reporting, data collection, and analysis that is increasingly seen as requisite proof of professionalism in organizations seeking funds or other support.

This story claims a special affinity between social innovation and American culture and values: "Entrepreneurship is deeply embedded in our nation's DNA. . . . The spirit of individual entrepreneurship undergirds the national experience, whether it is immigrants fleeing Europe for the United States or pioneers settling the American West. Entrepreneurial values inform our culture and psyche" (Keohane 2013, 3). Nevertheless, over time the focus on the heroic individual seems to have evolved. Ashoka has now moved its focus "beyond catalyzing individual entrepreneurs to enabling an 'everyone a changemaker' world . . . setting in motion the people, resources and eco-systems that will bring about a social revolution where everyone contributes to change for the good of all" (Ashoka n. d.-a). The Skoll Foundation specifically identifies the importance of partnerships to achieve large-scale change (Skoll Foundation 2015a), and works with several other similar organizations, both in delivering projects and in supporting research. Like the Skoll Foundation, the Gates Foundation emphasizes the importance of partnership, although this appears to be particularly focused on identifying projects in its key priority areas that can be implemented through those partners, on either a contract or a grant basis. Increasingly, the conversation amongst these actors is about networks, connections and collaboration, sometimes with each other and sometimes with other types of organization that are less involved in supporting entrepreneurs or projects, but act more as fora, bringing together leaders of industry and government to examine the big issues and ideas of the day and, in some measure, to set an agenda for social innovation. Examples have included the Clinton Global Initiative (Clinton Foundation 2016) and the World Economic Forum (World Economic Forum 2016). The Aspen Network of Development Entrepreneurs

(Aspen Network of Development Entrepreneurs 2016) specifically focusses on researching, connecting and supporting smaller businesses and entrepreneurs, and is itself a program of the eponymous institute, which acts as a forum for the exchange of ideas and ". . . for values-based leadership" (Aspen Institute 2016).

This diverse system of actors is able to amplify its already considerable direct impact by mobilizing connections with major global corporations and political leaders, connecting key institutions and organizations in the global economy with "social" issues and developing ways of leveraging their power and resources to address those issues. Eggers and Macmillan call this sort of assemblage of actors around an issue as an "ecosystem". For instance, they describe the way that the multinational Unilever is said to have contributed significantly to improving public sanitation in India by orchestrating collaboration around three focal points: firstly, painstakingly promoting the development of linkages between micro-finance systems and "organic networks of local female entrepreneurs" (2013, 170) to enable the distribution of soap at a village level; secondly, by establishing a partnership with a major "private hygiene education program" (171) to market a specifically branded product through grass-roots activity involving children and villagers; thirdly, by involving government agencies to get support for the initiative through schools. The successful formation of this ecosystem is attributed to the abandonment of traditional "silos" in favor of new collaborative relationships that are focused on the problem at hand, creating demand where none had existed before (174).

Far from seeing social innovation as growing out of protest or social movements that had been temporarily obscured by the rise of market ideology, but have reemerged invigorated by recent challenges to neoliberal models of society, this narrative presents it as a culmination of this same system, a triumphant extension of the new capabilities forged in response to a period of dramatic economic and technological change. Jenkins suggests that Philanthrocapitalism displays three features: "(1) the application of business principles to grantmaking, (2) high engagement by the funder, and (3) the tendency of funders to seek leverage to expand their spheres of influence" (2011, 764). Philanthrocapitalism presents social innovation as a movement that competes with both government and older forms of philanthropy in solving a range of problems, usually related to hunger, poverty, disease or education that, for one reason or another, other institutions have been unable or unwilling to solve. Although this project is presented as pragmatic and practical, and in some sense fundamentally apolitical, it achieves this only by ignoring the political value of market ideologies. Moreover, it assumes that powerful actors who become directly engaged in setting priorities and modalities of social interventions express rational, rather than political judgements, even when they attempt to influence government policy, as several have explicitly committed to do.

Reform

The Philanthrocapitalistic depiction of social innovation as essentially a process of socializing capitalism can be contrasted with another presentation that might be characterized as focused on reforming the system (and particularly government) as an adaptation to changed conditions. Rather than being the natural outgrowth of a capitalist system that is newly able to apply its innovative genius to long-standing problems that government has been unable to solve, this narrative presents social innovation as arising out of a failure of the system (encompassing all sectors—private, public and civil) to develop the capabilities required to meet unprecedented challenges. Social innovation in this "Reform" narrative is credited with a long history. In fact, even institutions such as trade unions, collective insurance for health care, kindergartens and sports clubs are claimed as social innovations that have now been normalized (Mulgan 2006, 145). However, although this narrative treats social innovation as being by no means a new phenomenon, in recent times it is claimed to have "moved centre stage" (Murray, Caulier-Grice, and Mulgan 2010, 3), because neither markets nor governments have been able to respond to challenges of the nature and magnitude that we now face. Where markets have failed, government has not been able to respond effectively because it is organized in traditional ways that cannot address complex problems that cross sectoral and national boundaries; and civil society has been ineffective because it has neither the resources nor the skills to generate solutions of sufficient scale (4). These are essentially problems of organization and institutions. Social innovation addresses newly identified issues such as climate change or chronic disease (3) that are "some of the most pressing issues of our time", a new category of problem for which our existing institutions find themselves maladapted.

A specific class of actor is associated with the Reform narrative, often established by or even within government, or with a focus on government policy or operations. In addition to the Young Foundation already mentioned, another key related organization is NESTA, which began as a public body in the United Kingdom in 1997, with a focus on innovation of all sorts (its original name was the National Endowment for Science, Technology and the Arts). In 2012 it became an independent charity under its current name (NESTA n.d.-a). In addition to its work promoting social innovation, it undertakes a wide variety of research activity, with a significant proportion devoted to making recommendations for government innovation and policy development across business, economy and public services (NESTA n.d.-c). Organizations like these play a key role in both supporting and establishing projects, sometimes financially or by brokering financial solutions, but also by providing non-financial resources, research capability and intellectual leadership, and participating in networks of social innovation practitioners around the world, such as the Social Innovation Exchange (SIX). Originally established in 2008 and "incubated" by the Young Foundation,

SIX became a UK registered charity in 2013, supported by the Calouste Gulbenkian Foundation (SIX 2016). It brings together individual and organizational promoters of social innovation on every continent, by linking regional networks in Africa, Asia, Australia, Canada, Europe, India, Latin America and the Nordic countries, and working with a range of partners in each region. These actors are engaged in developing the practice of social innovation globally, not so much because they claim to have the answers and the resources, but as an emerging body of knowledge and practice that others can bring to bear on their problems. Their problem focus is often more domestic, rather than international; the international aspect of their work is developed by connecting similar groups practicing social innovation across the world so they can learn from each other.

A closely related class of actor is the "laboratory", several of which are represented in the SIX Network. There is a vibrant efflorescence of "social labs" across the world, occupied with all manner of social issues (Hassan 2014), but some are particularly visible and long-lasting. MindLab in Denmark, for instance, is a cooperation between three government ministries and one municipality (Odense), "which involves citizens and businesses in creating new solutions for society" (MindLab n.d.). There are also organizations like PolicyLab UK, a unit within the Cabinet Office in the UK (see Kimbell [2015]), or La 27e Région in France, whose "partners are regional and local authorities, public administrations and private stakeholders" and which defines its role as being "to produce and pool knowledge, proposals and feedback to be shared simply for the common good" (La 27e Région n.d.). This type of actor may engage in the work of social innovation in its own right, or as a facilitator or trainer, supporting others to apply social innovation techniques. They very frequently work with public sector organizations, and may even be units within government. Far from being consigned to an essentially back-seat role, in the Reform narrative government is a key player and a central focus of reform efforts, a concern almost entirely absent in the Philanthrocapitalistic narrative.

There is a sense of urgency in the Reform narrative, because the challenges being faced by the system are generating sharply increased costs, which risk becoming so large that they eventually cannot be managed at all (Murray, Caulier-Grice, and Mulgan 2010, 4). Because of the powerful forces in play, and the need to reinvent major existing institutions and their interrelationships, social innovation is presented as part of a social transformation, delivering a new paradigm of society (22), rather than as a previously unrealized entelechy of business. It is described as a "new kind of economy . . . a 'social economy'", that emphasizes networks and collaboration over production and consumption, in a more "values-driven" world (4–5). Technology enables the networks and collaboration: the values transformation signals a cultural shift towards valuing the human over the system. Business is seen as an equal player, but not one that has privileged answers to the problems being addressed. Although it can contribute to social innovation, "it's misleading to translate business models directly into the social field. . . . But public structures can be equally inhibiting if they try to squeeze a new idea into the logic of siloed departments or professions" (7). Social innovation occurs particularly in ". . . fields in which commercial, voluntary and public organisations deliver services, in which public policy plays a key role and in which consumers co-create value alongside producers. . . . For all of these reasons traditional business models of innovation are of only limited use. Much of the most important innovation of the next few decades is set to follow the patterns of social innovation rather than the patterns familiar from sectors like IT or insurance" (Mulgan *et al.* 2007, 12).

This rather more pragmatic (not to say eclectic) attitude with regard to the sources and nature of appropriate models for innovation seems well-adapted to encompass forms of action that might be seen as hybrid, where business models operate within a broader view of society. For instance, in recent years NESTA has established a fund, NESTA Impact Investments, together with other investors Big Society Capital and the Omidyar Network (NESTA n.d.-c), and also established an "Innovation Growth Lab", which aims to "increase(e) the use of experiments (in particular RCTs) to build the evidence base on the most effective approaches to increase innovation, support high-growth entrepreneurship, and accelerate business growth" (NESTA n.d.-b). Another interesting application of "business" models within a broader conception of social innovation is Groupe SOS, based in France. It operates as a social enterprise in five sectors: youth, employment, aged care, health and "solidarity",[2] directly employing 15,000 people in 405 sites across thirty-five countries, with a turnover of EUR 750 million (Groupe SOS 2016b). Groupe SOS was formed in 1995 with government support, as a cooperative between three social organizations,[3] to consolidate the real estate needs of social organizations and contribute to innovation in housing policy, as well as professionalizing the management of their activities and finances (Groupe SOS 2016a). It makes a strong assertion of the importance of partnership: "To respond to the major economic, social and environmental challenges, it is best to open up to others, to work together . . . to co-construct solutions. . . . Let's mobilize public authorities, small and medium enterprises, community partners, the academic world and citizens to build solutions to the challenges of tomorrow's world together" (Groupe SOS 2016a, own translation).[4] Here, business thinking is applied to achieve efficiency and professionalize the operations of social innovators, without itself necessarily being a model for the innovation.

In its Reform version, then, the practice of social innovation is catholic as to its sources of expertise and methodologies, coalescing many ideas and approaches into new juxtapositions that qualify it as an emerging body of knowledge in its own right, not merely an extension of what has been learned by the private sector. Instead of being a demonstration of newly acquired capabilities, it seeks to develop and apply a body of knowledge and practices to problems that are new and different in nature from the problems of the past, achieving progress by changing the institutions of society and their relationships with each other.

Social Justice and Democracy

The Reform narrative's focus on reconfiguring institutions, and its belief that social innovation can be achieved by the development of a set of practices and expertise to be applied within and through those institutions, distinguishes itself not only from the Philanthrocapitalistic narrative, but also from perspectives that locate social innovation more in resistance and political struggle, and grow out of the sociological perspective already mentioned. This latter narrative is more pre-occupied with social justice and inequality (both economic and more broadly), which are seen to underlie and perhaps perpetuate the problems on which the other narratives focus. Rather than being associated with epochal changes or developments of the recent past, in this portrayal social innovation is placed in a broad historical context, relative to fundamental debates around the nature of social change and the relationship between the "social", the "economic" and the "technological". Like the Reform narrative, this "Social Justice" narrative engages the concept of the social economy but, rather than seeing it as an indication of a paradigmatic, transformational shift in society itself, presents it as the reassertion of the priority of social concerns over economic activity, particularly in the form of locally driven "associationism" (Moulaert *et al.* 2005, 1971), or "the (re)introduction of social justice into production and allocation systems" (Moulaert and Ailenei 2005, 2037). In either case, ". . . social economy, mainly the new social economy, appears unique as the organizational forms such as cooperative, mutuality and not-for-profit organisations are flourishing" (Jenson and Harrisson 2013, 17). Social innovation is presented as a vital expression of an on-going battle to assert the social and the collective, in opposition to alienating and hegemonic market ideologies, and one that produces new forms of organization and new institutions. It is depicted as a force for the development of a more equitable, inclusive, sustainable (usually in the environmental sense) and democratic society, in an enterprise that has significant moral dimensions, and is perceived to a greater or lesser degree in terms of a contest between conservative and progressive forces. This is a struggle for inclusion and empowerment: "Social innovation . . . refers to those changes in agendas, agency and institutions that lead to a better inclusion of excluded groups and individuals in various spheres of society at various spatial scales" (Moulaert *et al.* 2005, 1978). Whereas the Philanthrocapitalistic narrative, where it examines society at all, tends to accept it uncritically as a fact that is not really subject to ethical examination, the Social Justice narrative places ethical and political issues at the very center of what drives social innovation.

This depiction of social innovation also emphasizes its role in enabling communities and collectives to resolve concerns in their own way and on their own initiative. Going much further than simply enjoining "collaboration" between social innovators, or between them and the beneficiaries of "their" work, in the Social Justice narrative beneficiaries are to be specifically empowered to determine their own direction, often through the establishment of some form of association or collective structure that is able to project voice even in the face of attempts to suppress it. The manifestation of the social problems we face may (or may not) be new, but the underlying dynamic of society that gives rise to them essentially demands a continuing struggle to resist power, to assert the interests, voice and perspectives of the voiceless or less powerful. Social innovation's role is not so much "reforming" society or its institutions, as it is about asserting, even if only provisionally and *ad interim*, the interests and identity of underprivileged or excluded groups within it, rather than allowing them to be suppressed by or absorbed into the dominant mainstream.

Such an understanding evokes an ineluctable tension between community and society, or *Gemeinschaft* and *Gesellschaft* (Moulaert *et al.* 2005, 1972), which plays into a very different, and quite ambivalent, way of viewing either private sector or public institutions than in either of the other narratives. In the Social Justice narrative, government is, on the one hand, the default funder,[5] and so a risk to sustainability if social innovation becomes dependent on it (Grimm *et al.* 2013, 444); but is also an authority that might stifle or suppress the work of innovation (Moulaert *et al.* 2005, 1971). The private sector, on the other hand, is an inevitable part of the local interactions that are the focus of innovation, and often a source of livelihood for its beneficiaries; but is also (particularly when it takes the form of a large corporation) a conservative and potentially oppressive force that risks either reducing all benefit to economic terms or enforcing its own economic interests to the detriment of the underprivileged. However, by placing "community" at the heart of social innovation, the Social Justice narrative also seems to propose a radical reinvention of *Gemeinschaft*, which is more traditionally associated with "a context that is clearly inhospitable to innovation. *Gemeinschaft* is characterized by strong loyalty to insiders, high barriers to outsiders, and low tolerance for diversity, whereas an impressive body of research has shown that innovation thrives on difference and diversity (DiTomaso, Post, and Parks-Yancy 2007, Gulley and Lakhani 2010, Jehn *et al.* 2008, Page 2008, Van Knippenberg, De Dreu, and Homan 2004) and on a dispersed network of weak ties (Granovetter 1982, Ruef 2002)" (Adler 2015, 447).

Manzini presents a similar paradox between the "local" and the "open". The former allows one "to have a place to refer to and to have the possibility to participate to [sic] the definition of your everyday life context", which is a central feature "of a sustainable quality of life". However, promoting the local can also "lead people to jail themselves in closed communities. To isolate themselves . . . against all others". There is therefore a need to be "both local and open": "[b]ut maybe, it is exactly from dealing with this kind of quasi-oxymoron that a sustainable society will find the ground to emerge. A society that is based on a multiplicity of interconnected communities and places will appear as a large ecology of people, animals, plants, places and products" (Manzini, quoted in Brooks 2011).

This tension between the local and broader perspectives can be seen as echoing a concern that is deeply held in both the Philanthrocapitalistic and Reform narratives; the need to move from small-scale success in social innovation to something that has impact across the widest possible horizon of need. However, where the former narratives frame this primarily as a technical challenge, a matter of finding the right models and tools, the Social Justice narrative seems to present the answer as more likely existing in new forms of social organization, as being more about "connecting" than "replicating", so implying that significant changes may be required in the way both business and the public sectors fulfil their roles.

Tensions

Of course, these three stories do not encompass the field of social innovation entirely: actors are not bound to a particular narrative, but may borrow from some or all of them when speaking to different audiences in different contexts. Over time, as has been noted, there has been a shift away from depictions of heroic individual entrepreneurs in favor of more collaborative and systemic depictions, at least on the part of those actually undertaking social innovation (perhaps less so amongst some who comment on and promote it). Nevertheless, there seem to be some deeper contradictions between the narratives that cannot simply be ignored, because they may affect how actors are able to collaborate, and so ultimately impact on the development of the field. These can be seen as the fault lines by which the terrain of social innovation is riven, and from which, from time to time, minor or major disturbances or dislocations emanate. They are presented here as zones of contention, as four disputed dimensions that, employed together, allow approaches to social innovation to be understood and related to each other, and that will allow the practice of co-design to be more readily contextualized.

Contention 1: Can "Market Solutions" Be Value Free?

Beliefs in the superiority of the market model are not only deeply integrated into the Philanthrocapitalistic explanation of social innovation, but their rejection is also close to the heart of the Social Justice narrative. One effect of a belief in the superiority of markets is an assumption that social innovation is working towards a known form of solution: ". . . you can create markets—or at least market mechanisms—around problems like environmental cleanup, transitioning from welfare to work, and even fighting human trafficking. In fact, markets and economic ecosystems are developing around all manner of societal problems" (Eggers and Macmillan 2013, 6). In addition to the question of the intrinsic acceptability of market solutions, there is an apparently related belief, strongly held by many proponents of the Philanthrocapitalistic narrative, that business methods are inherently more effective than those in use in either the not-for-profit or public sectors, and that it is possible to distinguish between methods based on their sectoral origins. Of course, this belief is implicit in the idea that social innovation has mushroomed because of the availability of new techniques developed by business, but at a subtler level it is reflected in the managerial language adopted by many practitioners of social innovation. This language is not specific to social innovation, but reflects a dominant discourse designed to demonstrate the competence of the people concerned. For example, "Ashoka understands and serves a historical process, the transformation of the citizen half of the world's operations from a pre-modern to the same entrepreneurial and competitive architecture that has driven business ahead over the last three centuries. Such fundamental structural change is historically extremely rare" (Drayton 2003, 1).

This sense of manifest destiny is notably in harmony with the allusions made by the Philanthrocapitalistic narrative to the inevitability and, by implication, the desirability of "disruptive" innovation, as a presentation of modernity triumphal. However, the Philanthrocapitalistic community appears over time to have become aware of the need to move away from too uncritical an acceptance of the market, at least insofar as they are able to assert that they are building an acceptable face of capitalism. Hence, we see Acumen valuing "investing as a means, not an end, daring to go where markets have failed and aid has fallen short. It makes capital work for us, not control us" (Acumen 2016b). This is fully in line with ideas advanced in favor of reinventing capitalism, very prominently espoused by Porter and Kramer in their paper "Creating Shared Value" (2011); interestingly, this conceptualization can actually be seen as establishing social innovation (or at least social enterprise) as being at the forefront of rethinking business (Nicholls 2011, 2).

Of course, the ideological battle to either enshrine "the market" as an unchallenged good, or to dethrone it from its tyrannical and myopic rule over society, is such a general feature of any contemporary discourse that it would be surprising not to encounter it in the context of social innovation, and there is little value in attempting to map such well-trodden paths anew. Although some players take a clear position on market pre-eminence or inherent danger, a subtler tension appears to exist around whether, or to what extent, business and markets can be taken as value-free. The Philanthrocapitalistic narrative tends to present markets as being rational technological means to an end; there is also no shortage of examples of markets being presented as inherently negative, particularly within the Social Justice narrative, sometimes to the extent of delegitimizing actors who propose market solutions. There are also examples in both the Reform and the Social Justice narratives that treat the value of market solutions as a contextual question, one to be dealt with by solution design and implementation, rather than one that is open to *a priori* or in principle evaluation. This affects not only what sort of solutions to social problems can be considered by practitioners, but also with whom it is seen as acceptable to cooperate.

Contention 2: Can Social Problems Be Directly Addressed, or Do They Demand Intervention at Systemic or Institutional Level?

Although all approaches to social innovation seek to make a positive impact on the lives of some group of beneficiaries, there are significant differences in the emphasis different practitioner groups place on whether that impact is aimed directly at some "objective" problem, such as hunger or clean water supply, or whether a choice is made to attempt to influence the perceived systemic drivers of the problems, which are then presented as being symptomatic. In particular, some market-based approaches to poverty and development-related problems seem uninterested as to whether the way markets have operated may have contributed to that poverty. Likewise, some Social Justice narratives appear to focus much more on relatively abstract conceptualizations of problems, such as "inclusion", and treat issues that might be linked to them, such as unemployment, as somewhat subsidiary. The distinction between innovation that delivers "solutions" in the form of measurable progress against particular problems and innovation that accepts the possibility that value might be inherent in the process of innovation itself, is also related to the question of the level at which impact is sought, and to the divergences we have noted in perspectives on what social innovation produces. The notion of "practical solutions to real problems", particularly when it treats the societal and systemic context of the problem as imponderable or unproblematic, is congenial to, and is widely evinced in, the Philanthrocapitalistic narrative. It is concrete, immediate, measurable and "hard-nosed", and in quite overt tension with the perspectives of much of the Reform and the Social Justice narratives, which assume that each context is in large measure unknown and that dealing with it will likely require approaches that may not yet have been conceived of, and that may have effects beyond that context and over time.

To the extent that it is assumed that change needs to occur at a systemic level, the question then arises as to whether the target is to reform existing institutions, or whether they are to be treated as essentially problematic and bypassed. For example, the main focus of the Reform narrative is on developing new ways for the government, private and non-governmental sectors to work together, so a focus on reform within or across the sectors is taken as being a major vector of social innovation. The Philanthrocapitalistic narrative, on the other hand, if it considers the systemic level at all, may see the task of social innovation as being about bypassing or replacing government and establishing markets as sustainable solutions. The Social Justice narrative may also seek to reform government, or it may see it as inherently problematic and seek spaces free from its authority by focusing on developing citizen- or community-led action. This contention can also be expressed in terms of a predilection for either universal or local solutions, a preference that we will see has far-reaching consequences.

Contention 3: Is Social Innovation Expert-Driven or A Matter of Empowerment?

The impetus for any specific social innovation process can be variously presented as arising from a particularly perceptive, committed or competent individual or organizational entrepreneur, or as arising from successfully establishing the agency of those who are living the problem. In the former case, this tends to present the beneficiary of social innovation as relatively passive or lacking in capability; in the latter case, it is necessary to deal with the question of how to enable agency in systemic or political contexts where beneficiaries are significantly disadvantaged. Privileging the "entrepreneur" is, as noted, much more common in the Philanthrocapitalistic narrative, and completely absent in the Social Justice narrative, reflecting the different ideological positions of the proponents of both with regard to individual agency versus social bases of behavior. The Reform narrative, on the other hand, tends to adopt a more holistic view of the role of individual influence as a potential trigger, but also as embedded within and drawing from the networks of relationships and contextual institutional structures that the narrative seeks to reform. Such views are consistent with sophisticated conceptualizations of the social innovation process that draw on complexity theory (see, for example, Westley, Zimmerman, and Patton 2007). There is, of course, a fundamental ethical question inherent in both of these positions; the extent to which an external agent of change is entitled to act on behalf of others and potentially without their understanding or consent, or to determine on their behalf how to "liberate" their agency. It is possible to resolve this by recognizing that networks of actors may set off or influence a process that empowers a community or group to address their own concerns. However, the question of what is acceptable influence remains open at every stage of that process.

Contention 4: Stable State Solution or On-Going Change?

Both the Philanthrocapitalistic and Reform narratives profess ambitious goals, solving the "big problems" faced by the world today. Both therefore need to mobilize very significant resources and to demonstrate that any success has the potential to affect very large numbers of beneficiaries. Furthermore, solutions must be long-lasting, not merely providing transitory relief. On the other hand, the Social Justice narrative seems more ready to seek local solutions that may not necessarily be easy to extend beyond their original site, and accept them as valuable in their own right. In all three narratives, measuring success usually implies that an end-state can be reached. However, if social innovation is seen more as an on-going process, fixing an evaluation at a specific point of time risks distorting or misrepresenting what has or has not been achieved. Moreover, if "solutions" are considered as provisional waypoints in an ever-evolving process, the issue of whether and how it is possible to influence and possibly even govern the direction of that process becomes a vital one.

With these broad axes of tension in mind, we can now proceed to examine how the field of design in general, and co-design specifically, relates to social innovation.

Notes

1 " '[L]e retour de l'innovation sociale' s'est manifesté par l'utilisation du concept comme alternative à la logique du marché et au mouvement généralisé de privatisation des systèmes d'allocation économique, et s'exprime ainsi en termes de solidarité et de réciprocité (Nyssens 2000)"
2 Chiefly emergency medical and housing services for addicts.
3 SOS Drogue International, later Prévention et Soin des Addictions; Habitat et Soins; and Insertion et Alternatives.
4 "Pour relever de grands défis économiques, sociaux et environnementaux, mieux vaut s'ouvrir aux autres, travailler ensemble . . . co-construire des solutions. . . . Mobilisons pouvoirs publics, PME, grandes entreprises, partenaires associatifs, monde académique et citoyens pour construire ensemble les solutions aux enjeux du monde de demain" (SOS 2016a).
5 Indeed, much of this narrative is voiced in various reports produced for the European Commission.

References

Acumen. 2016a. "About Acumen: Who We Are, What We Do, How We Do It, and Why," accessed 20/7/16. http://acumen.org/about/.
Acumen. 2016b. "We Believe in Choice, Not Charity," accessed 15/7/16. http://acumen.org/manifesto/.
Adler, Paul S. 2015. "Community and Innovation: From Tönnies to Marx." *Organization Studies* 36 (4):445–471. doi: 10.1177/0170840614561566.
Ashoka. n. d.-a. "About Us," accessed 20/7/16. http://edit.ashoka.org/about.
Ashoka. n. d.-b. "Venture and Fellowship," accessed 4/10/16. https://www.ashoka.org/en/program/venture-and-fellowship.
Aspen Institute. 2016. "Aspen Institute," accessed 20/7/16. https://www.aspeninstitute.org/.
Aspen Network of Development Entrepreneurs. 2016. "Aspen Network of Development Entrepreneurs," accessed 20/7/16. http://www.andeglobal.org/.
Bates, Sandra M. 2012. *The Social Innovation Imperative: Create Winning Products, Services, and Programs that Solve Society's Most Pressing Challenges.* New York: McGraw-Hill.
Borzaga, Carlo, and Riccardo Bodini. 2012. What to Make of Social Innovation? Towards a Framework for Policy Development. *Euricse Working Paper No. 36/12.* Trento, Italy: European Reasearch Institute on Cooperative and Social Enterprises.

Brooks, Sarah. 2011. "Ezio Manzini on the Economics of Design for Social Innovation." *Shareable,* accessed 10/7/16. http://www.shareable.net/blog/the-economics-of-designing-for-social-innovation.

Caulier-Grice, Julie, Anna Davies, Robert Patrick, and Will Norman. 2012. *Defining Social Innovation. A Deliverable of the Project: "The Theoretical, Empirical and Policy Foundations for Building Social Innovation in Europe" (TEPSIE), European Commission—7th Framework Programme.* Brussels: European Commission, DG Research.

Christensen, Clayton M. 2003. *The Innovator's Dilemma: The Revolutionary Book that Will Change the Way You Do Business.* New York: HarperBusiness Essentials.

Christensen, Clayton M., Heiner Baumann, Rudy Ruggles, and Thomas M. Sadtler. 2006. "Disruptive Innovation for Social Change." *Harvard Business Review* 84 (12):94–101.

Christensen, Clayton M., and Stuart L. Hart. 2002. "The Great Leap: Driving Innovation from the Base of the Pyramid." *MIT Sloan Management Review* 44 (1):51.

Christensen, Clayton M., Michael Raynor, and Rory McDonald. 2015. *Disruptive Innovation? Twenty Years after the Introduction of the Theory, We Revisit What It Does—and Doesn't—Explain.* Boston, MA: Harvard Business School Press.

Clinton Foundation. 2016. "Clinton Foundation: Clinton Global Initiative," accessed 4/10/16. https://www.clintonfoundation.org/clinton-global-initiative.

Dart, Raymond. 2004. "The Legitimacy of Social Enterprise." *Nonprofit Management & Leadership* 14 (4):411–424.

Dey, Pascal, and Chris Steyaert. 2010. "The Politics of Narrating Social Entrepreneurship." *Journal of Enterprising Communities: People and Places in the Global Economy* 4 (1):85–108. doi: 10.1108/17506201011029528.

DiTomaso, N., C. Post, and R. Parks-Yancy. 2007. "Workforce diversity and inequality: Power, status, and numbers." *Annual Review of Sociology* 33:473–501.

Drayton, Bill. 2003. "Ashoka's Theory of Change." *SSRN,* accessed 19/1/17. http://ssrn.com/abstract=980092 or http://dx.doi.org/10.2139/ssrn.980092.

The Economist. 2006. "The Birth of Philanthrocapitalism." *The Economist,* 23/2/06.

Eggers, William D., and Paul Macmillan. 2013. *The Solution Revolution.* Boston, MA: Harvard Business Review Press.

Foundation Center. 2016. "Foundation Stats," accessed 3/10/16. http://data.foundationcenter.org/.

Gates Foundation. 2016a. "Who We Are: Foundation Fact Sheet," accessed 20/7/16. http://www.gatesfoundation.org/Who-We-Are/General-Information/Foundation-Factsheet.

Gates Foundation. 2016b. "Who We Are: Letter from Bill and Melinda Gates," accessed 20/7/16. http://www.gatesfoundation.org/Who-We-Are/General-Information/Letter-from-Bill-and-Melinda-Gates.

Granovetter, M. (1982). "The Strength of Weak Ties: A Network Theory Revisited." In *Social structure and network analysis,* edited by P. V. Marsden & N. Lin, 105–130. Beverly Hills, CA: SAGE.

Grimm, Robert, Christopher Fox, Susan Baines, and Kevin Albertson. 2013. "Social Innovation, an Answer to Contemporary Societal Challenges? Locating the Concept in Theory and Practice." *Innovation-the European Journal of Social Science Research* 26 (4):436–455. doi: 10.1080/13511610.2013.848163.

Groupe SOS. 2016a. "Notre Histoire," accessed 4/10/16. http://www.groupe-sos.org/310/notre_histoire.

Groupe SOS. 2016b. "Qui Sommes-Nous?" accessed 4/10/16. http://www.groupe-sos.org/309/qui_sommes_nous%20Access%2020/7/16.

Gulley, Ned and Lakhani, Karim R. 2010. The Determinants of Individual Performance and Collective Value in Private-Collective Software Innovation. *Harvard Business School Technology & Operations Mgt. Unit Working Paper No. 10-065.* Boston, MA: Harvard Business School.

Hassan, Zaid. 2014. *The Social Labs Revolution: A New Approach to Solving Our Most Complex Challenges.* San Francisco, CA: Berrett-Koehler.

Howaldt, Jürgen, and Michael Schwarz. 2010. "Social Innovation: Concepts, Research Fields and International Trends." In *Studies for Innovation in a Modern Working Environment—International Monitoring,* edited by Klaus Henning and Frank Hees. Aachen: IMA/ZLW.

Hubert, Agnès. 2011. *Empowering People, Driving Change: Social Innovation in the European Union.* Luxembourg: BEPA (Bureau of European Policy Advisors).

Huybrechts, Benjamin, and Alex Nicholls. 2012. "Social Entrepreneurship: Definitions, Drivers and Challenges." In *Social Entrepreneurship and Social Business: An Introduction and Discussion with Case Studies,* edited by Christine K. Volkmann, Kim Oliver Tokarski and Kati Ernst, 31–45. Wiesbaden: Gabler Verlag.

Iwanowski, David. 2012. "How in the World Are Ashoka Fellows Chosen?" *Ashoka: Youth Venture,* accessed 10/7/16. https://www.youthventure.org/how-world-are-ashoka-fellows-chosen.

Jehn, Karen A., Lindred Greer, Sheen Levine, and Gabriel Szulanski. 2008. "The Effects of Conflict Types, Dimensions, and Emergent States on Group Outcomes." *Group Decision and Negotiation* 17 (6):465–495. doi: 10.1007/s10726-008-9107-0.

Jenkins, Garry W. 2011. "Who's Afraid of Philanthrocapitalism?" *Case Western Reserve Law Review* 61 (3):753.

Jenson, Jane, and Denis Harrisson. 2013. *Social Innovation Research in the European Union. Approaches, Findings and Future Directions. Policy Review.* Luxembourg: European Union.

Keohane, Georgia Levenson. 2013. *Social Entrepreneurship for the 21st Century: Innovation across the Nonprofit, Private, and Public Sectors.* New York: McGraw-Hill.

Kim, W. Chan, and Renée Mauborgne. 2004. "Blue Ocean Strategy." *Harvard Business Review* 82 (10):76–84.

Kimbell, Lucy. 2015. *Applying Design Approaches to Policy Making: Discovering Policy Lab.* Brighton: University of Brighton.

La 27e Région. n.d. "A Lab to Transform Public Policies," accessed 20/7/16. http://www.la27eregion.fr/en/. La 27e Région.

Mezue, Bryan C., Clayton M. Christensen, and Derek van Bever. 2015. *The Power of Market Creation: How Innovation Can Spur Development.* New York: Council on Foreign Relations.

MindLab. n.d. "About MindLab," accessed 20/7/16. http://mind-lab.dk/en/om-mindlab/.

Moulaert, Frank. 2005. *Social Innovation, Governance and Community Building: SINGOCOM.* Luxembourg: European Communities.

Moulaert, Frank, and Oana Ailenei. 2005. "Social Economy, Third Sector and Solidarity Relations: A Conceptual Synthesis from History to Present." *Urban Studies* 42 (11):2037–2053. doi: 10.1080/00420980500279794.

Moulaert, Frank, Flavia Martinelli, Erik Swyngedouw, and Sara Gonzalez. 2005. "Towards Alternative Model(s) of Local Innovation." *Urban Studies* 42 (11):1969–1990. doi: 10.1080/00420980500279893.

Mulgan, Geoff. 2006. "The Process of Social Innovation." *Innovations* 1:145–162.

Mulgan, Geoff, Simon Tucker, Rushnara Ali, and Ben Sanders. 2007. *Social Innovation: What It Is, Why It Matters and How It Can Be Accelerated*. Oxford: Skoll Centre for Social Entrepreneurship, Saïd Business School, University of Oxford.

Murray, Robin, Julie Caulier-Grice, and Geoff Mulgan. 2010. *The Open Book of Social Innovation*. London: NESTA.

NESTA. n.d.-a. *A Brief History of NESTA*. London: NESTA.

NESTA. n.d.-b. "Innovation Growth Lab (IGL)," accessed 4/10/16. https://www.nesta.org.uk/project/innovation-growth-lab-igl.

NESTA. n.d.-c. "Publications," accessed 20/7/2016. https://www.nesta.org.uk/publications.

Nicholls, Alex. 2010. "The Legitimacy of Social Entrepreneurship: Reflexive Isomorphism in a Pre-Paradigmatic Field." *Entrepreneurship Theory and Practice* 34 (4):611–633. doi: 10.1111/j.1540–6520.2010.00397.x.

Nicholls, Alex. 2011. "Editorial: Social Enterprise—At the Forefront of Rethinking Business?" *Journal of Social Entrepreneurship* 2 (1):1–5. doi: 10.1080/19420676.2011.566764.

Nicholls, Alex, Julie Simon, and Madeleine Gabriel. 2015. "Introduction: Dimensions of Social Innovation." In *New Frontiers in Social Innovation Research*, edited by Alex Nicholls, Julie Simon, and Madeleine Gabriel, 1–26. Basingstoke: Palgrave Macmillan.

Nussbaumer, Jacques, and Frank Moulaert. 2006. "L'Innovation Sociale au Cœur des Débats Publics et Scientifiques." In *L'innovation sociale: Émergence et effets sur la transformation des sociétés*, edited by Juan-Luis Klein and Denis Harrisson, 71–88. Québec: Les Presses de l'Université du Québec.

Nyssens, Marthe. 2000. "Les approches économiques du tiers secteur." *Sociologie du Travail* 42 (4):551–565. doi: http://dx.doi.org/10.1016/S0038–0296(00)01102-X.

Omidyar Network. 2016. "Omidyar Network: Who We Are," accessed 20/7/16. https://www.omidyar.com/who-we-are.

Page, Scott E. 2008. *The difference: How the Power of Diversity Creates Better Groups, Firms, Schools, and Societies*. Princeton, NJ: Princeton University Press.

Phills, James A. Jr., Kriss Deiglmeier, and Dale T. Miller. 2008. "Rediscovering Social Innovation." *Stanford Social Innovation Review* 6 (4):34–43.

Picciotto, Robert. 2012. "Experimentalism and Development Evaluation: Will the Bubble Burst?" *Evaluation* 18 (2):213–229. doi: 10.1177/1356389012440915.

Pol, Eduardo, and Simon Ville. 2009. "Social Innovation: Buzz Word or Enduring Term?" *The Journal of Socio-Economics* 38 (6):878–885. doi: http://dx.doi.org/10.1016/j.socec.2009.02.011.

Porter, Michael E., and Mark R. Kramer. 2011. "Creating Shared Value." *Harvard Business Review* 89 (1/2):62–77.

Prahalad, C. K., and Venkatram Ramaswamy. 2000. "Co-Opting Customer Competence." *Harvard Business Review* 78 (1):79–87.

Ruef, Martin. 2002. "Strong ties, weak ties and islands: structural and cultural predictors of organizational innovation." *Industrial and Corporate Change* 11 (3): 427–449. doi: 10.1093/icc/11.3.427.

SIX. 2016. "About SIX," accessed 20/7/16. http://www.socialinnovationexchange. org/about#about.

Skoll Foundation. 2015a. "About: Approach," accessed 20/7/16. http://skoll.org/about/ approach/.

Skoll Foundation. 2015b. "Skoll Foundation," accessed 20/7/16. http://skoll.org/.

Ulwick, Anthony W. 2005. *What Customers want: Using Outcome-Driven Innovation to Create Breakthrough Products and Services.* New York: McGraw-Hill.

Ulwick, Anthony W., and Dorothy Leonard. 2002. "Turn Customer Input into Innovation." *Harvard Business Review* 80 (1):91–97.

van Knippenberg, Daan, Carsten K. W. De Dreu, and Astrid C. Homan. 2004. "Work Group Diversity and Group Performance: An Integrative Model and Research Agenda." *Journal of Applied Psychology* 89 (6):1008–1022. doi: 10.1037/0021-9010.89.6.1008.

Westley, Frances, Brenda Zimmerman, and Michael Q. Patton. 2007. *Getting to Maybe.* Toronto: Vintage Canada.

World Economic Forum. 2016. "World Economic Forum," accessed 20/7/16. https:// www.weforum.org/.

Young Foundation. 2016. "About Us: History," accessed 10/7/16. http://youngfoun dation.org/about-us/history/.

2 Co-Design as Innovation

Design as a discipline and a recognized practice is said to have its roots in the Bauhaus movement that emerged after World War I (Bannon and Ehn 2013, 38), which explicitly started to relate social objectives to art and technology, and bring them together in objects or artifacts that were seen as engendering change. Hence, even though the practice of design in industrial and commercial contexts may not always have recognized this heritage, it has always been linked to the social and to social change. The Design Council in the United Kingdom was "[e]stablished in 1944 to demonstrate the value of industrial design in reviving post-war Britain, . . . [and] is now an enterprising charity which works to improve people's lives through the use of design" (Design Council 2016a). It initially started to apply design approaches to social issues through its RED unit, which later became the social enterprise Participle (Hillgren, Seravalli, and Emilson 2011, 171), and still "use[s] design as a strategic tool to tackle major societal challenges, drive economic growth and innovation, and improve the quality of the built environment" (Design Council 2016b). These, and other design-oriented actors in the United Kingdom, have established an active community promoting the use of design approaches in social innovation, particularly with NESTA and the Young Foundation, mentioned in chapter 1. In the US, the design company IDEO has played, and continues to play, a key role in the practice of "human-centered design" focused particularly on poor and vulnerable communities (IDEO.org n.d.). As the social mission of design has been promoted and developed, the boundaries between design and social innovation appear to have blurred, to the extent that they seem at times to be virtually inextricably interwoven.

Although the importance of design and "design thinking" is widely, if not universally, recognized within social innovation communities, the world of the designer has been evolving and itself contains multiple strands of practice and perspective. Kimbell observes that "design researchers have moved over several decades from conceiving of giving form to artifacts, to problem solving, to a generalisable 'design thinking' that can be applied to many different kinds of human activity, towards an attentiveness to practices, rather than individuals, including the practices of non-designers involved in shaping designs" (2010, 6). This movement can be seen as triple decentering. First, there is a decentering of design as a discipline, as design work is performed across increasingly diverse domains, such as architecture, management, information technology, fashion and policy formulation. A second decentering applies to the artifact as the object of design, as the human user becomes more central to the understanding of design. Third is the decentering of designers themselves, as the influence of known or unknown stakeholders, including beneficiaries, is recognized in shaping the design as it is conceived and as it is enacted.

User as Subject and User as Partner

These moves are intertwined and mutually supporting, but take place against the background of quite different underlying discourses or assumptions about the purpose and nature of design. On the one hand, there are perspectives that remain more or less resolutely modernist. These perspectives present design as being about responding rationally to some need (recognized or not) that can be more or less objectively defined, even if this definition requires the adoption of the user's perspective in order to achieve a better understanding of what is required. From this perspective, the three moves are all motivated by developing *better solutions*. The extension of design thinking across multiple domains is essentially about replicating techniques in one domain that have been shown to work in another. The involvement of end-users is useful because it generates a better understanding or insight into "their world" and the outcomes they are seeking, so that these can be met more effectively or efficiently. Being more human-centered, from this perspective, is primarily about ensuring the "right" focus on the outcomes end-users are seeking, and suggests that engagement with them would be most valuable in the early stages of the design process, before the experts proceed to build the best response to them. This delimiting of user involvement also sets a boundary beyond which the role of the expert designers (and, indeed, the organizations for which they are working) is preserved: experts retain control of the process as a whole, even if they relinquish their primacy in part of it, in exchange for better data.

Participatory Design

However, this sort of limited end-user engagement is increasingly challenged by more radical approaches that place the end-user into a much more equal relationship with other participants in the design process, particularly the designer. Burns *et al.*, having recognized the shift towards " 'user-centered' design", detect a further shift "in *who* is actually doing the designing" (2006, 10). Sanders and Stappers contrast the "user-centered" (or "user as subject") tradition, described above, with the "user as partner" approach of Participatory Design (2008, 5), which they identify as ". . . the terminology used until the recent obsession with what is now called co-creation/co-design" (7). Participatory Design originated as an approach to information technology design in Scandinavia during the 1980s, growing out of the workplace democracy movement of the 1970s, the social movements of those (and earlier) years (Kensing and Greenbaum 2013, Robertson and Simonsen 2013, 1–2), which are related to the Social Justice narrative of social innovation, and "the Scandinavian Cooperative design tradition, where researchers engaged with workers and unions to explore alternatives to how technology might be designed for skilled workers" (Iversen and Dindler 2014, 154), "supplementing representative democracy with democracy at work" (Binder, Brant, and Halse 2015, 156). Although Participatory Design has itself evolved much over these decades, together with the technologies it has worked on, it retains some key preoccupations that contrast it quite markedly with user as subject approaches that may also frequently be described as co-design. Bannon and Ehn stress the "overarching concern within the 'Participatory Design tradition', if we can call it that, on the 'how' of designing, i.e. a focus on the practice of design—the nature of design activities, the need for providing means for people to be able to be involved, the need for respect for different voices, the engagement of modes other than the technical or verbal, the concern with improvisation and ongoing evaluation throughout the design process, etc." (2013, 41).

Three aspects of design practice demonstrate the particular concerns of the Participatory Design tradition, and contrast it markedly with "user-as-subject" approaches.

Genuine Participation

Firstly, Participatory Design is concerned with achieving *genuine participation*, not as a means to an end, but as an expression of fundamental values that are embedded in its heritage, values of emancipation or the "giving of voice", and of locally expressed democracy. This intent goes well beyond merely extending an invitation to collaborate, although the invitation is a key concern: the impact of power imbalances on participants' willingness and ability to engage in either framing the discussion or contributing to it demands the development of a sophisticated array of approaches and techniques to actively enable participation. In Participatory Design, participation must also extend not only to the achievement of some pre-defined goal, but to the definition of the goals themselves (Blomberg and Karasti 2013, 89), without which the very basis for democratic claims is undermined.

Prototyping

An important part of enabling genuine participation is finding ways to grapple with the different languages of "experts" and "naïve" participants, which might exclude the latter or inhibit their contributions. One part of a response to this problem has been the development of "design-by-doing" methods (Björgvinsson 2008), such as mock-ups and prototypes, which act as concrete, present exemplars of ways forward, and are as amenable to practical as to expert responses. Versions of prototyping are core practice across all types of design practice, but in Participatory Design they have a specific place, because of their role in bridging power and expertise imbalances and enabling *mutual learning*, which is seen as the archetypal form of interaction in this tradition. The existence of concrete artifacts as foci for discussion, critique and collaboration, as well as the application of an array of other tools and processes, enables progress to be made that not only draws on the expertise of all contributors, but also allows new solutions to emerge that might not have been visible to any, or that might not have been authorized by the experts. Hence, the focus of Participatory Design on achieving mutual learning around provisional artifacts is also a key way of enabling innovation, rather than being bound by pre-conceived constraints.

Ethnography and Action

A third pre-occupation of Participatory Design is to achieve action in the everyday context of the people who occupy it, in ways that are meaningful to them. In this, Participatory Design can be seen as being close to ethnographic traditions, which focus on "studying phenomena in their *everyday settings*, taking a *holistic* view, providing a *descriptive understanding* and taking a *members' perspective*" (Blomberg and Karasti 2013, 88, emphasis in original). The ethnographic tradition resonates well with Participatory Design's commitment to treating all participants, and their contributions, as equal, in a respectful way; it also establishes a predisposition to curiosity about alternative ways of seeing that strongly supports the value of mutual learning. Moreover, the commitment to adopting the participant's perspective points to the ethnographic practice of immersion in the life of the community in focus, instead of attempting to observe it from the exterior.

The juxtaposition of ethnography and Participatory Design draws attention to some less obvious aspects of Participatory Design. Firstly, ethnography's commitment to developing a holistic view reminds us of Participatory Design's own early connections and conflicts with the world of systems thinking. On the one hand, Participatory Design arose in part as a critique of the socio-technical systems approaches being developed in the UK (Mumford 1972, 1993a, b). Although this critique was based on the rejection of the notion that participation could be enabled without attention to power relations, and the rejection of the primacy of the technical goal over the achievement of social and political objectives (Kensing and Greenbaum 2013, 25), there was also agreement that activity has to be seen in its broader, systemic context. Indeed, Participatory Design was significantly influenced by the work of Checkland on soft systems, and of systems theorist C West Churchman (Bannon and Ehn 2013, 43).

There is also an apparent tension between ethnography's fundamentally descriptive focus and the avowedly interventionist orientation of Participatory Design. In this respect, Participatory Design shares much with Action Research (and Participatory Action Research) (Bannon and Ehn 2013, 44), and in particular with the idea that research not only may, but should, change the context in which it is taking place, and for the benefit of its participants. Participatory Design's concern to enable change, and give voice to participants, challenges perspectives on ethnography that present communities as unchanging and would deprive community members of willingness to change and adapt. It also challenges practitioners of Participatory Design to ensure that the purpose or change that they seek to support is, indeed, the purpose of the people with whom they are working, and not an aspiration imported from an exterior that knows better, the "god-like" perspective that ethnography attempts to subvert. Moreover, we might observe that "description" is not necessarily conservative, or even neutral: particularly when multiple perspectives are brought together to develop a new, joint understanding of a context, insights that were not available to any one participant may emerge and serve to alter the views of others. The act of describing *together* becomes creative and potentially disruptive. Hence, adopting an ethnographic orientation in a process of mutual learning might actually become a vital source of dialogue around purposes, ideas and motivation.

While user as subject approaches also use ethnography, they mobilize it in a fundamentally different way: as a source of information *about* the end-user, for *use by* the designer, rather than as a means to directly implicate the user's community and context in the design process and make the product of the design relevant within that broader system. User as subject approaches are partly defined by the way they reserve the prerogative of action to the "expert" or owner of the process, in effect enforcing a strictly descriptive version of ethnography that is in direct contradiction to the way it is deployed in Participatory Design. Sanders and Stappers propose that, in Participatory Design, ". . . the person who will eventually be served through the design process is given the position of 'expert of his/her experience', and plays a large role in knowledge development, idea generation and concept development" (2008, 12).

In this way, we see that in Participatory Design the move away from a designer-centered to a user as partner orientation implies a fundamental reframing of relationships and an opening up of questions of influence and intent. It gives full effect to the decentering of the designer.

The Nature of Solutions

Redström notes that ". . . the object as such—the thing-design—appears to be less important in design centred on participation and collaboration, at least in terms of how finished it has to be as a designed thing. It seems that its primary concern is not with the perfection of form and aesthetics, but rather how it opens up for acts of defining use" (2008, 415). Ehn sees it as possible to seek to design not only as "use before use", where prototypes and objects serve to bring the future use of the object into the design process through acts of testing and checking, but also as "design after design", where the process of designing continues after use commences (Ehn 2008). This draws a conceptual distinction between the way design encompasses not only the acts that users take to develop something and put it to its intended work, but also the way users effectively continue to design after they start to use objects by developing new, unforeseen ways to act with and towards them. Redström sees the shift to "design after design" as implying not so much a change of the role of the designer and the user, but as a change "in the relation between, and relative importance of, 'definitions of use through design' and 'definitions of use through use' in the design process" (2008, 416, 421). This constitutes the decentering of the artifact/object in favor of the human user that we have noted, and seems to be consistent with the concern of the Participatory Design tradition to promote the agency of users: agency continues after design is complete, and users may therefore modify the purpose to which the design is put or the way it is applied. In this way, design solutions in Participatory Design are always in some sense provisional.

Infrastructuring

This notion of the provisional nature of design solutions can be related to the idea that that the process of design is not only about solving a particular challenge, represented by the "thing-design", but can also be seen as a form of "infrastructuring", because the practices in which design solutions arise and become embedded are themselves constantly evolving in co-relation with them (Björgvinsson 2008, 87). In the same way as the attention of design has shifted from the object of design to incorporate the humans undertaking and utilizing the design, this shifts attention to the relationships that are constructed in the design process, and that endure after and outside it, as a potential for further action, "creating enduring, self-sustaining collaborations" (Iversen and Dindler 2014, 155), so connecting to the contention over whether social innovation is to be seen as a defined solution to a defined problem, or whether it occurs at the systemic level, where on-going value is created in the process of innovation itself. This need not imply a permanent alliance, or a full alignment of interests, but is more likely to be shifting, partial and continuous (Björgvinsson, Ehn, and Hillgren 2012, 130). "Infrastructuring" has also been taken as the transfer of skills and capacities to users, so they have "the tools, skills and organisational capacity for ongoing change" (Burns *et al.* 2006, 21). It is possible that this "residual" benefit of the design process could occur unintentionally, but it might also be actively promoted as part of the design process, although this requires a different approach "focuse(d) on long-term commitment, . . . characterised by a continuous process of building relations with diverse actors and by a flexible allotment of time and resources" (Hillgren, Seravalli, and Emilson 2011, 180). However, intentionally promoting infrastructuring can be challenging: "Although the infrastructuring process has proved to be valuable in revealing possibilities that could not emerge with a more structured project approach, it also has its disadvantages: being flexible means that we need to continuously plan and replan the activities according to the situation, which can become complex, with several opportunities emerging at the same time or at a moment when we lack the resources to develop them" (181).

The concept of "metadesign", lifting the scope of the design process from the creation of content to the creation of context (Giaccardi 2005, 343), appears to be closely related to "infrastructuring", at least where it is associated with an intention to influence at this higher (or longer term) level. In both cases, attention is inevitably drawn to an awareness and interrogation of the nature of the developing collaboration: ". . . metadesign has been conceived as co-creation: a shared design endeavor aimed at sustaining emergence, evolution and adaptation. According to this development, the operational terms and potential of designing at a higher-order level must be joined to a more reflexive and collaborative practice of design" (347).

This shift from understanding design as being focused on its object, or product, to focusing on the relations it produces, both as they emerge and in anticipation of their potential for future action, challenges us to re-conceptualize the activity of design: "participatory design practices are particularly well suited for renouncing the obsession with 'objects', so dominant within design, and replacing it with *things* or *thinging* as socio-material assemblies that evolve over time" (Binder *et al.* 2015, 152, emphasis added). Adopting this formulation builds on the etymological roots of the word "*thing*", referring as it did in ancient European languages to quasi-judiciary assemblies of people to discuss matters of communal importance (Björgvinsson, Ehn, and Hillgren 2012, Ehn 2008, Latour 2004, 232–233). In this context, it is even more necessary that the outcome, or product, of Participatory Design should be seen as a prototype at some level or over some time frame—an artifact that emerges from an artificially (and possibly interested or randomly) bounded collaboration, which is itself prone to further adaptation and contestation, and that may itself also be an focus of design. The object and the collaboration can only be understood in relationship to each other. It is not a matter of choice whether to design in this way, but a decision about what and whom to pay attention to or ignore, recognizing that the outcomes of a collaboration that has excluded some interested parties will almost inevitably be subject to scrutiny by those excluded after it is "completed". The results of one collaboration will form the basis for further work in a future assessment of what came out of it, in a context that has also evolved from the one that prevailed when it was conceived. Furthermore, the product of a Participatory Design process will not only modify the possibilities of what can be further designed, but will also open up new collaborations that may not have been previously possible.

Contrasting the Approaches

User as subject approaches, then, start from the notion that needs can be objectively identified and, with the right methods, knowledge and capabilities, satisfied. The problem they try to solve is a technical one; one in which the user is a potentially vital source of data and insight, but not necessarily able to bring much to the table in resolving the issues they face. In this way, the "problem" remains the designer's: "Product designers traditionally 'own' the solution, it is 'their' product and they measure their success through a variety of mostly market-driven agendas. Not only is this contrary to the co-design or Participatory Design process where the most desirable outcome is a solution owned by the user and their community, thus requiring designers to let go of their personal product agendas, but also the very process of value adding becomes significantly redundant in a functionality-driven solution" (Melles, de Vere, and Misic 2011, 149).

User as partner approaches, in contrast, center the act of design on the purposes and perspectives of the eventual beneficiaries of its output by finding ways to enable their genuine participation in defining intent and developing responses; the act of design itself becomes a process of mutual learning and discovery, where new ways forward are generated collaboratively and where the "ownership" of those ideas or directions is therefore shared, and new relationships are established that potentiate further change. However, although at the conceptual level user as subject and user as partner approaches are starkly different, the practices in which they typically engage may look very similar. User as subject approaches frequently apply ethnographic methods to assist in identifying the needs of a user group, and prototyping is a common phase of virtually all design processes, whatever their tradition. For example, the "Field Guide to Human-Centered Design", published by IDEO.org, seems to speak to individuals, whom it hopes to inspire and equip with tools to bring about social innovation: "Creative confidence . . . [is] the belief that you can and will come up with creative solutions to big problems and the confidence that all it takes is rolling up your sleeves and diving in. . . . As you start with small successes and then build to bigger ones, you'll see your creative confidence grow and before long you'll find yourself in the mindset that you are a wildly creative person" (2015, 19) This sounds fully consonant with both heroic entrepreneur views of the world and with user as subject perspectives. However, another of the "key mindsets" proposed to enable Human-Centered Design is "empathy", defined as "the capacity to step into other people's shoes, to understand their lives, and start to solve problems from their perspectives. Human-centered design is premised on empathy, on the idea that the people you're designing for are your roadmap to innovative solutions. All you have to do is empathize, understand them, and bring them along with you in the design process. . . . Empathizing with the people you're designing for is the best route to truly grasping the context and complexities of their lives. But most importantly, it keeps the people you're designing for squarely grounded in the center of your work" (22). Although this formulation mixes instrumental language ("your roadmap"), it clearly does so with the intention of engaging beneficiaries centrally in the design process. It seems likely that the distinction between user as subject and user as partner within such frameworks will only become evident in practice, dependent on the specifics of the application of these "mindsets" in context, and on the predilections of the "designer" involved.

As in the world of social innovation, there is intense interest in the study of cases and examples across both user as subject and user as partner traditions. It is therefore possible to take techniques and methods from one tradition into the other, a possibility that in a sense conceals the ideological and political differences inherent in their different origins. As has been noted, from the user as subject perspective, the extension of successful design methods from one domain to another is simply a case of making good use of tools that have become available. In the Participatory Design world, by contrast, the triple decentering that has occurred is not about solutions or techniques (although these have developed as practice has evolved): it is fundamentally about exploring the extension of a set of democratic and inclusive values into new domains of application, empowering the beneficiary of the design process to take control of their world and challenging the pre-eminence of expertise as the driver of the process.

It has been noted that some writers see Participatory Design as coterminous with co-design. But where does this leave the related terms, co-creation and co-production? On the face of it, co-design seems to uncontroversially point to the engagement, to at least some extent, of beneficiaries in the design phase of a project. Kimbell defines it as "[i]nvolving people with relevant (often first-hand) experience of an issue in generating and exploring potential solutions to it" (2015, 80). However, as we have seen, this leaves several questions open. Is the beneficiary being engaged as a source of data or as a genuine partner in the process? By whom are the purposes of the project defined? What are the limits placed on the influence of the beneficiary and how long does the design phase endure before becoming in some way more fixed or "complete"? Co-creation appears to be the broadest of the three terms in its application, but Voorberg *et. al.* (2015), in a survey of 122 papers using the terms "co-creation" and "co-production", found that they are used almost interchangeably. In contrast, Bason suggests that "[w]hile co-creation is about the development, or *creation*, of new solutions *with* people, co-production is about the leveraging of people's own resources and engagement to enhance public service *delivery*" (Bason 2010, 157, emphasis in original). Likewise, Boyle and Harris locate co-production in the collaboration between the public and professionals in the delivery of services (Boyle and Harris 2009, 11).

One possible way to achieve clarity in the use of the terms might be to build on the apparent generality of co-creation and use it to encompass both design and delivery, with design assumed to precede delivery (Sanders and Stappers 2008, 7). Under this formulation, co-design and co-production become subsidiary to co-creation. However, as we have seen, as users become more engaged in the act of creation, and therefore able to promote or enact modifications to what is designed after it is put into use, the delineation of design and delivery phases appears much harder to maintain (see Björgvinsson 2008, 87–88, Kimbell 2010, 12). A similar concern attaches to "co-production", which is only unproblematic to the extent that it is possible to identify a relatively stable end-state process, product or interaction, in the delivery of which both provider and the end-user collaborate, a contention familiar from the social innovation perspective. Bearing in mind that co-production is usually applied to the delivery of services, it has also been pointed out that services differ in fundamental ways from products, in that they are effectively created anew each time they are delivered, and are substantively (re)-produced as a pattern of social interactions (Osborne, Radnor, and Nasi 2013). As soon as we accept that there may be agency exerted by the end-user in changing what is delivered, we are able to assert that there is an on-going collaboration on design. On the other hand, if we observe that there are limits or controls placed on the end-user's ability to influence what is delivered by the provider, we might consider the notion of participation itself to be under threat, and "co-production" loses its distinction from production.

It seems, then, that the essence of co-design lies less in its attachment to a specific "phase" of a process that encompasses the conception, elaboration and delivery of a solution, than in its recognition of shared agency or collaboration between those involved in the initial and on-going configuration of the service or product in question. This would allow, then, that co-design continues even during delivery, as the various parties monitor and adapt their practice. In a very real sense, co-design seen in this way is no longer a specific technique, a tool one might choose to use during one or more design phases (although user as subject practitioners will continue to use it in this way), but an analytical concept that interrogates the extent to which participants in a design process (including beneficiaries) are able to influence what is being conceived, developed and delivered for their purported benefit(s).

Dimensions of Co-Design

Understanding co-design in this way suggests examining certain dimensions of design as it is enacted within social innovation. One might be the *scope of influence* that beneficiaries are permitted to have on the process; is it limited to providing data to implement a solution already defined or, at the other extreme, is it possible for the collaboration to influence even the purposes being addressed? A second dimension that might be considered is the *temporal scope*; what is the time frame over which the design activity is being observed? Is the focus on a project, which is completed when a model or "solution" is put in place, or is there on-going engagement over several iterations of design *things*, as experience is gained during use, new parties engage and further modifications are made? Karasti has suggested that there has been a shift away from treating the project as the unit of focus, "extending design towards more open-ended, long-term processes (Björgvinsson, Ehn, and Hillgren 2010, 2012). Interests in non-professional design in communities have opened possibilities for the exploration of longitudinal infrastructuring efforts as they unfold 'in the wild' (Karasti and Baker 2008, Karasti and Syrjänen 2004), and the juxtaposing of 'project time' with 'infrastructure time' in support of the argument that long-term matters in infrastructuring (Karasti, Baker, and Millerand 2010)" (Karasti 2014, 146–147).

However, these short-term, "project-time" boundaries are what make it possible to claim that design is a controlled and rational process, one of the tensions already evident in our discussion of social innovation. What if project boundaries are, in fact, a handy fiction, an analytical convenience or tactical device, that allows us to preserve the modernist illusion that we are masters of the process? Furthermore, if we are forced to accept that each of our neatly bounded projects, with their specific goals and measures of success, are in fact only interim waypoints in an on-going and evolving process, might it not also be necessary to challenge the notion that we can, at least over time, limit the scope of influence of beneficiaries? In this sense, attempts to limit participation in a design process; to limit the influence that collaboration may have on the purpose (as in user as subject approaches); or to fix a result at a certain point in time, although they may not be futile in their own terms or for immediate purposes, are never sustainable beyond those ephemeral boundaries. While beneficiaries might be excluded from contributing to the purpose and the work of design, locked out of "use before use", this might be seen as merely postponing their assertion of agency. This speculation suggests that we might rather consider user as subject approaches as a limited sub-category of design processes that, for whatever reasons, choose to deny both the inherently provisional nature of innovation and the inevitability that beneficiaries will exert agency in "design after design". It may be possible, or even appropriate, to adopt these limited approaches in order to achieve some result that is considered to have an overriding justification, but such a decision will carry not only ethical and political costs, but also force trade-offs in terms of sub-optimal infrastructuring and probably (and ironically) of the stability of the solution they produce. Our suggestion is that, as we extend the scope of influence to recognize the agency of beneficiaries, we also inevitably move towards seeing design as an unbounded and evolving process, a process that is to be conceived of as an intertwining of "socio-material assemblies", or *things*, and the provisional constructed meanings that their design work creates. Conversely, it is possible to limit the scope of influence, but only by also limiting the temporal scope of our view of the process.

It is this broad understanding of co-design, in its full development as Participatory Design, that we henceforth intend when we use the term. The term may, of course, be used in more restricted "user as subject" or project-based ways, but these, based on the above discussion, can now be considered as specific applications that fail to activate the full range of implications or possibilities that the broader usage enables. Likewise, design can only be made something other than co-design by setting the same artificial boundaries on participation and limiting the time horizon we choose to apply.

Connecting Co-Design and Social Innovation

From a Participatory Design point of view, social innovation can be seen as a "contemporary design approach that can challenge and inspire . . ." (Bannon and Ehn 2013, 55). From a social innovation point of view, "design methods . . . catalyse people to see issues and possibilities in a fresh way. They spark creativity and help us to spot the possible connections between things, which so often become obscured by the silos of daily life which dominate governments and businesses alike" (Mulgan 2014, 6). From both perspectives, the engagement of co-design and social innovation is exciting and potentially productive. However, a number of questions need to be clarified.

First amongst these is what is actually being "designed" when social innovation is undertaken. Franz *et al.* propose that social innovation should be seen as consisting of changes in social practices (Franz, Hochgerner, and Howaldt 2012, 6), while pointing out that this is tautological (we will return to the question of the nature of the "social" in chapter 4). Accepting this as a working solution, the application of design in the context of social innovation is, therefore, the modification of social practices in an intentional way, in order to achieve some purpose: in the case of co-design, furthermore, it addresses the involvement of those who are expected to perform the social practices resulting from the design activity in both the design and the definition of purpose. The possibility that social innovation should have both an immediate effect and a longer-lasting value in the form of greater social capacity or social capital appears, then, as a straightforward interpretation of "infrastructuring" in the language of social innovation: "The process of the establishment of connections between diverse actors, focused on development of design objectives, often itself constitutes the greatest legacy in terms of capacity building among networks of actors so that they can sustain progress towards achievement of (further) societal goals . . ." (Thorpe and Gamman 2011, 226). In effect, co-design in the context of social innovation becomes a way of describing the intent to deliberately shape the process of social innovation, and the form of social innovation reflects the features of the co-design process, together with its call to recognize the agency of beneficiaries, the provisional and emergent nature of its outcomes and their dual character, as at once responses to specific engagements of actors with issues and as infrastructuring that enables future engagement. The provisional nature of social innovation, and the way communities coalesce around issues to produce it into the future, is inherent in the co-design process ". . . entail[ing] a shift from treating designed systems as fixed products to treating them as ongoing infrastructure, socio-technical processes that relate different contexts (Star and Ruhleder 1996). Infrastructuring, then, is the work of creating socio-technical resources that intentionally enable adoption and appropriation beyond the initial scope of the design, a process that might include participants not present during the initial design (Le Dantec and DiSalvo 2013, 247)" (Karasti 2014, 144).

As another key aspect of design practice, prototyping raises specific issues when placed in the context of social innovation: "Contemporary design practices are mainly construed to support creating objects, interactive devices, spaces and intelligent systems, but these practices give designers little help in the area of abstract social entities and how to work with them" (Yang and Sung 2016, 3). If a prototype is some form of a precursor to a final form of solution (Sanders and Stappers 2014, 1), what status does this have when applied to social practices? Björgvinsson, from the perspective of Participatory Design applied in the workplace, proposes that design be seen "as a joint inquiry into prototypical practices . . . [that are] new in the sense that they are perceived by the practitioners to extend existing communicative practices [and] . . . exemplary in the sense that they are constructive and of value to the practice being designed for; they contribute to sustaining as well as developing the practice. . . . [E]merging communicative practices are part of an encompassing competent engagement within communities of practice including its members' identities" (Björgvinsson 2008, 88–89). This formulation suggests that co-design of social practices involves experimentation with new ways of relating, which engage people who already interact with each other in known ways that in part help to constitute their identity, and that the results of this experimentation may be seen as prototypical and to some extent normative models for future interactions.

It is vital to note that when we talk about co-design of social practices, we are considering them as inextricably woven into the fabric of interpersonal interaction, not as transactions between isolated individuals. Some user as subject views of co-design propose understanding what modern customers want as being changes to themselves, that they are willing to pay for "transformation": ". . . we will increasingly ask companies to stage experiences that change us. Human beings have always sought out new and exciting experiences to learn and grow, develop and improve, mend and reform. But as the world progresses further into the Experience Economy, much that was previously obtained through noneconomic activity will increasingly be found in the domain of commerce. That represents a significant change. It means that what we once sought for free, we now pay a fee" (Pine and Gilmore 1999, 163). Quite apart from the extreme (and rather chilling) view of the possible scope of market models, such an approach proposes a commodification of our identity itself, and not just branded artifacts that might help express what we think we want. This seems to be a completely individualized conception of humanity, totally at odds with the underlying assumption of this work, that we become who we are in interaction with others, and therefore only exist in a social web.

The view of co-design that we have developed, as it is enacted in the social space, seems to favor a systemic view of social innovation, rather than a problem-focused one. It also seems to favor understanding social innovation as an on-going process of adaptation, rather than as a specific stable or fixed outcome. Finally, it seems that the design of social relations must inevitably be seen as co-design, even when, for whatever reason, we decide to pretend otherwise. In the sense in which we intend to use co-design, when put to work as social innovation, these features can therefore be seen as necessary effects of favoring the empowerment of beneficiaries over an "expert-driven" process.

* * *

Understanding co-design in the context of social innovation calls upon us, then, to first investigate our beliefs about the extent to which the people who will ultimately "perform" the practices our design produces should be involved in the definition of those practices. To the extent that we accept that these beneficiaries of the design process should be able to influence it, and even negotiate its purpose, we are then called on to understand the process as a mutual exploration of new ways of relating, ones that may challenge participants' ideas (including the designer's) about who they are and how they relate, and that are provisional, and so also enable further, previously unforeseen, development. Our attention is turned, not so much to whether a particular technique is being used to achieve innovation, but to understanding how intention is being developed and expressed in the process of prototyping new practices, who is involved in what ways in that process and how the new relational configurations might open up new possibilities. It renders questions about how to "manage" or influence the process problematic, since this would imply that human action both can (and can ethically) be manipulated to achieve an ulterior purpose. Rather than focusing on the process in this instrumental dimension, this emerging understanding suggests we should instead turn our attention to enabling voice and finding ways for participants to achieve even a provisional or limited way forward. Co-design of this type becomes a process of relational prototyping to achieve social innovation; a process of mutual learning and the achievement of mutual awareness of what has been learned and what it means in practical and relational terms. Hence, co-design also implies a level of reflexivity, the development of some form of collective understanding of what is occurring and to what it might lead.

In a very real sense, this displaces the "external" impetus of user as subject approaches, in favor of the development of a locus of understanding and awareness that is internal to the collaboration. It also challenges models that present themselves as rational problem-solving, at least in terms of the existence of an external rationality: the focus instead must become the generation of an internal logic, very reminiscent of Weick's "sensemaking" (Weick 1995, 2001, 2009, 2012, Weick, Sutcliffe, and Obstfeld 2005). The process suggested is not one of organizing reality into a neat and manageable series of steps, as it is said Simon proposed, but rather of immersing ourselves in the reality of the lives of those who are implicated in it: "While Simon suggests ways to transform and reduce this messiness into a stable design space where systems thinking, standard logic and mathematics can be applied, Schön suggests that we pay attention to the ways professionals in their practice master this messiness and complexity 'in the swamp', acknowledging that a stable state is an illusion. The concepts of *reflection-in-action* and *conversations-with-the-material-of-the-situation*—as ways of understanding the professional designers' practice—have become standard references in the Participatory Design community" (Bannon and Ehn 2013, 46, emphasis in original). It also engages us not just with the substance of the conversation, but with the constitution of the parliament, or *thing*. Binder describes it as "design *thinging* . . . a flickering between processes of collective decision making and collaborative material making, between 'parliamentary' and 'laboratory' practices, between engagements with objects of worry as 'matters of concern' (Latour 1999) and the transformation of objective matter as 'circulating references' (Latour 1999), forging strategies and tactics of participation and representation across these practices" (Binder *et al.* 2015, 154). This encapsulates the intertwining and interdependency of awareness of the collective *thing*, the "object of worry" and the "objective matter" that constitute the substance of co-design when it is enacted as social innovation. Iedema *et al.* (2010, 79) describe it, in a clinical context, in terms of "four discursive domains": as a "deliberative" process; a "reflexive" process that confronts actors with the outcomes of their actions; as a "research methodological capacity-building process", or a way for those involved to learn from their experience; and as a "dialogic process through which practical solutions can be derived".

In this chapter, we have developed a view of co-design as a term that is widely (perhaps too widely) used to minimally indicate some form of engagement with beneficiaries, but whose use may conceal significant ideological and conceptual distinctions. At its most limited, it may refer to a formalized and tightly constrained engagement of end-users in providing information to guide design tasks being performed by experts. At its broadest, it can be used to represent the on-going relationship between gatherings of people around issues of concern to them, intentionally attempting to develop approaches to them in an on-going process of reflective assessment of where they have got to, engagement in developing and trialing new, but largely provisional solutions, and adjusting to contextual conditions that their own actions change. This goes beyond the anodyne ideal of collaboration: it is something that deals with the development of intention and the establishment of relationships that form a foundation to meet future challenges. It also provides a paradigm within which some of the key features of social innovation can be understood; its differing levels and the relationship between (provisionally) resolving immediate problems and building capability for the future and the nature of social innovation as being the establishment of new social practices.

References

Bannon, Liam J., and Pelle Ehn. 2013. "Design: Design Matters in Participatory Design." In *Routledge International Handbook of Participatory Design*, edited by Jesper Simonsen and Toni Robertson, 37–63. New York: Routledge.

Bason, Christian. 2010. *Leading Public Sector Innovation: Co-Creating for a Better Society*. Bristol: Policy Press.

Binder, Thomas, Eva Brandt, Pelle Ehn, and Joachim Halse. 2015. "Democratic Design Experiments: Between Parliament and Laboratory." *CoDesign* 11 (3–4):152–165. doi: 10.1080/15710882.2015.1081248.

Björgvinsson, Erling Bjarki. 2008. "Open-Ended Participatory Design as Prototypical Practice." *CoDesign* 4 (2):85–99. doi: 10.1080/15710880802095400.

Björgvinsson, Erling Bjarki, Pelle Ehn, and Per-Anders Hillgren. 2010. "Participatory Design and 'Democratizing Innovation'." Proceedings of the 11th Biennial Participatory Design Conference, Sydney, Australia.

Björgvinsson, Erling Bjarki, Pelle Ehn, and Per-Anders Hillgren. 2012. "Design Things and Design Thinking: Contemporary Participatory Design Challenges." *Design Issues* 28 (3):101–116.

Blomberg, Jeanette, and Helena Karasti. 2013. "Ethnography: Positioning Ethnography within Participatory Design." In *Routledge International Handbook of Participatory Design*, edited by Jesper Simonsen and Toni Robertson, 86–116. New York: Routledge.

Boyle, David, and Michael Harris. 2009. *The Challenge of Co-Production: How Equal Partnerships between Professionals and the Public Are Crucial to Improving Public Services*. London: NESTA.

Burns, Colin, Hilary Cottam, Chris Vanstone, and Jennie Winhall. 2006. *Red Paper 02: Transformation Design*. London: Design Council.

Design Council. 2016a. "About Us," accessed 22/8/16. http://www.designcouncil.org.uk/about-us.

Design Council. 2016b. "Design Council," accessed 22/8/16. http://www.designcouncil.org.uk/.

Ehn, Pelle. 2008. "Participation in Design Things." Proceedings of the Tenth Anniversary Conference on Participatory Design 2008, Bloomington, IN.

Franz, Hans-Werner, Josef Hochgerner, and Jürgen Howaldt, eds. 2012. *Challenge Social Innovation: Potentials for Business, Social Entrepreneurship, Welfare and Civil Society*. 1st ed. Berlin: Springer.

Giaccardi, Elisa. 2005. "Metadesign as Emergent Design Culture." *Leonardo* 38 (4):342–349.

Hillgren, Per-Anders, Anna Seravalli, and Anders Emilson. 2011. "Prototyping and Infrastructuring in Design for Social Innovation." *CoDesign* 7 (3–4):169–183. doi: 10.1080/15710882.2011.630474.

IDEO.org. 2015. *The Field Guide to Human-Centered Design*. IDEO.org.

IDEO.org. n.d. "IDEO.org," accessed 15/8/16. http://www.ideo.org/.

Iedema, Rick, Eamon Merrick, Donella Piper, Kate Britton, Jane Gray, Raj Verma, and Nicole Manning. 2010. "Codesigning as a Discursive Practice in Emergency Health Services: The Architecture of Deliberation." *The Journal of Applied Behavioral Science* 46 (1):73–91. doi: 10.1177/0021886309357544.

Iversen, Ole Sejer, and Christian Dindler. 2014. "Sustaining Participatory Design Initiatives." *CoDesign* 10 (3–4):153–170. doi: 10.1080/15710882.2014.963124.

Karasti, Helena. 2014. "Infrastructuring in Participatory Design." Proceedings of the 13th Participatory Design Conference: Research Papers—Volume 1, Windhoek, Namibia.

Karasti, Helena, and Karen S. Baker. 2008. "Community Design: Growing One's Own Information Infrastructure." Proceedings of the Tenth Anniversary Conference on Participatory Design 2008, Bloomington, IN.

Karasti, Helena, Karen S. Baker, and Florence Millerand. 2010. "Infrastructure Time: Long-term Matters in Collaborative Development." *Computer Supported Cooperative Work (CSCW)* 19 (3):377–415. doi: 10.1007/s10606-010-9113-z.

Karasti, Helena, and Anna-Liisa Syrjänen. 2004. "Artful Infrastructuring in Two Cases of Community PD." Proceedings of the Eighth Conference on Participatory Design: Artful Integration: Interweaving Media, Materials and Practices—Volume 1, ACM, Toronto, Ontario, Canada.

Kensing, Finn, and Joan Greenbaum. 2013. "Heritage: Having a Say." In *Routledge International Handbook of Participatory Design*, edited by Jesper Simonsen and Toni Robertson, 21–36. New York: Routledge.

Kimbell, Lucy. 2010. "Design Practices in Design Thinking." *University of Oxford Saïd Business School*, accessed 17/2/16. http://www.lucykimbell.com/stuff/DesignPractices_Kimbell.pdf.

Kimbell, Lucy. 2015. *Applying Design Approaches to Policy Making: Discovering Policy Lab*. Brighton: University of Brighton.

Latour, Bruno. 1999. *Pandora's Hope: Essays on the Reality of Science Studies*. Cambridge, MA: Harvard University Press.

Latour, Bruno. 2004. "Why Has Critique Run Out of Steam? From Matters of Fact to Matters of Concern." *Critical Inquiry* 30 (2):225–248.

Le Dantec, Christopher A. Le, and Carl DiSalvo. 2013. "Infrastructuring and the Formation of Publics in Participatory Design." *Social Studies of Science* 43 (2):241–264. doi: 10.1177/0306312712471581.

Melles, Gavin, Ian de Vere, and Vanja Misic. 2011. "Socially Responsible Design: Thinking Beyond the Triple Bottom Line to Socially Responsive and Sustainable Product Design." *CoDesign* 7 (3–4):143–154. doi: 10.1080/15710882.2011.630473.

Mulgan, Geoff. 2014. *Design in Public and Social Innovation: What Works and What Could Work Better*. London: NESTA.

Mumford, Enid. 1972. "Job Satisfaction: A Method of Analysis." *Personnel Review* 1 (3):48–57. doi: 10.1108/eb055207.

Mumford, Enid. 1993a. "The ETHICS Approach." *Commun. ACM* 36 (6):82. doi: 10.1145/153571.214824.

Mumford, Enid. 1993b. "The Participation of Users in System Design: An Account of the Origin, Evolution, and Use of the ETHICS Method." In *Participatory Design: Principles and Practices*, edited by Douglas Schuler and Aki Namioka, 257–270. Hillsdale, NJ: Lawrence Erlbaum Associates.

Osborne, Stephen P., Zoe Radnor, and Greta Nasi. 2013. "A New Theory for Public Service Management? Toward a (Public) Service-Dominant Approach." *The American Review of Public Administration* 43 (2):135–158. doi: 10.1177/0275074012466935.

Pine, B. Joseph, and James H. Gilmore. 1999. *The Experience Economy: Work Is Theatre & Every Business a Stage.* Boston, MA: Harvard Business School Press.

Redström, Johan. 2008. "RE:Definitions of Use." *Design Studies* 29 (4):410–423. doi: http://dx.doi.org/10.1016/j.destud.2008.05.001.

Robertson, Toni, and Jesper Simonsen. 2013. "Participatory Design: An introduction." In *Routledge International Handbook of Participatory Design*, edited by Jesper Simonsen and Toni Robertson, 1–17. New York: Routledge.

Sanders, Elizabeth B. N., and Pieter Jan Stappers. 2008. "Co-Creation and the New Landscapes of Design." *CoDesign* 4 (1):5–18. doi: 10.1080/15710880701875068.

Sanders, Elizabeth B. N., and Pieter Jan Stappers. 2014. "Editorial." *International Journal of CoCreation in Design and the Arts* 10 (1):1–4. doi: 10.1080/15710882.2014.896584.

Star, Susan Leigh, and Karen Ruhleder. 1996. "Steps toward an Ecology of Infrastructure: Design and Access for Large Information Spaces." *Information Systems Research* 7 (1):111–134.

Thorpe, Adam, and Lorraine Gamman. 2011. "Design with Society: Why Socially Responsive Design Is Good Enough." *CoDesign* 7 (3–4):217–230. doi: 10.1080/15710882.2011.630477.

Voorberg, W. H., V. J. J. M. Bekkers, and L. G. Tummers. 2015. "A Systematic Review of Co-Creation and Co-Production: Embarking on the social innovation journey." *Public Management Review* 17 (9):1333–1357. doi: 10.1080/14719037.2014.930505.

Weick, Karl E. 1995. *Sensemaking in Organizations.* Thousand Oaks, CA: Sage.

Weick, Karl E. 2001. *Making Sense of the Organization.* Malden, MA: Blackwell Publishers.

Weick, Karl E. 2009. *Making Sense of the Organization: Vol. 2 The Impermanent Organization, Impermanent Organization.* Chichester: Wiley.

Weick, Karl E. 2012. "Organized Sensemaking: A Commentary on Processes of Interpretive Work." *Human Relations* 65 (1):141–153. doi: 10.1177/0018726711424235.

Weick, Karl E., Kathleen M. Sutcliffe, and David Obstfeld. 2005. "Organizing and the Process of Sensemaking." *Organization Science* 16 (4):409–421.

Yang, Chen-Fu, and Tung-Jung Sung. 2016. "Service Design for Social Innovation through Participatory Action Research." *International Journal of Design* 10 (1):21–36.

3   Taking Co-Design Seriously

The preceding chapters have proposed an underlying connection between conceptions of Participatory Design, or co-design in its fullest expression, and social innovation, a connection that grows out of the obligation and necessity to empower those who are to eventually enact new social practices. Examining the implications of this connection has suggested that social innovation should be seen as a fundamentally emergent, radically unresolved and evolving process that connects socio-material assemblies or *things* to the meanings that they construct and, in the same movement, creates the focus for further work and builds the relational infrastructure that allows and directs that work. It has also suggested that, although it is possible to delimit this process, temporally and in terms of the influence that interested actors may have in its outcomes, this is always a temporary convenience, and that it comes at a cost to the outcomes of the process.

This emerging understanding of what social innovation actually consists of seems quite far removed from our examination of the various ways in which it is depicted. What of the ambition to change the world? The new-found power lent to humankind by technology, and its own inventiveness, that allows us to challenge problems that until recently would have been seen as the concerns of higher beings? Can any of this be maintained if social innovation is now essentially a matter of enabling those affected to chart their own course? We will continue the development of the idea that co-design is at the very heart of social innovation with a mind to answer these and related questions. However, we need first to revisit some remaining aspects of the way social innovation is being framed that cut across the narratives that we have identified, and clarify what sort of description we would like to produce.

Let's start by revisiting the exuberance that permeates so many of the reports on social innovation.

Novelty

Social innovation, and many of the "techniques" associated with it, have been presented with glowing references by its recent practitioners, even risking the label of "policy chic" (Larsson and Brandsen 2016, 293). Of course, there is an understandable drive to promote their efforts, generate partners and supporters and cement access to resources that will enable further efforts. However, it is implicit (and sometimes explicit) in the presentation of some proponents that they have "discovered" a new and better way to achieve results that it was previously not possible to achieve. The very newness of their efforts is presented as inevitably exciting and superior to past efforts. As Larsson and Brandsen say, "there is even talk of a 'social innovation movement', though there is no convincing evidence to suggest that there is more social innovation now than 50 or 100 years ago, nor that it is part of a coherent movement. It appears to be ideology more than a serious assessment" (2016, 294). The problem with this hubris is that it is not without effect, in its dismissal of the existing networks, experience and expertise of actors that do not spring from the same roots or talk the same language as the promoters of social innovation, or design thinking, or any one of the multitude of other "paradigm-breaking" new ideas. Social practices have been the subject of deliberate, and presumably at least occasionally successful, attempts at change, probably since the beginning of human society: none of the traditions that make up the "social innovation movement" have developed in a vacuum. There are large-scale community-based organizations that have been working at local (and sometimes broader) levels to achieve social goals—the 35,000 clubs that constitute an organization like Rotary International are a case in point. Chasing the chimera of the wondrous new at best risks distracting from the substance of the issues that are being faced; at worst, it represents an active displacement of significant reserves of social capital that could otherwise be put to work. There is significant potential for conflict between social innovators as the new seeks to supplant the less new, particularly given the widely divergent ideological roots of the various communities:

> The artificial unity that seems to be indicated by the meeting of community actors and social enterprises under one banner, the ESS [the French Chamber of Social and Solidarity-based Economy], conceals the hostility of entrepreneurial discourse towards community-based associations. These two actors do not represent two approaches to 'social' action that can live together. The very legitimacy of the community model is constantly denied in every line of the social entrepreneurs' discourse: ineffective, dependent on public authorities, paralyzed by ideology— for them, community associations are the past and so destined to die. Jean-Marc Borello, president of Groupe SOS, the giant of social entrepreneurship, likes to repeat that 'in ten years, there will be 10 times fewer community associations in France'. With friends like these, the community sector doesn't need enemies.
>
> (Sevilla 2016, own translation)[1]

There are also tensions within the social innovation field around the role of design and design thinking in social innovation. Mulgan (2014), while noting the contributions made by design thinking to social innovation, most notably in assisting to understand user experiences, ideation and the provision of useful tools, also identifies them with high-paid consultants who are more adept at creating than implementing, and who do not recognize that they do not have a monopoly on expertise. Although there is a sense that Mulgan may here be particularly concerned with design practices in the user as subject tradition, both of these examples remind us that social innovation is being carried out by a diverse set of communities, with different preoccupations and perspectives, and that the social dynamics between those communities are likely to be significant determinants of how the field develops.

The potential for this sort of hegemonic conflict appears to be a particularly strong concern in the case of the Philanthrocapitalistic narrative, no doubt at least in part because of the very significant resources and powerful networks through which it is maintained and promoted. "While perhaps not intentional, the new muscular philanthropy casts most nonprofit organizations as crisis-prone, desperately poor, starry-eyed, even witless do-gooders. This characterization can lead to condescension and fractured relationships" (Jenkins 2011, 793). Unsurprisingly, this has led to resistance: "The philanthrocapitalists are drinking from a heady and seductive cocktail, one part 'irrational exuberance' that is characteristic of market thinking, two parts believing that success in business equips them to make a similar impact on social change, a dash or two of the excitement that accompanies any new solution, and an extra degree of fizz from the oxygen of publicity" (Edwards 2008, 23–24). However, this is more than empty sarcasm: substantive concerns are raised about the way that the promotion of the values and techniques associated with Philanthrocapitalism may distort the purpose towards which they are working and undermine both existing philanthropic actors and more appropriate ways of working. These effects arise both from the approaches developed by the Philanthrocapitalists and from the way they are reshaping the philanthropic sector and relations between funders and operators: "Philanthrocapitalism . . . is nothing short of an effort to remodel the prevailing philanthropic patterns by supplying a new language, a new mindset, and new techniques for addressing social problems. . . . It places the foundation at the center of the social problem-solving endeavor, relegating grantees to the role of subcontractors expected to execute the grand vision of the private foundation funder" (Jenkins 2011, 768–769).

These impacts have the potential to extend well beyond the American philanthropic system. The adoption of the language of business; of tightly controlled measurement systems that focus on pre-defined standards of "impact"; of emphasis on being "strategic", by developing high-level plans that are then implemented in a disciplined fashion, are all visible in the work of organizations across the world, and have often been adopted by government funding bodies as self-evidently best practice ways of ensuring efficiency in spending. Of course, this reflects the power of the managerial discourse behind Philanthrocapitalism, and its penetration of much broader spheres, through movements like New Public Management, as part of a broader agenda that might be called neoliberal: "Business structures and market models have become organizing models sine qua non (Kuttner 1997), and sociopolitical or moral legitimacy is accorded to social-enterprise initiatives that mimic them" (Dart 2004). However, its impact on social innovation is not solely political; it has practical impacts on the way innovators act and the risks they are willing to take, as well as favoring some (generally larger) organizations and suppressing others. "By demanding that philanthropy be impact-oriented, market-savvy and cost-effective, the new philanthropy explicitly assumes a moral hierarchy of philanthropic value that is structured according to measurable financial benefit" (McGoey 2012, 193). Moreover, it turns the attention of the system to the funders' requirements, strategies and capabilities, and away from the specificities of the people by and for whom the work is being done. In fact, the novelty of the Philanthrocapitalistic wave is questionable: not only did John D. Rockefeller III use the term "venture philanthropy", "a distinctive but compatible concept to philanthrocapitalism, . . . as early as 1969" (McGoey 2012, 189), long before the technological revolution that was supposed to have created a new business world, but "[b]oth John D. Rockefeller or [sic] Andrew Carnegie . . . claimed to apply the modern, rational methods of business to the administration of charitable deeds, which they considered to be outdated and deficient" (Guilhot 2007, 451).

Emphasizing novelty also carries with it risks of being seen to serve topical agendas. This is particularly the case where there is a close link between the promoters of social innovation and government, as in the case of the United Kingdom: "More than £350 million of public money has been spent on social entrepreneurship, charity capacity-building and social ventures (Mulgan 2007), helping to develop an estimated £24 billion social enterprise sector that now employs 800,000 people. In the UK, particularly in England, social enterprise has become elided with delivery of public services under contract to state agencies (Teasdale, Alcock, and Smith 2012)" (Grimm *et al.* 2013, 443). This heavy and very visible investment is connected with the UK government's "Big Society" initiatives, including the "Big Society Bank", creating a significant risk that the social innovation agenda, and related ideas such as "co-production", come to be seen as synonymous with austerity and as a cloak for the extension of ideological moves to reduce the scale and influence of the public sector in favor of the private sector. Although these initiatives appear to be consistent with moves towards local empowerment and autonomy, their prescriptions are not grounded in any specific understanding of the concerns of any particular community, but rather in a belief *a priori* that such institutions are appropriate ways to respond to a diagnosis of "what is wrong" with society as a whole. This appears to be in tension with actually relinquishing even some control over purpose and direction to beneficiaries of the process. The ability of social innovation and co-design to build social capacity are nevertheless particularly important in these contexts. If power is "handed back" to communities, in the absence of capability building at the individual, family and community levels, merely informing citizens and communities that they are now able to take charge of their lives is likely to set off a process that will be controlled and dominated by those who already have the capabilities and resources to act, potentially disenfranchising the intended beneficiaries and in no way increasing social capital. Indeed, the rush by large service contractor companies to take over service delivery in the UK under the banner of the Big Society might be seen as a very precise demonstration of this phenomenon (Elliott, Stone, and Beverley 2013), and one which directly disadvantages existing charities and community groups. This concern is reminiscent of the ambivalence of the Social Justice narrative towards government: mitigating the risk of becoming dependent, while still receiving funding to operate, and balancing the concern that state power might smother local volition, is not a negligible project.

Of course, the Philanthrocapitalistic narrative can also be seen as a subterfuge for establishing private sector hegemony over social innovation, or for minimizing public sector expenditure in pursuit of a neoliberal ideological model of society: "Today, philanthropic foundations invest in companies shown to radically exacerbate the very ill-health outcomes and economic inequalities they aim to battle, even as they acknowledge that their investment decisions may be perpetuating the problems they attempt to remedy. Central to their efforts is less the denial or the masking of self-interest, but instead the capitalization of self-interest itself, the questionable upholding of self-interest as something indistinguishable from collective abundance" (McGoey 2012, 197).

Novelty, in the form of claims to miraculous new capabilities or discovering a mother-lode of silver bullets, then, is not without its risks, and on the whole appears potentially antagonistic to the sort of social innovation we describe, which is much more oriented to learning, questioning and local invention. It is not that social innovation is not discovering new ways of working, but rather that it should be seen as an on-going expression of everyday people's desire for change, and that making it the centerpiece of a polished, corporatized exposition of the latest managerial technology, or placing it at the core of an ideological push to remodel society, seems unlikely to connect at the right level with those needs, if anyone remembers to listen to them at all as the movers and shakers leap onto the stage. It also risks displacing the long-term commitment and experience of people and organizations who know the terrain very well. Without assuming that every existing organization in the social innovation has a right to continue to exist, it would seem potentially counterproductive to simply sweep aside existing knowledge and relationships without inspecting them thoroughly for what they may enable.

Scaling

The ambition of social innovation, then, also seems to be under attack. It has been pointed out that both the Philanthrocapitalistic and the Reform narratives look for major impact across social systems, generally expressed as a need for "scaling". This is one of the main supports advanced for the claimed superiority of business approaches, which are seen to be inherently well-adapted to achieving large-scale impact, particularly when able to access the resources of major multi-national corporations. Larsson and Brandsen, however, challenge the idea that scaling (or "rolling-out") is a "logical final step for a mature innovation" (2016, 294), the absence of which represents failure. They suggest that it is a concept imported from business and government which carries normative implications that "deny alternative conceptions of systemic change that rely less on big breakthroughs and more on incremental groundswell delivery (Garcia and Calantone 2002, Osborne 1998) [and] . . . consistently undervalue the role of alternative providers such as voluntary organisations and informal initiatives . . ." (295). In addition to reflecting the current dominant discourse of organizations with which we are familiar, the assumption behind the drive for "scale" seems to be that, in order to be worthy of investment, an innovation should have a significant impact on the long-term well-being of a significant number of beneficiaries, and to generate sufficient support because of this for it to continue to function without further contributions. This is a form of sustainability—but it is not the only form. From the Participatory Design tradition, Iversen and Dindler (2014) propose four "ideal typical forms" of sustainability, adding "maintaining, replicating and evolving" to scaling. In maintaining, "initiatives . . . exist in the same way, and within the same context, after the project is completed"; scaling occurs where the ". . . initiative . . . remains relatively stable, but the context changes, typically from a small group to a larger group or organisation" (157); replicating occurs when the ". . . initiative . . . remains relatively stable, but the context of this initiative is changed"; and evolving occurs where the ". . . initiative is subject to change or acts as a catalyst for new processes. The context of the initiative may also be subject to change, as ideas develop beyond organizational boundaries" (158).

These distinctions offer more precision in describing the possible paths of expansion of innovation, where it expands at all. Each type of sustainability carries with it different implications for the engagement of agency as innovation spreads. In maintaining, the original participants remain in control; in scaling, more participants are involved without having the opportunity to change the design, as occurs with replication. Evolution, on the other hand, offers the possibility that the innovation will be adapted to each new context to which it is extended. Scaling and replication imply that no further adaptation is needed before an innovation is "rolled out", and therefore bear the marks of the non-participative approaches we have discussed. This highlights the tension between the ambition of both the Philanthrocapitalistic and the Reform narratives and the establishment of the sort of "authentic" participation called for in co-design, particularly on longer-term time scales or across multiple locations.[2] "Despite paying lip service to innovation, authorities tend to prefer what is known and tested—be it in the tradition of state regulation and standard-setting or through a swing towards approaches that are believed to work well in the business sector" (Brandsen, Evers, *et al.* 2016, 310). The tension is also manifest in the conceptualization of the outcome of innovation as a model, and the idea that it can be applied elsewhere, based on initial co-design, and without further investigation or adaptation. Except for the "business knows best" proponents, who bring their models with them, co-designing models is not inconsistent with any of the narratives. However, driven by the desire for impact and scale these models may still be presented, once established, as being unproblematically applicable in other contexts without further involvement of beneficiaries at the new site. This seems just as true for those who believe they are demonstrating a new form of capitalism as those who see themselves as reshaping government: perhaps, therefore, the "major distinction in society must not always be between market and state but could also be between universal and contextualised perspectives (Scott 1998)" (Larsson and Brandsen 2016, 296).

The question of scaling can also be seen as a challenge to the professional boundaries of design: "if we want to solve big social problem [sic] we need more than design thinking. . . . We need the critical questioning of social policy alongside the creative freshness of design. Indeed, if we want to achieve long-term social transformation, we must be equipped to develop, test and spread robust theories of change" (Schulman 2010, cited in Hillgren, Seravalli, and Emilson 2011, 172). Again, this reflects the desire to achieve major change and the confidence that models can be developed to achieve that. However, the tension between local and universal, between standardized scale and adaptive localism is also evident. Indeed, the former approach, even if it is assumed to be the only way to achieve significant results, may not actually be as practical as the latter: "The repeated 'success, scale, fail' experience of the last 20 years of development practice suggests something super boring: Development projects thrive or tank according to the specific dynamics of the place in which they're applied. It's not that you test something in one place, then scale it up to 50. It's that you test it in one place, then test it in another, then another" (Hobbes 2014, 61).

Of course, we should also acknowledge that learning accumulates across multiple sites, as solutions are tried out, adapted and evaluated. The point is not whether this might, or might not, lead to faster implementation of solutions when they are introduced to new sites. It is to recognize that each time a solution developed somewhere else is introduced to a new context, it should be opened up to co-design and adaptation to the needs of people in that context.

Inherent Value

Even with these points in mind, we might still remain convinced of the inherent value of social innovation. The Philanthrocapitalistic narrative offers never before seen levels of efficiency and impact, and cutting-edge tools; the Reform narrative holds out the promise of a newly adaptive and resilient society where outmoded institutional forms have been replaced with flexible, responsive ones; and the Social Justice narrative champions empowerment, inclusion, voice and justice. How could collaboration to achieve these attractive results be seen in a bad light, particularly when it is dressed in its modern form of "co-design"? Depending on your value preferences, surely there is something here for anyone?

Of course, such a discursively constructed blind spot does not resist scrutiny for very long. The apparent inherent good of social innovation rests on shaky foundations. The illusion is sometimes established by defining social innovation to exclude negative evaluations: social innovation is not just novel, but "more effective, efficient, sustainable or just" than present arrangements (Phills, Deiglmeier, and Miller 2008, 36). By definition, if positive outcomes are not achieved, neither is social innovation. There is also an implicit bias towards the positive in the terms "social" and "innovation" themselves. "Social" seems to indicate a more human alternative to innovation that is merely "economic", and "innovation" alludes to both progress and creativity. However, any attempt to distinguish "social" innovation from other forms of innovation leads inexorably to a conclusion that all the aspects of innovation, technological, economic or social, are inextricably entwined with each other ". . . and can only be completely captured in their interaction with one another" (Howaldt and Schwarz 2010, 21). Even innovation itself, following Schumpeter, destroys as it creates. If social innovation is indeed about change in social practices, often accompanying, enabling or shaping other forms of innovation (and vice versa), then it is inherently contested: ". . . social innovations are necessarily also conflict-ridden and political by nature. . . . Resistance and opposition, risks and dangers, as well as negative effects and misuse need to be taken seriously" (Larsson and Brandsen 2016, 297). As pointed out by Howaldt and Schwarz, "the commonly found normative link between social innovation and socially esteemed values overlooks the fact that different purposes and interests can indeed be pursued with a social innovation depending on the related utility and prevailing rationale and that these accordingly by no means have to be regarded as 'good' per se . . ." (2010, 31, see also Nicholls, Simon, and Gabriel 2015, 5). Because changes in social practices involve the cessation of existing ways of doing things, and because they are intended to bring about consequences that may be valued differently by different groups, neither the purposes of social innovation, nor the changes that arise consequent to the taking of action, can be considered inherently positive. The value of an innovation is also recognized in a context that, over time, may not remain the same as when it was initiated and so will always be subject to renegotiation, both with reference to its original intent and from the point of view of the different groups implicated in or affected by the change as it occurred. Furthermore, by definition, innovation is uncertain; as a risky matter, it may not produce the desired results, and there is no guarantee it will produce anything of value at all—"failure" must be a possibility, and may have negative consequences for those involved (Larsson and Brandsen 2016, 296). The chain of causality that leads from good intentions to eventual results is also very difficult to map out even retrospectively, and impossible to chart in advance. Not only are social arrangements by definition too complex to predict, particularly when they are in interaction with the technological and economic aspects of innovation, but there are multiple contextual and historical factors that will affect the way an innovation is received and modified by those it impacts.

Bearing in mind the provisional nature of the outcomes of social innovation, it is also not possible to achieve a fixed evaluation, even at the individual project level. The concepts of failure and success are themselves contestable. "Failure" is attributed: it is not an objective, deontological quality, nor is it self-evidently present or absent in any situation. Different groups may hold different views on what is desirable or good, or choose to apply different standards, in order to assert that failure has occurred or to deny such a claim. Hence, the attribution of failure is often controversial. A failure declared may form the basis of future success, either because lessons are learned or because new conditions emerge that allow novel action to occur; a success may turn out to have unintended consequences that led some to later regret its achievement. Even if we focus on co-design as the mechanism by which social innovation comes about, and by which relational capital is built, we cannot attribute any essentially positive quality to it, since the new relationships are only a potential for future innovation; no particular value inheres in them until they are put to use. A limited sense of control can be maintained by defining performance indicators or other "objective" standards by which to assess what is achieved; but these are only meaningful in the context in which they were conceived, and different perspectives and changing contexts may make them irrelevant or even deceptive. Such "measures" assert the priority of a certain set of purposes, but at the same time exclude both competing intentions and new directions that may become possible as the context of the activity evolves. The implication is that social innovation can only be evaluated based on its outcomes, including the potential it creates for further action, as seen from a particular situated perspective. Social innovation is neither inherently positive nor neutral; indeed, its evaluation cannot be fixed, but will be the subject of on-going negotiation, in each context in which it is taking place, as new interlocutors join existing ones and review their evolving perspectives on social practices, institutions and purposes in a changing environment.

Intentionality

Social innovation is indisputably well-intentioned, regardless of the complexities it may experience in delivering on those intentions. The commitment of social innovators to strive for something of value can even be seen as partially definitive of social innovation. Franz *et al.* state that "[t]he intentionality of social innovation is what distinguishes it from social change. Social change just happens" (Franz, Hochgerner, and Howaldt 2012, 4). Innovation constitutes purposive action, which brings about observable outcomes, and the term may be used to refer either to the process or action being taken (as long as it produces tangible results), or to the "new" state of social practices. But when is the "intention" that drives social innovation formed? Is it a problem-solution dyad emerging more or less fully formed in an entrepreneur's head? Or does it begin with a more or less unformed area of interest or attention, which is then subject to an iterative and largely unpredictable process of refinement and possibly action, until some sort of fully developed design emerges? Many of the design models adopted in social innovation and co-design have just such an iterative, convergent, experimental process at their heart. Does the application of these processes constitute social innovation in its own right, or must that label be reserved for when an observable effect justifies a declaration that it has occurred? Moreover, does intention apply to the new practices, or to the changed relationships which represent the "infrastructuring" resulting from social innovation? How is intention to be operationalized in a context where purpose is considered as arising from an open-ended negotiation between stakeholders with conflicting interests and perspectives?

In the design world, Sanders and Stappers attribute the slowness with which co-design has been able to influence "the man-made world" to the way it challenges existing power structures and consumerism, as well as its perceived irrelevance to the logic of the marketplace (2008, 9–10). These tensions seem inevitable when co-design is placed in the context of an ideology of rational progress that underlies the Philanthrocapitalistic narrative: the ceding of control which is inherent in the values of genuine participation challenges not only the priority of the "rational purpose" and the supremacy of the "technological expertise" that motivates this ideology, but also appears to unacceptably dissipate attention (and therefore resources and time) towards matters that the "project owners" may not consider relevant to solving the problem at hand. It may also threaten to blur the project boundaries, making it impossible to know when the project is complete and therefore to evaluate whether "success" has been achieved. For rationalists (or managerialists), responding to the challenges raised by participation in social innovation is likely to be seen as confusion and lack of vision, lack of accountability or transparent performance measures, as well as inefficiency and impracticality.

The situation is not very different when co-design is considered from the perspective of the Reform narrative. The same tension remains around the ceding of control over purpose, in the sense that the expressed aim is to respond to concerns of the state, or respond to "macro-trends" that are taken as self-evidently demanding action. The tension around technological mastery is less and of a different nature: whereas the Philanthrocapitalistic narrative relies on a foundational story that new technologies, whether they are physical, managerial or economic, have enabled solutions that were only recently inconceivable, and therefore not within the capability of communities to solve for themselves, the Reform narrative is centrally concerned with the establishment of a recognized body of practice—almost a profession—to drive social innovation. While this perspective seems much more prone to accept the participation of beneficiaries and other participants, it still relies on at least a partial appropriation of credit for the process, or ownership, to demonstrate the value of the profession. Nevertheless, it is possible to imagine a more comprehensive co-design process occurring under the Reform ideology, particularly where government explicitly allows power to be transferred to communities, or where government has intentionally or unintentionally vacated that space. The possibility even exists that the institutions supporting social innovation, including enabling institutions such as funders and expert laboratories of thought leaders, might be convinced to use their emerging power and credibility to negotiate space for co-design to occur. Beyond these negotiated bounds, it is likely that similar criticisms of co-design as those arising in the rational progress world would apply, particularly where a process extends beyond the space negotiated for it, at which stage it is likely to be declared "out of control" or out of scope.

Even from the perspective of the Social Justice narrative, which at first sight seems to be consistent with, and possibly even congenial to co-design, there is still a risk that the social innovator will see the values of democracy, equality and voice that underpin it as incontestable and not open to interpretation by participants. However, these need to be brought to life in a specific context, particularly with regard to the means by which voice is exerted, which may have strong cultural implications, and also in terms of what actors are acceptable collaborators (such as commercial interests). Even the specifics of trade-offs between economic, social and environmental concerns need to be subject to the co-design process. The risk for practitioners in this tradition is that they attempt to influence the process to achieve their particular interpretations of these values, rather than truly relinquishing control of the process to end-users.

The problem of trade-offs between values, where co-design is being sought, is a challenge for all the narratives of social innovation. Even though some intentions, such as eradication of disease or adequate food supply, are universal, there are still frequently compromises to be made between them, or with other values that may not be the same as those of the social innovator. It is tempting to suggest that the focus should be on particular priority issues—indeed this makes up a significant part of the "business-like" methods of the philanthropic foundations. Of course, at a high level, no one would deny the importance of maternal health or safe water supply, but the ways that those are delivered at the local level will still require value judgments, and so must be achieved holistically. This at best complicates the intentional nature of the social innovation. It also has significant implications for the organization of "implementation" of projects—if controls are set to ensure that the high-level goal is prioritized, and that what is implemented is reliably what was designed, the risk cannot be ignored that a program designed to achieve it will not be accepted, or that it causes unexpected negative consequences.

The question of intention is also relevant when considering the different levels of social innovation. Even if it is possible to manage, plan and implement change at the social level in a controlled way, it is very difficult to apply the same sort of concept of planning and control (and therefore of accountability) to societal or systemic change, even more so when the inevitable interaction occurring between the levels is considered. Is it necessary to seek to control all levels of the social level intervention to ensure that they contribute as intended to societal programs and systemic goals? How can the impact of increased social capacity be foreseen when social conditions are constantly evolving in unpredictable ways? This appears, at the very least, to be a significant organizational or management challenge, and leaves the hint of a question as to how far it is necessary or feasible to direct and control social innovation. This issue brings us back to the concept of "meta-design", which "represents a cultural shift from design as 'planning' to design as 'seeding' . . . with the goal of producing more open and evolving systems of interaction" (Giaccardi 2005, 348).

Responding to the challenge of co-design in social innovation therefore requires that "intention" not be taken as fixed or absolute, but as something to be negotiated over time and between participants in the process, even as the participants and context may themselves be changing. Intention becomes an accomplishment, indeed the central accomplishment of co-design, rather than external reality: it is part of the design process, and must co-evolve with the (provisional) solutions that are produced. It also requires that we admit the presence of politics in the process, since these open-ended negotiations are inevitably also negotiations between differing preferences and values, leading to the view of "design things . . . as a space for what DiSalvo (2010) calls 'political design,' and the possibility that heterogeneous stakeholders could 'make decisions about the projects we choose to take on, the people we choose to work with, and the solutions we co-create'" (Emilson 2014, 28).

The Challenge

If we are to respond to the challenge raised by placing co-design in its fullest expression at the heart of social innovation, this discussion suggests that we will need to achieve a number of things. The fundamental question to be answered is if, and how, it might be possible to continuously and practically enable and preserve agency as the driver of social innovation. Given that the process of innovation cannot itself be seen as inherently positive, we also need to understand how to deal with the ethical questions that will inevitably arise in achieving this project, as different interests, perspectives and preferences must be reconciled. Since the process we are seeking to understand and promote is essentially a local process, we also need to understand how it might achieve effects beyond the local level, while still remaining true to the principle of agency which defines the approach, and how the effect of local agency and local ethical decisions might nevertheless lead to broader change in areas of interest at the societal and systemic level—in some sense a change in the context that affects global interactions in significant ways. How can intention be enacted at this broader level? Despite its local focus, the vision of social innovation being developed here seems to be reflected in what Unger calls a "maximal solution", aimed at change at the level of the whole of society, its institutional arrangements and its dominant form of consciousness: ". . . the social innovation movement must undertake the small initiatives that have the greatest potential to foreshadow, by persuasive example, the transformation of those arrangements and of that consciousness. It must launch such initiatives even as it seeks to redress recognised and immediate problems in a particular piece of society" (Unger 2015, 237). This process is inherently political and radically unresolved: it is contextually, institutionally and temporally situated and co-evolving with social and material structures, institutions and arrangements, "an open-ended exploration where prototypical practices are explored that engender favourable conditions for the on-going negotiation of meaning" (Björgvinsson 2008, 85).

By extending our attention beyond the "outcomes" of social innovation, to encompass the social interaction that is actually producing it, we open up a need for new ways to understand those interactions. What should they look like? How are they to be influenced to be productive? Who determines what productive means? It would be tempting at this point to assume that some form of consensus and fellow-feeling might be necessary to enable the best form of collaboration: "Infrastructuring also provides the ground for building the 'relational qualities' that Jégou and Manzini (2008) stress as a precondition for collaborative organisations: 'Peer-to-peer collaboration calls for trust, and trust calls for relational qualities: no relational qualities means no trust and no collaboration' (p. 33)" (Hillgren, Seravalli, and Emilson 2011, 180). However, such a harmonious, or at least non-conflictual, process seems likely to be the exception rather than the rule. Indeed, it might be suggested that it is the very contrasts in positions and interests that enable innovation to arise from the co-design process: "the motivations for social innovation will usually come from tensions; contradictions; dissatisfactions; and the negation of what exists. . . . these tensions are not unfortunate by-products of innovation; they are part of its nature . . ." (Mulgan 2012, 21). The picture is one where the activity of the "struggle", far from hindering innovation, is actually its chief enabler. The question, then, is what sort of relationship can preserve that difference while enabling joint production?

Björgvinsson *et al.*, drawing on Mouffe, propose seeing it as an "agonistic struggle" that ". . . does not presuppose the possibility of consensus and rational conflict resolution, but rather proposes a polyphony of voices and mutually vigorous but tolerant disputes among groups united by passionate engagement" (2012, 129). They examine their experience of a series of workshops that took place while establishing a social innovation incubator. These had been designed to allow significant input from marginalized social groups, and Björgvinsson *et al.* note that their resulting proposals would have been unacceptable to the authorities, except that some participants (representing the authorities) were able to "translate" them in a way that could be funded and carried forward. In this case, the conflict in perspectives was never "resolved": no-one yielded to an adversary, and authority remained (at least apparently) in place. However, the application of different perspectives and skills allowed the work to proceed in a way that preserved at least some of its potentially subversive intent. The "outcome" was in no sense final—it was another step on a pathway that led in a general direction, that was being laid down as the work progressed, and which could not have been known in advance—a progress through a sequence of "adjacent possibles" (Kauffman 1995). Björgvinsson *et al.* propose that "[t]o capture this change we think it may be useful to shift the frame of reference from design politics for democracy at work towards democratisation as political design in an agonistic public framework" (2012, 129).

The view of social innovation that is developing in this work is one that rejects grand solutions and adopts a realistic, but nevertheless hopeful, orientation to enable action, in a style described by Mulgan (drawing on Unger) as

> . . . advocating systematic experimentation, a model of social change as self-aware but also cautious about the hubris of grand plans and reforms. Its core is a belief in people as struggling with constraint and contingency, but able to create entirely new ideas and things; a belief in permanent innovation so that 'we rethink and redesign our productive tasks in the course of executing them' using 'the smaller variations that are at hand to produce the bigger variations that do not yet exist'; and a practical commitment to making change internal to social and political institutions, through permanent experimentation. In this, cooperation and innovation are seen as twins, but also in tension with each other since innovation will tend to disrupt.
>
> (2012, 34)

Notes

1 "L'unité factice que semble indiquer la réunion des acteurs associatifs et des entreprises sociales au sein d'un même ensemble, l'ESS, dissimule l'hostilité du discours entrepreneurial envers les associations. Ces deux acteurs ne représentent pas deux approches de l'action « sociale » qui pourraient cohabiter. La légitimité même du modèle associatif est constamment niée à chaque ligne du discours des entrepreneurs sociaux: inefficaces, dépendantes des pouvoirs publics, paralysées par l'idéologie—pour ces derniers, les associés sont le passé et sont donc voués à mourir. Jean-Marc Borello, président du groupe SOS, géant de l'entrepreneuriat social, aime ainsi à répéter que « dans dix ans, il y aura 10 fois moins d'associations en France ». Avec de tels amis, le secteur associatif n'a pas besoin d'ennemis" (Sevilla 2016).

2 It should be noted that we, as Iversen and Dindler, are using these terms in their pure sense, for conceptual clarity. We recognize that in practice many social innovators will speak of replication, understanding full well the need to adapt to local conditions, and therefore, in practice, intending what we would call evolution. The use of the term replication in such circumstances probably has more to do with conforming to beliefs about how businesses should be seen to develop and roll out solutions than as a description of empirical reality. However, the concern still exists that real attempts may be made, based on this language, to efficiently "replicate" solutions, when evolution is really the objective.

References

Björgvinsson, Erling Bjarki. 2008. "Open-Ended Participatory Design as Prototypical Practice." *CoDesign* 4 (2):85–99. doi: 10.1080/15710880802095400.

Björgvinsson, Erling Bjarki, Pelle Ehn, and Per-Anders Hillgren. 2012. "Agonistic Participatory Design: Working with Marginalised Social Movements." *CoDesign* 8 (2–3):127–144. doi: 10.1080/15710882.2012.672577.

Brandsen, T., A. Evers, S. Cattacin, and A. Zimmer. 2016. "The Good, the Bad and the Ugly in Social Innovation." In *Social Innovations in the Urban Context*, edited by T. Brandsen, S. Cattacin, A. Evers, and A. Zimmer, 303–310. Dordrecht: Springer.

Dart, Raymond. 2004. "The Legitimacy of Social Enterprise." *Nonprofit Management & Leadership* 14 (4):411–424.

DiSalvo, Carl. 2010. "Design, Democracy and Agonistic Pluralism." DRS 2010, Montreal.

Edwards, Michael. 2008. "Philanthrocapitalism and Its Limits." *International Journal of Not-for-Profit Law* 10 (2):22–29.

Elliott, Cameron, Christopher Stone, and Stephen Beverley. 2013. *Whatever Happened to the Big Society?* Sydney: Centre for Policy Development.

Emilson, Anders. 2014. "Designing Conditions for the Social." In *Making Futures: Marginal Notes on Innovation, Design, and Democracy*, edited by Pelle Ehn, Elisabet M. Nilsson, and Richard Topgaard, 17–33. Cambridge, MA: MIT Press.

Franz, Hans-Werner, Josef Hochgerner, and Jürgen Howaldt, eds. 2012. *Challenge Social Innovation: Potentials for Business, Social Entrepreneurship, Welfare and Civil Society.* 1st ed. Berlin: Springer.

Garcia, Rosanna, and Roger Calantone. 2002. "A Critical Look at Technological Innovation Typology and Innovativeness Terminology: A Literature Review." *Journal of Product Innovation Management* 19 (2):110–132. doi: 10.1111/1540–5885.1920110.

Giaccardi, Elisa. 2005. "Metadesign as Emergent Design Culture." *Leonardo* 38 (4):342–349.

Grimm, Robert, Christopher Fox, Susan Baines, and Kevin Albertson. 2013. "Social Innovation, an Answer to Contemporary Societal Challenges? Locating the Concept in Theory and Practice." *Innovation-the European Journal of Social Science Research* 26 (4):436–455. doi: 10.1080/13511610.2013.848163.

Guilhot, Nicolas. 2007. "Reforming the World: George Soros, Global Capitalism and the Philanthropic Management of the Social Sciences1." *Critical Sociology* 33 (3):447–477. doi: 10.1163/156916307x188988.

Hillgren, Per-Anders, Anna Seravalli, and Anders Emilson. 2011. "Prototyping and infrastructuring in design for social innovation." *CoDesign* 7 (3–4):169–183. doi: 10.1080/15710882.2011.630474.

Hobbes, Michael. 2014. "How to Save the World." *The New Republic* 245 (19):52.

Howaldt, Jürgen, and Michael Schwarz. 2010. "Social Innovation: Concepts, Research Fields and International Trends." In *Studies for Innovation in a Modern Working Environment—International Monitoring*, edited by Klaus Henning and Frank Hees. Aachen: IMA/ZLW.

Iversen, Ole Sejer, and Christian Dindler. 2014. "Sustaining Participatory Design Initiatives." *CoDesign* 10 (3–4):153–170. doi: 10.1080/15710882.2014.963124.

Jégou, François, and Ezio Manzini. 2008. *Collaborative Services: Social Innovation and Design for Sustainability*. Milan: Edizioni POLI.design.

Jenkins, Garry W. 2011. "Who's Afraid of Philanthrocapitalism?" *Case Western Reserve Law Review* 61 (3):753.

Kauffman, Stuart A. 1995. *At Home in the Universe: The Search for the Laws of Self-Organization and Complexity*. New York: Oxford University Press.

Kuttner, Robert. 1997. *Everything for Sale: The Virtues and Limits of Markets*. 1st ed. New York: Alfred A. Knopf.

Larsson, O. S., and T. Brandsen. 2016. "The Implicit Normative Assumptions of Social Innovation Research: Embracing the Dark Side." In *Social Innovations in the Urban Context*, edited by T. Brandsen, S. Cattacin, A. Evers, and A. Zimmer, 293–302. Dordrecht: Springer.

McGoey, Linsey. 2012. "Philanthrocapitalism and Its Critics." *Poetics* 40 (2):185–199. doi: 10.1016/j.poetic.2012.02.006.

Mulgan, Geoff. 2012. "Social Innovation Theories: Can Theory Catch Up with Practice?" In *Challenge Social Innovation: Potentials for Business, Social Entrepreneurship, Welfare and Civil Society*, edited by Hans-Werner Franz, Josef Hochgerner, and Jürgen Howaldt, 19–42. Berlin: Springer.

Mulgan, Geoff. 2014. *Design in Public and Social Innovation: What Works and What Could Work Better*. London: NESTA.

Mulgan, Geoff, Simon Tucker, Rushnara Ali, and Ben Sanders. 2007. *Social Innovation: What It Is, Why It Matters and How It Can Be Accelerated*. Oxford: Skoll Centre for Social Entrepreneurship, Saïd Business School, University of Oxford.

Nicholls, Alex, Julie Simon, and Madeleine Gabriel. 2015. "Introduction: Dimensions of Social Innovation." In *New Frontiers in Social Innovation Research*, edited by Alex Nicholls, Julie Simon, and Madeleine Gabriel, 1–26. Basingstoke: Palgrave Macmillan.

Osborne, Stephen P. 1998. "Naming the Beast: Defining and Classifying Service Innovations in Social Policy." *Human Relations* 51 (9):1133–1154. doi: 10.1177/001872679805100902.

Phills, James A. Jr., Kriss Deiglmeier, and Dale T. Miller. 2008. "Rediscovering Social Innovation." *Stanford Social Innovation Review* 6 (4):34–43.

Sanders, Elizabeth B. N., and Pieter Jan Stappers. 2008. "Co-Creation and the New Landscapes of Design." *CoDesign* 4 (1):5–18. doi: 10.1080/15710880701875068.

Schulman, Sarah. 2010. "Design Thinking Is Not Enough." http://www.inwithfor. org/2010/01/design-thinking-is-not-enough/.

Scott, James C. 1998. *Seeing Like a State: How Certain Schemes to Improve the Human Condition Have Failed, Yale ISPS Series*. New Haven, CT: Yale University Press.

Sevilla, Pablo. 2016. "Associations: faire face à l'offensive des entrepreneurs sociaux," accessed 6/6/16. http://www.revue-ballast.fr/associations-face-a-loffensive-des-entre preneurs-sociaux.

Teasdale, Simon, Pete Alcock, and Graham Smith. 2012. "Legislating for the Big Society? The Case of the Public Services (Social Value) Bill." *Public Money & Management* 32 (3):201–208. doi: 10.1080/09540962.2012.676277.

Unger, Roberto Mangabeira. 2015. "Conclusion: The Task of the Social Innovation Movement." In *New Frontiers in Social Innovation Research*, edited by Alex Nicholls, Julie Simon, and Madeleine Gabriel, 233–251. Basingstoke: Palgrave Macmillan.

Young Foundation. 2007. *Social Innovation: What It Is, Why It Matters and How It Can Be Accelerated*. Oxford: Skoll Centre for Social Entrepreneurship, Saïd Business School, University of Oxford.

Part 2

An Integrating Proposition

The next part of this book will offer a proposal that might meet the challenge outlined in chapter 3. It will proceed in three steps. First, there will be an examination of the ontology of the co-designed social innovation process we are attempting to understand, as a local phenomenon that gives rise to the "social", in a form of agonistic, relational sense-making. This will address the question of how power and constraint are exerted by institutions and actors, but at the same time how actors find space for agency and room to subvert these constraints. In chapter 5, we will examine the epistemology of the process: how actors in the process of social innovation might become aware of the progress that they are making, where they are going and where they came from: how a collective, reflexive awareness of action and reaction might be developed and how that might be seen as a form of infrastructuring. Chapter 6 will examine how direction is formed in this process and how it gives rise to larger patterns and macro-processes.

We will not propose a further elaboration of tools, techniques or the articulation of a process that "should" be followed, but a more descriptive approach, which orients us to the general nature of social innovation and suggests a set of conceptual levers or heuristics to understand and influence it. These might be seen as "sensitizing concepts" (Blumer 1954), that ". . . can be used to 'remind' (Wittgenstein 1953, 127) us of specific events and features in that situation that might be of importance, that might otherwise pass us by unnoticed" (Shotter 2009, 138); that are alive in the act and allow us to more satisfactorily grasp options to move forward in the moment. This approach respects the unique nature of each situation in which social innovation is generated, and the need to co-design solutions anew in every context in which it is sought. It also resists the idea that social innovation can be pinned down to a defined process that, properly enacted, will reliably bring about results desired by any of the parties. Instead, we assume that every *thing* that brings about social innovation is established *de novo*, inventing its own rules, but that it also draws upon and is constrained by what has gone before. More than this, it reserves for participants in this process the status of agents capable of reframing perspectives on a situation, contesting alternative views of it and creating new proposals for ways forward. We do not believe that the agency of any individual in a social innovation process can be promoted by subjecting them, even with their consent, to a prescribed process that was developed without awareness of any of the specificities of the context in which they are working. However, we do believe that exposing people to possibilities that existed in the past, or speculations that might be made, can assist them in developing new futures that might become the dreams or meet the needs of people who may not yet have articulated them, and enable the active exploration of how to bring those futures to life.

4 Actors and Structure

It has been asserted that social innovation is a portrayal of the process(es) by which social practices are changed (Franz, Hochgerner, and Howaldt 2012, 6). This formulation, as useful as it is, remains problematic on several levels, not only because it is tautological. Firstly, it sets up an apparent opposition between the process of change and the subject of that change, which tends to suggest that "social practices" are themselves normally stable. However, it is clear that these practices are themselves constructs, labels attached to actions that must be (re)produced in order to be brought into existence. They are by nature semiotic and subject to interpretation. Hence, they are at once variable in their repetition, and in their (re)construction, either through changes in the practices themselves, or through the attachment of different significance to them. Understanding social practices is a process of sensemaking that emphasizes the necessity of seeing them in their context and as resulting from strategic acts of framing and interpretation. Secondly, the meaning of "social" must be investigated: what is included and excluded in this term? Are changed organizational configurations around a new technology to be considered social and separate from the technological change, or should they be seen together? How can we distinguish economic practices from social practices—are not the former merely a class of the latter, a subset that happens to involve the exchange of value as its object? But then should that exchange of value not be understood in a broader relational context, which needs to include an explanation of how value is assigned differentially in different societies or cultures? Certainly, economic and technological change appear to be linked, if we consider the growth of the information technology and communication industries over the past thirty years. But this growth seems to have had dramatic social effects as well, including significantly impacting the practice of social innovation itself. Is it possible, or even desirable, to distinguish between these forms of change?

Some argue that it is essential to acknowledge social innovation as a unique form of innovation in order to "make the systemic connection and interdependence of social and technological innovation processes comprehensible", even though the end being sought is still "an integrated theory of socio-technological innovation" (Howaldt and Schwarz 2010, 8). This seems to be a reaction against the idea that social innovation is something that follows technological innovation, an assertion that the social should not be seen as subsidiary. However, and without in any way diminishing the necessity of recognizing a social dimension of innovation, the very act of separating the social out from the technical or economic facets of innovation can be seen as erecting an unnecessary opposition that encourages the differential evaluation of the social, economic and technological spheres. On what basis can we make this distinction, and why would we wish to introduce it if not absolutely necessary?

In addition to the problematic nature of the "social" aspect of the practices that we seek to understand, we lack a framework to understand the actions that (re)produce or constitute them. Are these actions to be understood as solely the acts of individuals? Or do we have to take into account that they must be performed, and only have meaning, in a relational context: that is, in the context of others, both individual and collective? In this latter case, though, what is the substance of the collective? And how does a relational context deal with inanimate objects that are nevertheless vital to performing and understanding practices, such as the computer; or the welfare office; or abstract, but nevertheless powerful, institutional "actors", such as "the law"?

Actor-Network Theory

In our discussion of design approaches, we observed that there has been a triple decentering: of design as a discipline; of the artifact as the focus of design; and of the designer, as non-expert participants become involved in the practice of design. Attempting to understand what this means for how design is done, and how it influences those who participate in it, either in "use before use" or "design after design", has led to a view of what is occurring as an on-going, always provisional interplay between artifacts, which are often themselves abstract or "proto-typical practices", and human participants. As the interactions proceed, both the artifacts and the relationships between the human actors change or co-evolve, as experiments are made and participants strive to reach the stage where they can go on. Design is envisaged as a process that no longer has either an object or an expert at its center, but which has become a "socio-material assembly" (Binder *et al.* 2015). This conceptualization is redolent of actor-network theory (ANT) (Callon and Latour 1981, Latour 1987), which has strongly influenced a number of researchers in the Participatory Design tradition, and we propose now to explore more fully the implications of seeing social innovation through this lens.

Before listing some key aspects of ANT for our purposes, it is important to note that it is a complex, diverse, shifting and multivalent body of work, which would defy a comprehensive survey that did not reveal its diversity as much as its coherence, even if we intended to give one. Law says "I've talked of 'it', an actor-network theory, but there is no 'it'. Rather it is a diaspora that overlaps with other intellectual traditions. As I have already hinted, it is better to talk of 'material semiotics' rather than 'actor-network theory'. This better catches the openness, uncertainty, revisability and diversity of the most interesting work" (Law 2007). It offers no explanations: "it is better understood as a toolkit for telling interesting stories about, and interfering in, those relations. More profoundly, it is a sensibility to the messy practices of relationality and materiality of the world" (2). It is built on three methodological principles: agnosticism towards the claims of anyone engaged in a controversy; "generalized symmetry", or the use of "a single repertoire" to describe "considerations concerning both Society and Nature"; and "free association", which ". . . abandon[s] all a priori distinctions between natural and social events" (Callon 1986, 4). It is this particular disregard for the distinction between human and non-human that has become one of the most commonly recognized features of ANT, and which makes it particularly congenial to understanding the "socio-material assemblies" or *things* that we propose as the central site of social innovation. However, of more interest at this point in our discussion is the way it develops its understanding of the "social". Latour proposes that "the social cannot be construed as a kind of material or domain" and challenges the status of a " 'social explanation' of some other state of affairs" (2005, 1). Instead, he understands the issue in terms of the constitution of "actor-networks" which manifest action. These are assemblages[1] of actors, that may be either human or non-human, and therefore do not belong to or exhibit a special "social" class or attribute. In this conceptualization, an actor is "something that acts or to which activity is granted by others. It implies *no* special motivation of *human individual* actors, nor of humans in general" (Latour 1996, 373, emphasis in original). An actor is defined by its associations, or is a figuration of them (prior to figuration, actors are better seen as "actants" [Latour 2005, 71]). Action is a relational achievement, a movement that may or may not become "stabilized" and therefore endure for a period. Actor-networks are at once maps of material associations and semiotic associations, and their character relies on both these aspects. They are "ontological definitions" of themselves (Latour 1996, 372) rather than stable "facts"—"not a thing but the recorded movement of a thing". The act of connecting them is therefore an act of explanation—indeed, the "only explanation" possible in ANT is "[t]he attachment of a set of practices that control or interfere in one another. No explanation is stronger or more powerful than providing connections among unrelated elements or showing how one element holds many others" (375).

This approach has several advantages from an innovation point of view. It ". . . allows us to look at innovation from a formal perspective as the creation of new actor-networks that are, in the accounts of the human actors, linked to intentional change. One of the general and key characteristics of innovation processes is that they involve new entities or new combinations of entities, that is, in ANT terms, evolving associations of mediators to chains and actor-networks" (Degelsegger and Kesselring 2012, 63).

Here, we note the particular terminology of ANT, which distinguishes between "mediators" and "intermediaries", the latter being "what transports meaning or force without transformation: defining its inputs is enough to define its outputs" whereas, for the former, "their input is never a good predictor of their output . . . [they] transform, translate, distort and modify the meaning or the elements they are meant to carry" (Latour 2005, 39). For ANT, the process by which associations evolve is called "translation": a process which accomplishes the difficult task of "inducing two mediators into co-existing" (107). Translations are always precarious: "All it takes is for one translation to fail and the whole web of reality unravels" (Law 2007, 5). Social innovation, from this perspective, then, is about actor-networks that the human actors recognize as having been constructed in response to their action, a self-referential project of building insight into associations between multiple actors, whether human or non-human. No external substance, force or institution is needed to produce such an actor-network (or for it to produce itself). Furthermore, the actor-network is irreducibly specific. It arises from "background/foreground reversal: instead of starting from universal laws—social or natural—and taking local contingencies as so many queer particularities that should either be eliminated or protected, [ANT] starts from irreducible, incommensurable, unconnected localities which then, at a great price, sometimes end into provisionally commensurable connections. . . . Universality or order are not the rule but the exceptions that have to be accounted for. Loci, contingencies or clusters are more like archipelagos on a sea than like lakes dotting a solid land" (Latour 1996, 370).

An innovation, in this frame, is the working out of new actor-networks, or new connections between existing ones, in a specific context, not a particular case of a more general phenomenon. It is also inherently a provisional accomplishment. Neither is an actor-network amenable to "replication": it may connect to new networks, but is always created anew, so the whole concept of building "models" and then "implementing" them in order to eventually "achieve innovation" is rendered meaningless (even if actor-networks were the creations of intentional beings, in complete contradiction to the principles outlined). However, "models" might be considered as non-human actors or quasi-objects that, in relationship with other actors, bring about or fail to bring about action: they are not the action itself, and the actions arising cannot be represented by them, in the absence of the other actors, or in the context of different actors. The approach also gives a very different status to decisions that include or exclude actors from *things*. Inclusion or exclusion are simply different qualities of association—just as conflict is as much a form of association as collaboration (and both are different from unawareness). Co-existence, as indicated by agreement of a common way forward, is not only an on-going accomplishment, but also a transitory one, reminding us that actor-networks are dynamic and evolving. In all these aspects, then, ANT resonates with the view of social innovation developed so far.

Actor-network theory distinguishes different phases in the formation of actor-networks, as they emerge, engage actors and evolve into coexistence or disappear. In his classic study of an attempt by a group of researchers to get a group of French fishermen to explore a way of increasing the population of scallops in their area (or, in his words "attempts . . . to impose themselves and their definition of the situation on others"), Callon (1986) defines four "moments of translation": "Problematization", where one actor tried to establish the nature of the problem in a way which made that actor central to its resolution; "interessement", where this actor attempted to "lock other actors into the roles that had been proposed for them"; "enrolment", where the actor then tried to define the roles and how they related to each other; and "mobilisation", in which the actor tried to ensure that there were reliable spokespeople for different collectivities, who would not be undermined by their base. This shows various attempts to bring about stable actor-networks through translations that together make up a higher-level translation—in this case, a decision to "pass by" the project. Rather than seeing these phases as sequential, it seems more plausible to consider them as intertwined and strategic negotiations, as actors attempt, successfully or unsuccessfully, to find a suitable basis for each, experimenting, rejecting and revising.

The case of the scallop fishermen presented by Callon, and particularly the associated definitions of problematization and interessement, have been criticized as enshrining a "managerialist" approach, where the perspectives and interests of one actor are the focus (Storni 2015, 172). Although this does not seem to be the only way to read the case, it does draw attention to the need to see each of the proposed translations as at least potentially contested maneuvers, rather than as moves made by a powerful actor. It seems quite plausible to see problematization as a contest between actors to establish what is in focus, and towards what any possible action should be oriented. Seen in this way, no "managerial" assumption is needed. Establishing Callon's "Obligatory Passage Point" (OPP), at which he sees a set of actors defining themselves as indispensable by framing an issue in a certain way, and which constitutes problematization (1986, 6), appears to demand only the achievement of a common understanding of what should be the focus of further action, perhaps by the formation of a new constellation of actors, rather than advancing a normative requirement that a particular actor should prevail. Although this might occur, it does not seem to be the only possible solution, and assuming that it is draws attention away from the very process of contestation and negotiation that generates the activity of the actor-network in this phase. It also risks ignoring the possibility of resistance and subversion arising around the OPP in later phases, so imposing an unnecessary and unrealistic linear form on the process.

With this in mind, we propose to understand problematization as a dynamic, contested process in which actors negotiate a common understanding of what should form the basis for their future action, or what associations should prevail. It can be seen as being about how to turn "matters of fact", which are unquestioned universal claims, into "matters of concern" (Björgvinsson, Ehn, and Hillgren 2012, Dewey 1927), in which these claims are opened up to question (Latour 2004). This transformation is not merely an intellectual one; it produces action. Latour points out that, while "matters of fact" might be seen as "stones, rugs, mugs and hammers", "matters of concern" are no less real but, because they are defined by dispute and uncertainty "are taken not exactly as object but rather as *gatherings*" (Latour 2005, 114). Hence, "matters of concern" bring with them the uncertainty, openness and contest around, and in relation to, which actors array themselves. They also, and in the same move, identify those actors and challenge their associations with each other. Problematization, then, is a process by which actors gather around "matters for concern", making some things visible and others invisible, and foreshadowing directions for action: all the other phases of translation descend from this *thing*, in that it makes actors available for the moves of interessement, enrolment and mobilization. The process of turning a matter of fact into a matter of concern becomes an operational definition of participation (Andersen *et al.* 2015).

Problematization forces the lifting of attention from a defined, constrained object to bring in all its connections and contexts: "A matter of concern is what happens to a matter of fact when you add to it its whole scenography, much like you would do by shifting your attention from the stage to the whole machinery of a theatre" (Latour 2008, 39). This appears to approximate descriptions of the first stages of the innovation process as "the fuzzy front end" (Bason 2010, 175), where uncertainty and ambiguity are particularly pronounced, a situation much project-oriented methodology works to exit as fast as possible. However, its importance is made clear if we understand it as is proposed by ANT, for it is this space that draws actors in, to debate what is to be dealt with and in what direction to move, and it does so not by narrowing down options, but by opening them up to examination and contest. Rather than paring an issue down to its minimal statement, and consequently separating it from its broad human and systemic context, it is also possible to encourage broad engagement by diverse voices with what is (and is not) known, in an agonistic process of mutual learning, encompassing not only what might be done, but also opening up to debate the purposes of that action and who is engaged in that action.

Adopting an ANT perspective on co-design and social innovation, then, helps to clarify the nature of *things*, how they form and how they relate issues and actors. From a co-design perspective, the focus becomes how "to shape a new aesthetic of matters of concern, to devise new ways to problematise and be interested and to represent and being re-presented" (Storni 2015, 168). Design is no longer just about the production of design objects, in the most efficient way, but also about the processes behind design, the "design *thing*", that need to be made visible and public, including the decisions taken about who to invite into the *thing* and how to do so. The task is to ". . . better support the formation of publics, the articulation of issues and the possibility to disagree" (171). The techniques and activities of the design process become more than means to facilitate and regulate interactions: they also involve making evidence of those interactions available to all to critique, support or build on. This is an open process, in sharp contrast to what occurs in "proprietary design networks" that ". . . often end(s) up replacing the *thing* behind a design (Storni 2012) with mute black boxes" (Storni 2015, 170), making the trade-offs and decisions about who to include and exclude impossible to trace. Social innovation, driven by co-design, is not only about a collaboration internal to a group of participants, but also about opening outwards, to engage people in the framing and critique of the work.

PlayPumps

We will now attempt to re-read a story of "social innovation" from an ANT perspective, to see where it might lead. We start at the end—in 2013, with the use of the PlayPumps project as a case study on failure by Ken Stern (2013, loc 443–458). At first sight, the central actor in this story is a piece of equipment, a rotary pump intended to be driven by African children running as they play, which lifts water from a bore to an overhead storage tank, whence it becomes available at the turn of a tap by gravity feed. The storage tank is a medium for the display of advertising, some intended for social purposes (an HIV/AIDS prevention campaign) and the rest available for commercial sale to generate funds to maintain the pumps. According to Stern, "The concept thus kneads together several enticing ingredients: the provision of a clean and easily accessible water supply, the building of community playgrounds for children, prominent messaging on matters of public importance, and a business model cleverly built on local advertising. It's a charity marketer's dream" (loc 445).

As Stern tells the story, PlayPumps were the product of an organization that burst into prominence after receiving a commitment for a major grant from First Lady Laura Bush at the Clinton Global Initiative in 2006. It then spent the next four years installing PlayPumps across Africa until a series of blog posts (Owen 2009a, b, c) revealed that the pumps were not maintained and so often not functioning; that the advertising revenue was chimerical; and that the kids did not use them as intended, preferring other pastimes. Stern makes this actor, a whistle-blowing aid-worker, the hero of a broader exposé of the failure of the "water charity industry" to make a difference to the water crisis in Africa. He attributes this failure to a "misallocation of resources, a lack of accountability, and a perverse incentive system", which focuses on maintaining the flow of donations rather than achieving impact. According to Stern, the PlayPump failure ". . . could have been easily averted by research and field testing, an approach that is all too rare in the charitable world" (2013, loc 453). Stern's prescription for change is focused on establishing proper (market) incentives and accountabilities ("all institutions are creatures of economic forces" [loc 471]) which, once established, will ensure a return to rational behavior by all the actors. The responsibility for this, in the broader charitable context, is ultimately with the donor public, which ". . . must begin to see donations as investments—investments with social rather than individual returns—and people must take charitable giving as seriously as they do investing in the stock market. This is the critical first step toward creating a new market discipline, a new culture of effectiveness, and efficient, results-oriented service" (loc 3109).

The first point to note here is that Stern is bringing the PlayPump story to bear to problematize the workings of the charitable industry, particularly in the US. The story is populated with actors of varying qualities: a charitable industry that is wasting money donated by a naïve public, which is in turn being seduced by heartwarming pictures of the transformation they can bring about for poor children on another continent; the PlayPump itself, an unloved mix of toy and unwieldy pump that should have been revealed as an impostor, but instead was able to hide behind the incompetence and venality of the water charity industry; good, clean water which is left inaccessible to thirsty, poor children because of the PlayPump, which often ejects perfectly useable existing hand pumps from their places in the villages of Africa; and a whistleblower worker who is the eyes and ears of rationality on the ground. This is a morality tale, designed to warn readers that charity might not be as good as it seems and to justify the assertion of hard-nosed business solutions. The phases of interessement, enrolment and mobilization are visible in the admonishment to the donor public to avoid being fooled and recognize that they should conform to models of responsible investment in organizations that are run by competent business-people, and to institutional players to reassert values of discipline and accountability by properly executing the roles assigned to them by market discipline. The PlayPump is to be abandoned, and the children in need of drinking water are to be represented, not by advertising, but by reliable managers who will finally ensure they have access to water, in a further mobilization where the children become silent beneficiaries of the appropriate system. Hence, this story is much less about the PlayPumps project than it is about making the philanthropic industry a matter of concern, and establishing an actor-network that conforms to certain prescriptions for that industry. This is an actor-network that has been formed by translating a concern about getting water to African children into an attempt to mobilize the American philanthropic sector in a certain direction. The PlayPumps project has become a black box, an actor in an actor-network far from its original home.

Although it is impossible to pick up all the traces of what occurred at the time, it is possible to uncover some hints that allow a different reading, one that focuses more on the PlayPumps project *in vivo* (or that opens up the black box), and make some observations about the way that actor-network evolved. In 2000, six years before Stern's story starts, the advertising company that developed the PlayPump won the World Bank Development Marketplace award and began to be promoted to water supply programs across sub-Saharan Africa (UNICEF 2007, 5). By October 2005, when a report on the TV show Frontline, produced by the PBS network in the US, gave a glowing report of the project, it was well-established, at least in South Africa (Frontline n.d.). In this show, the PlayPump was presented as the invention of a successful South African adverting executive, of English origin, turned social entrepreneur. PlayPump is a heroic character, potentially enabling the provision of clean water with little investment to millions of people who either did not have access to reticulated water at all, or who collected it from "leaky, contaminated hand pumps" (Frontline 2005). PlayPump releases women and girls from the burden of collection and carrying of water, which is in any case often unsafe, and which distracts them from performing their duties as "loving mothers", carers and educators. This story and, no doubt, the on-going efforts of the social entrepreneur himself, resulted in the grant of $16.4 million in September 2006, mentioned by Stern, made up of $10 million from the US government and the remainder from donations by the Case Foundation and another foundation based in New Jersey, together forming the "PlayPumps Alliance" (Costello 2006). In December 2006, the wave of support from this and other sources, including popular music figures, allowed the conversion of the project into a company, PlayPumps International (PPI), with executive support from personnel drawn from both the Case Foundation and former International Finance Corporation staff (Frontline n.d.). The initiative now had offices in Washington and had established a clear-cut contractual structure between the not-for-profit installer of the pumps and two other companies, the for-profit manufacturer of the pumps and the company which sold the advertising displayed on the storage tanks.

What was the "matter of concern" here? It is possible that, on the ground, it was indeed how to give good clean water access to the people of Africa. Around this, a number of actors had gathered: an inventor, the PlayPump, a number of communities where the PlayPumps had been successfully installed, with all their children, mothers and other characters. However, the identification of an actor as a "social entrepreneur", whether this originated prior to the media story or was introduced by it, enrolled a variety of other actors in the actor-network, to whom good clean water was only one consideration, and possibly not the most important one. The matter of concern appears to have been displaced from being (to the extent it was ever) about good clean water in African communities to a heady story of how a clever idea can attract the support of the most powerful and literally change the world. This was a different sort of "black boxing" of the PlayPump from the one performed by Stern's actor-network, but one that nevertheless coopted the PlayPump to act in a different actor-network. Instead of drawing attention to the individual communities and schools, we find ourselves looking at world leaders, large charitable foundations, executives, roll-out plans, contracts, corporate structures: the articulation of a model that gives comfort to donors that their money will be well-spent (and which may approximate the actor-network that Stern black boxes as "the water charity industry"). Success was assumed—the story became a celebration of the power of the model. Support flowed and the goals grew more ambitious. A mini-campaign was launched on World Water Day in March 2007, to raise $1.4 million for PPI in 100 days, with the claimed support of Accenture, the Coca-Cola Company, Deutsche Bank, HP and JP Morgan (Frontline n.d.). In April, this was presented as part of a larger effort to provide clean water to ten million people. This web of connections between individuals, organizations, technologies; the flows of funding, images and values; and the performance of roles and ideologies it brought forth, might be called the Western PlayPump actor-network.

However, not everyone was carried away. In mid-2007, UNICEF noted that many government and non-governmental organizations in several countries were aware of the project, but wished to "know more about the technology before committing to it" (2007, 5), and so prepared an assessment. This found several advantages of the PlayPump system, in both social and technical terms, but also noted a number of deficiencies, including issues related to assessing the quality of existing boreholes; relatively low capacity of the pumps; and control of the contracted installation teams across a very wide geography, which had led to a number of deficient installations. Also, in some locations, adults resisted operating the pumps when children were not available. Despite the stated intention of PPI to only install PlayPumps where there was no existing useable service, in one country people at nearly two thirds of sites reported that an earlier technology, which had been preferred, had been removed without them being offered any choice (UNICEF 2007, 10). Furthermore, the PlayPump installation, because it was serviced by and produced advertising income for an entity external to the community, did not become part of the communities in which it was installed, and contributed to impressions of loss of control and dependence. It was also noted that the cost of an installation had increased dramatically over a short period, rather than reducing as expected (13–14). This meant that funding a PlayPump would now provide water for far fewer people than alternative hand pumps. Reports had been received that some governments were experiencing donor pressure to sign up with PlayPumps, and the articulation of connections with government water and sanitation development policies was often poor, weakening other efforts already in place in the countries concerned. It is not clear how widely this report was circulated, but it was neither the first nor the last indicator of issues in the implementation of the project. Also during 2007, Save the Children USA had reported issues with both reliability and community acceptance of pumps they were installing

(Frontline n.d.), and in 2008 the government of Mozambique commissioned its own detailed review (Obiols and Erpf 2008), reaching very similar conclusions to the UNICEF Report. It appears that, at about this time, the company that had formerly been PPI's South African company, Water for All, "broadened its mission to include multiple water solutions, and ceased fundraising for the PlayPump" as well as ceasing to work with the company that sold advertising for the PlayPump system and maintained the pumps (Frontline n.d.).

This story, not noted by Stern, presents the PlayPump as a different sort of character, as a newcomer in a context where there are already a number of professionals operating, and presents its organizational promoters[2] as outsiders who did not make much effort to connect with existing actors or respect the arrangements and connections already in place. Although not wishing to expel the intruders, the actors in this narrative formed around the question of how to integrate PlayPump into the development of water supply in Africa (the matter of concern), a translation that would have required a number of adaptations to be negotiated differentially across the actor-network in Africa. We can see this story as the connection of the PlayPump to an existing actor-network, already occupied with developing water supply in the context of overall community development, and involving many experienced actors on the ground, which we might call the African Water Community actor-network. This existed side by side with the Western Play-Pump actor-network, which had formed around a matter of concern that was initially (possibly) about raising philanthropic funds to provide drinking water in Africa, but seems to have evolved into being about proving how the new philanthropic institutions are able to change the world. These two actor-networks do not appear to have been connected with each other in any meaningful sense, but to have continued to operate quite oblivious of each other for some time, except for the unwelcome attempts by the Western PlayPump actor-network to coerce some actors in the African Water Community actor-network to treat PlayPump as a different character than they saw it to be (a contested translation). The publicity for PlayPumps continued, with more entertainment figures aligning themselves with fundraising initiatives, while in parallel the PlayPump was being associated with a different actor-network, integrating it with different but existing actors and their associated reports (also actors in ANT terms), in which the PlayPump looked much less attractive.

We cannot know if PPI or their partners knew about the emerging concerns and decided to conceal them in order to maintain the actor-network that constituted them, or whether they simply did not come into contact with the findings, but in many ways this is not an issue in the ANT framework—the effect is the same. However, connections would be made, regardless of intention. In mid-2009 the media, in the person of the Frontline show that had been a key actor in the initiation of the PlayPump phenomenon, became aware of the UNICEF and Mozambique reports, and effectively introduced them into the Western PlayPump actor-network, producing significant disturbance. It was about this time that the blog posts noted by Stern began to appear. While preparing a follow-up show, Frontline were unable to get access to the PPI organization for interviews, but PPI itself made a voluntary admission that it had been experiencing problems with the PlayPumps project, announcing the temporary suspension of PPI funding for new pumps and the establishment of a strategic review (Edson 2009). Only a month later, the remaining stock of PlayPumps was transferred to another US charity, with substantial cash and in-kind support, and PPI took down its website. A variety of critical media reports followed. In March 2010, PPI US ceased fundraising for PlayPumps, and its CEO moved on to a senior disaster relief position (Frontline n.d.). By the time the Frontline follow-up report aired in late June 2010, the project had effectively been dissolved, although the pumps are still being marketed "as a niche solution for schools in rural areas" (Hobbes 2014, 61). If the PlayPump could not be a hero, it could not continue to exist, because only heroes could support the Western actor-network's claims to superiority. Only silver bullets were good enough.

What caused the voluntary dismantlement of the Western PlayPump actor-network, and the rejection of the PlayPump by the African Water Community actor-network, in this way? In ANT, as we have noted, explanations take the form of making connections, and it is possible to see what happened in those terms. There appear to be at least two complementary influences: firstly, the emergence of data in the Western PlayPump actor-network suggesting that the heroic profile of PlayPump as a brilliant, self-sustaining and uniquely effective business model could not be sustained seems to have made it impossible to maintain support for the actor-network at all; secondly, the need for the PlayPump to integrate with other actors, to adapt and engage with both governments and NGOs, appears to have been a challenge that its supporters could not or would not rise to: they did not want to participate in that actor-network (perhaps they were not interested in the same matter of concern). It is important to note that neither the UNICEF nor the Mozambique governments reports recommended a cessation of the PlayPump project, merely its integration into a broader landscape of actors, communities, governments and organizations. This does not, however, seem to have been an acceptable solution to the Western PlayPump actors, and they preferred to exit the stage, leaving the PlayPump project as a duplicitous impostor that could be activated by Stern. However, telling the story in an ANT way suggests that the reason that the PlayPump failed to become part of the African Water Community actor-network had little to do with the PlayPump technology itself; and the demise of the Western PlayPump actor-network appears likewise to have more to do with it becoming impossible for the PlayPump to play its vital role as hero, rather than its inability to contribute in some practical, but not necessarily dominant, way to providing water for African communities.

Does this account overcomplicate the story? Is it possible to see this all much more simply—as Stern has proposed, as a clear matter of lack of accountability, perverse incentives and a failure to conduct basic market testing? Certainly, it does seem as if the focus of the Western PlayPump actor-network became one of continuing to raise funds, rather than ensuring impact. However, this attachment to fundraising has to be linked to the fiction of the PlayPump as a silver bullet solution: it appears that the latter was an essential condition for the former, rather than the more realistic understanding that launching a new response to a complex problem in a difficult and volatile environment was likely to experience some difficulties, and potentially to need adaptation, and managing donors' expectations accordingly. This appears to be less a matter of perverse incentives than of an inability or lack of desire to accept that resolving some issues is not simple or fast, even for powerful actors. It also challenges Stern's faith in accountability and market mechanisms as being "the solution"; in fact, accountability within the African Water Community actor-network was quite swift once the PlayPump project began to ramp up—the UNICEF report was available only six months after the first major funding, and provided a perfectly practical basis for learning and adjustment, had the players wished to follow that route. It appears however, that the Western PlayPump actor-network was not able to make this leap, away from stardom, towards the nitty-gritty, difficult, unpredictable, complex reality of working on such problems. In fact, based on this analysis, it appears as if Stern's suggested approach of introducing "true" market disciplines into the American philanthropic sector would have been at best likely to be irrelevant to the issues experienced by the PlayPump project, which had much more to do with how they failed to connect with the actor-network in Africa. The assertion that what occurred was all a matter of a failure to conduct market testing is clearly not born out on a more detailed examination—this was a project that had already been shown to work in some, but not all, situations and that, with a different set of expectations, more adaptable and less rigid governance, a more measured approach to integration on the ground and less of a felt obligation to save the world in one stroke, might have been much more effective than it was, and might still be contributing today. In the end, Stern's attempt to use the PlayPump case to promote "market discipline" appears somewhat beside the point: this analysis suggests that the bigger question is how to ensure that innovations are introduced into a bewildering variety of contexts, flexibly and in ways that generate the best results, and that respect the on-going work and progress already being made in those contexts, rather than trying to sweep them aside with another brand-new broom. As Hobbes says: "In 2010, 'Frontline' interviewed the director of PlayPump about its failures, and he said, 'It might have been a bit ambitious, but hey, you gotta dream big. Everyone's always said it's such a great idea.' And it was. But maybe when the next great idea comes along, we should all dream a little smaller" (Hobbes 2014, 61).

Critiques of ANT

The re-presentation of the PlayPumps story in ANT terms remains essentially descriptive: "ANT does not aim to act as a framework, theory or metalanguage to explain social phenomena; rather, it offers an approach, a language and a series of foundational principles to produce descriptions of them" (Storni 2015, 167). With respect to the usefulness of "mere" description, we have already pointed out that description is in no sense neutral, and ANT helps understand more specifically why this might be so. By its nature, description draws attention to some features of its subject and obscures or ignores others. The expression of differing descriptions therefore constitutes the proposal of competing strategies of exposure or concealment, functionally defining "matters of concern", whose attempted resolution animates an actor-network. The proposal that description is neutral relies on the idea that a description can be objective: indeed, that the goal of description is to produce a "matter of fact". As soon as a description is contested, the matter of fact is transformed into a matter of concern which, by definition, is not inert but which demands action. Description can be used to exclude actors and competing perspectives: this appears to be the strategy involved in treating the PlayPump case as being a matter of the organization of the American philanthropic system, rather than admitting the possibility that other actors and their understandings of the world needed to be engaged. Description is therefore not only interested but, and precisely because of that, strategic. What should raise suspicion is not an apparent affiliation between a description and a purpose or interest, but the exact reverse; any attempt to present a description as disinterested, since this is clearly an act of concealment. It is for this reason that Storni's call to make design things public is so potent: it confronts attempts to hide descriptions and so create "matters of fact" rather than "matters of concern".

We have already seen that ANT has been criticized for promoting a "managerialist" world-view. It has also been characterized as politically disinterested or even conservative (Whittle and Spicer 2008). One form of this critique suggests that, by equating human and non-human actors, ANT diminishes humans and removes from them their unique property of intentionality. In order to deal with this, it is important to observe the unique conception of agency in ANT, as a property not attached to any specific actor in an actor-network but instead as a property of the actor-network itself. ANT, therefore, neither asserts that non-human actors have intentions, nor that humans do not, because agency does not require intention, but is based on association. Another concern is that, in seeking to describe the process of stabilizing actor-networks, ANT risks merely reproducing existing hegemonies. Again, this reminds us that, in ANT, the social is by nature unfinalized, and that groups are on-going productions: ". . . social is not a place, a thing, a domain or a kind of stuff but a provisional movement of new associations" (Latour 2005, 238). While an actor-network may move towards stability, it is that movement that is of interest, rather than its end state: "ANT is not about *traced* networks, but about network-*tracing* activity" (1996, 378). It has also been said that, by focusing on the local, micro-actions within networks, ANT ignores the structures by which power is maintained and exerted. This calls up the particular relation that ANT proposes between the micro and macro. Latour, drawing on Tarde, says: ". . . we should not consider that the macro encompasses the micro, but that the micro is made up of a proliferation of incommensurable entities . . . 'monads'—which are simply lending one of their aspects, a 'façade of themselves' to make up a provisional whole. The small holds the big. Or rather the big could at any moment drown again in the small from which it emerged and to which it will return" (Latour 2005, 243). "Structures" are not denied, but are produced as entities that (together) consist of the micro, and are therefore inherently provisional. Power relationships are to be understood by "describing the way in which actors are defined, associated and simultaneously obliged to remain faithful to their alliances" (Callon 1986, 19).

Certainly, this does not treat "structure" or power as a fixed or exogenous reality, but that seems quite different from claiming it is not recognized at all. Translation specifically allows "an explanation of how a few obtain the right to express and to represent the many silent actors of the social and natural worlds they have mobilized" (Callon 1986, 19): the attempts by donors to pressure African governments in the PlayPump case can be seen in precisely this light. The issue, then, appears to be not so much whether ANT fails to recognize structure or power *per se*, but the way it treats them as inherent in, or arising from, rather than being external to, the connections that form the actor-network. While this represents a challenge to theories that treat social structure as "something" that exists outside and acts upon the local, this is not the same as denying the existence of structures or power relations: it simply provides a different explanation. In fact, Latour suggests provocatively that the assertion of the existence of the social as an external reality is itself anti-political: "[i]f there is a society, *then no politics is possible*" (Latour 2005, 250, emphasis in original), because that would locate agency outside actors and beyond hope of their influence and ". . . if you have to fight against a force that is invisible, untraceable, ubiquitous, and total, you will be roundly defeated". Instead, he locates political action at the level of "smaller ties that can be dealt with one by one". The accusation that this is "anti-political" seems difficult to sustain. However, we will propose an extension of this explanation in the next section.

Another concern, and one that is harder to answer, notes that ANT tends to produce accounts from a detached, objective observer's viewpoint, and therefore does not encourage a reflexive view that places the analysts within the action. Akama suggests that Latour's description of the Colombia space shuttle disaster (2010) "still takes a perspective of no-where and every-where, a presumed innocence and neutrality" (Akama 2015, 267). Not only does this risk falling into the trap of objectivity by concealment (of which the description of the PlayPumps case offered here might also be accused) but it also, and more importantly, fails to place the "observer" *within* the action. It is all very well when what has happened has happened, and the various traces of an actor-network can be inspected and reassembled at will, to present a version of "what really went on"—and this may even be valuable, if it stimulates those who read it to engage differently or more critically with future *things*, but it does not present the view from the heart of the controversy, which must surely be the point of view for which we need to prepare if we wish to be "oriented towards the emergence of futures" (264). This is not to make a case for asserting the "primacy" of the embodied individual or their perspective. Latour eloquently deals with the impossibility of separating the individual or the local from the collective or universal: "to believe in the existence either of individual or of society is simply a way to say that we have been deprived of information on the individuals we started with; that we have little knowledge about their interactions; that we have lost the *precise conduits* through which what we call 'the whole' actually circulates" (2010, 10, emphasis in original), a concept neatly expressed by the idea that an action's "universality is fully local" (7). Rather, it insists that neither can exist or be seen without the other, that they generate each other. This being the case, the experience of being in the moment of controversy, with all our associations available, might be seen as the *only* way to truly seize and be seized of the actor-network: every other position is in some way removed from the local which is the universal.

The Question of Structure and Constraint

Taking the perspective of the individual within the action opens up the question of the status of structures, constraints and entities, and how they influence action, if only as felt realities. How can the individual and collective construct, reproduce, be constrained by and subvert the structures and institutions that they are acting towards?

Let us start to propose an answer by considering the way that "protocols" in design—mundane formats and rules for presenting data and making visible the results of design things—actually constrain the design process itself. They can be placed within ANT as assemblages of quasi-objects, which exert agency by limiting or requiring what is to be made visible, as distinct from being treated as noise. For example, the specific requirements of documentation, the artistic records of what occurred in a design interaction or the need to present to outside audiences using PowerPoint or press release formats (to say nothing of accepted genre rules) can all channel, limit and control the design process, even in the absence of intentional human intervention. They therefore operationally define constraints, at least to the extent that the formats and media are accepted as "matters of fact" and remain unchallenged. Acceptance of protocols might simply indicate inattention; however, it is also possible that it reveals people's beliefs about what they can and cannot challenge—felt constraints. Palmås and von Busch (2015), recounting a brainstorming session, observe that participants felt unable to use Post-it notes during a session to record "negative" comments, because that might lead to the exclusion of the commentator and the note. In allowing this anticipation to affect their actions, participants were effectively bringing into being an external force to which they yielded. This might be seen as an "actor at a distance", with the Post-it note participating ". . . simultaneously . . . as an actor and as a network of other actors" (Andersen *et al.* 2015, 253). But how is the prohibition on the uttering of negative comments imported into the process even prior to their being written? If protocols are systems of rules governing communication, where do the rules exist prior to the communication, and how do they enforce themselves, sometimes invisibly?

I propose that this must be dealt with by making two extensions to the concepts brought to bear so far. First, we posit that humans individually and collectively construct "quasi-objects", both through acts they perform and that they fail to perform, and that these acts thereby present the quasi-object as an actor in the actor-network. This is not to allow that these are "grand forces" of "society" with any independent existence, against which Latour argues, but rather that human actors objectify perceived and invisible entities, and accept constraints, by acting *as if* these existed, and that the actor-network must consider them as actors, at the same level as human and non-human actors. Second, I propose that there is a process by which structures are constructed internal to the individual, which are expressed by action (or the absence of action) in the external world and, further, that individuals respond to the observation of actions in the external world as representing these structures. This concept is drawn from structuration theory (Giddens 1984) and addresses the question of how individuals negotiate ways forward with each other and with respect to structures they perceive to be real, thereby in a pragmatic sense making them real. This negotiation of ways forward essentially becomes a question of how the individuals involved in a process are able to at once exert agency and at the same time reproduce the constraints they are bound by, where both constraint and agency have external and internal manifestations at the level of the actor. Externally, individuals act in ways that are observed and interpreted by others and express both constraint and agency in doing so. However, individuals also perceive what is occurring externally and understand that through the lens of their individual histories and more generalized ways of understanding that are shared by other members of groups to which they belong (world-views, schema or cultures). In doing so, they develop different views of what actions are possible or appropriate, effectively internalizing constraint. The tension between constraint and agency, then, is played out both internally and externally, and both internal and external structures impact on each other in a "dual instantiation" (Stones 2005, 14): a "duality of agency and structure within the agent that is central both to structure as the medium of practices, and to the production of structure as the outcome of practices . . ." (81). Stones describes this as a "strong ontology" and conceives of it as a quadripartite process (84–85), linking:

- External structures as conditions of action "which have an existence that is autonomous from the agent in focus";
- Internal structures within the agent "which themselves can be divided analytically into . . . conjuncturally specific internal structures and general-dispositional structures or, following Bourdieu, habitus";
- Active agency/agent's practices, including the ways in which the actor either routinely and pre-reflectively, or strategically and critically, draws upon her internal structures;
- Outcomes (as external and internal structures and as events).[3]

Using this approach turns attention to observing behaviors and practices at an "intermediate zone of position practices", rather than at either the purely institutional or individual levels, a zone that is strongly reminiscent of the actor-network, since it connects the individual (human) actant to their context, in keeping with the principles of general symmetry. In non-ANT terms, it can be taken as a representation both of how agency and structure interact to produce action within an innovation or collaboration process, and how, at the same time, that activity mirrors, relates to and potentially subverts the (constructed) institutions within which the process occurs. It starts with individuals who are responding to the path-dependent world in which they find themselves, based on the tensions between internal structures that reflect their experience of the external world through the lens of their own individual history. In responding, they exert agency and produce outcomes that are themselves reproducing and modifying the external structures experienced by the individuals. These structures may be understood at the collective level as institutions and, because of micro-variations in the agency of the multiple individuals producing them, they are both sustained and modified in the one movement.

This approach, far from producing the effect Latour objects to (rightly in this writer's opinion), the usurping of any possibility of individual action by social forces that they are doomed to reproduce, allows for both direct rejection or rebellion against an institution (so bringing both it and its counterforce into existence), but also and perhaps more importantly the possibility of modification, subversion or mutation within every act, in the same moment as those acts reproduce the structure in focus. Moreover, it is quite possible that the institution might itself become a matter of concern: what does it or does it not require, what is its authority or legitimacy? The picture is one where resistance and subversion occur not only in direct rebellion, but in some way at the margins—through small accommodations, limited disobedience and trivial betrayals. Hence, collaboration may proceed, not only through cooperation and consensus, but through small concessions and transitory alignments that leave conflict intact, reflecting an "agonistic" dynamic. This conceptualization also suggests that the way the actor calculates what is in their interest is likely to be contextualized, contingent and inherently political: ". . . recurrently constructed and partially pursued, rather than affirmed and realised as a predetermined, essential destiny" (Willmott 2003, 86). Such a position, far from contradicting ANT, seems to have been foreshadowed by Callon: "This is a reflection of ANT's proposition of 'radical indeterminacy of the actor' (Callon 1999, 181), and the idea that interests are merely 'temporarily stabilised outcomes of previous processes of enrolment' (Callon and Law 1982, 662)" (Palmås and von Busch 2015, 240).

The proposal to adopt an ANT perspective on social innovation has been widely aired in both the social innovation and co-design space. Latour has himself drawn the connections between several of the key concepts: "If things, or rather Dinge, are gatherings, as Heidegger used to define them, then it is a short step from there to considering all things as the result of an activity called 'collaborative design' in Scandinavia. This activity is in fact the very definition of the politics of matters of concern since all designs are 'collaborative' designs—even if in some cases the 'collaborators' are not all visible, welcomed or willing" (Latour 2009, 6). The specific working out of the proposal that has been undertaken here has aimed to better connect the co-design and social innovation understandings of ANT, and to demonstrate that, by bringing its methodology to bear on social innovation, several of its key observed features can be explained. In particular, it presents a process by which action is at once created, performed and constitutes a gathering of human and non-human actors around matters of concern, a *thing*. The *thing* involves different actors attempting to translate meaning or elements of the actor-network they form, often disputing how this should occur, in order to stabilize it in ways they see as appropriate. Although this is the form of the activity from the exterior, the view from *within* the actor-network, the lived experience of a reflexive human actor, is one of attempting to negotiate an accepted way of understanding the matter of concern, an inter-subjective sense-making, in an agonistic space. It is in this space that "participants" in innovation come together, dispute, agree, propose, discard and go on. The negotiation surfaces shifting interests and conflicts within a context that is affected both by the awareness of constraints and of areas that are unregulated, where new ways of being can be developed, corresponding to the "weak ties" evoked by Latour (1996, 370). To the extent that actors are able to achieve collective meaning around the matter of concern, meaning as expressed in action that they themselves see as "new", they may claim to have "innovated", or agreed to act in ways or with others that they would not have done before they came together. These agreements, stabilized actor-networks, become "matters of fact" and effectively disappear as the actors move on to other matters of concern.

Machiavelli and Prometheus

Although it is no doubt true that most ANT studies, reporting as they do from the present on past events, tend to take a detached perspective, it is quite plausible to see ANT as potentially offering some useful "sensitizing concepts" for those who are living the action, even if this is not the point of view which most researchers using ANT have chosen to take. These would involve turning the attention of an actor towards the way they and other actors are being constituted by observing the associations being deployed, and towards detecting the attempts that are being made to translate these as they occur. The aim would be to offer a way or ways of seeing differently, or seeing the unexpected, that might suggest alternative ways forward. This is far from inconsistent with the aims of ANT which, as already noted, aims to encourage the development of interesting stories about the way relations are assembled, and to interfere in those relations in a messy world. It has been said that ANT must be translated into empirically grounded practices (Law 2007, 2): what seems to be called for in this context is to turn its attention not only to practices that generate research, but also towards practices that may influence action.

But where does the designer stand in this? Latour has proposed that we must move from conceiving of him as a "Machiavellian prince", manipulating the action in order to efficiently achieve goals in the modernist sense, to seeing her as a "cautious Prometheus"; cautious because design is inherently "obsessively" oriented towards details, craft, skills (2009, 3), in a way that is diametrically opposed to the "hubris" of the modernist grand project. In this, he echoes ANT's own focus on the reality of the specific local act, and rejection of the grand forces of society: "It is as though we had to combine the engineering tradition with the precautionary principle; it is as though we had to imagine Prometheus stealing fire from heaven in a cautious way!" (4). Refocusing this idea, Storni proposes that the designer take on the role of an *agnostic* Prometheus, producing "public maps" of actor-networks, "constantly circulated, updated, collected and made available to enable both engagement and reflection and the exploration of further additions and subtractions" (2015, 173), and which seek "co-habitation . . . enabl[ing] the actors themselves to look for ways to improve the state of things, knowing that it is not for the designer to determine whether a situation has improved as a result of a design intervention". Leaving aside the unappetizing prospect of the Olympian punishment the designer might attract under either metaphor, this seems to constitute an operational rather than an individual definition of the role of the designer, one which might be enacted at different times by different actors, and one that also allows the designer to exist at the heart of the actor-network, as a participant rather than remote manipulator. The defining "skill" of the designer becomes the ability to make publicly visible, and therefore open up to action, maps of actor-networks, and to do this in a way that encourages co-habitation, rather than consensus, that affords actors the possibility to develop ways to move forward. This is risky, but at least possible: "For all our actions we consider risk-taking and precaution-taking as synonymous: the more risk we take, the more careful we are. The potential danger in this instance is of antagonism between the actors who, when drawn together and given a visible public voice, might see themselves as enemies rather than legitimate adversaries designing things together" (Storni 2015, 176).

Developing the technologies to enable this role even provides some inkling of what "mapping controversies" might involve in practice. Venturini distinguishes between "positivistic 'first-degree' objectivity" and "'second-degree objectivity' (which is interested) . . . in revealing the full range of oppositions around matters of concern" (2012, 798). Rather than giving equal weight to every viewpoint, these are to be given "different visibility . . . according to, 1) their representativeness, 2) their influence, and 3) their interest". Seven principles are proposed to guide practice:

1. you shall listen to actors' voices more than to your own presumptions;
2. you shall observe from as many viewpoints as possible;
3. you shall not restrict your observation to any single theory or methodology;
4. you shall adjust your descriptions and observations recursively;
5. you shall simplify complexity respectfully;
6. you shall attribute to each actor a visibility proportional to its weight;
7. you shall provide descriptions that are adapted, redundant and flexible.

(800)

Of course, neither control nor certainty is any longer possible under this formulation of innovation; indeed, control would be inimical to the process and result only in mute matters of fact that displaced controversy and creativity elsewhere. However, although "success" cannot be guaranteed, failure is to be expected, participation may be subverted, compromise is inevitable and goals are bound to shift, there is equally a very real sense that hope is reasonable. Even though participation may proceed in small steps, defined by petty transgressions and acceptable betrayals, without directly challenging the status quo, "[t]he Machiavelli-inspired, micro-oriented conception of power proposed by ANT (Callon 1986, Clegg 1989, 203, Latour 1988) suggests that there the proverbial 'powers that be' may not always control citizens through the new modes of participatory governance" (Palmås and von Busch 2015, 241).

Notes

1 Note that Law calls "assemblage" an "awkward translation" of the French *agencement*, a term used by Deleuze, which he sees as being comparable to actor-network, and notes that Law has also called actor-networks "actant-rhizomes" (2007, 6).

2 For the sake of simplicity, we will treat these as one actor, although there were clearly several issues that worked out differently in different locations due to specific configurations of these actors.

3 There are several significant issues with the understanding of "internal" and "external" inherent in this formulation that are beyond the scope of this book to deal with. For an extended discussion of the status of "mind" and social relating, drawing on the ideas of Mead, see Stacey (2001).

References

Akama, Yoko. 2015. "Being Awake to Ma: Designing in between-ness as a Way of Becoming With." *CoDesign* 11 (3–4):262–274. doi: 10.1080/15710882.2015.1081243.

Andersen, Lars Bo, Peter Danholt, Kim Halskov, Nicolai Brodersen Hansen, and Peter Lauritsen. 2015. "Participation as a Matter of Concern in Participatory Design." *CoDesign* 11 (3–4):250–261. doi: 10.1080/15710882.2015.1081246.

Bason, Christian. 2010. *Leading public Sector Innovation: Co-Creating for a Better Society*. Bristol: Policy Press.

Binder, Thomas, Eva Brandt, Pelle Ehn, and Joachim Halse. 2015. "Democratic Design Experiments: Between Parliament and Laboratory." *CoDesign* 11 (3–4):152–165. doi: 10.1080/15710882.2015.1081248.

Björgvinsson, Erling Bjarki, Pelle Ehn, and Per-Anders Hillgren. 2012. "Design Things and Design Thinking: Contemporary Participatory Design Challenges." *Design Issues* 28 (3):101–116.

Blumer, Herbert. 1954. "What Is Wrong with Social Theory?" *American Sociological Review* 19 (1):3–10. doi: 10.2307/2088165.

Callon, Michel. 1986. "Some Elements of a Sociology of Translation—Domestication of the Scallops and the Fishermen of St-Brieuc Bay." *Sociological Review Monograph* 32:196–233.

Callon, Michel. 1999. "Actor-Network Theory-the Market Test." In *Actor Network Theory and After*, edited by John Law and John Hassard, 181–195. Boston, MA: Blackwell Publishers.

Callon, Michel, and B. Latour. 1981. "Unscrewing the Big Leviathan: How Actors Macrostructure Reality and How Sociologists Help Them to Do So." In *Advances in Social Theory and Methodology: Toward an Integration of Micro- and Macro-Sociologies*, edited by K. Knorr-Cetina and Aaron Victor Cicourel, 277–303. Boston, MA: Routledge & Kegan Paul.

Callon, Michel, and J. Law. 1982. "On Interests and Their Transformation—Enrollment and Counter-Enrollment." *Social Studies of Science* 12 (4):615–625. doi: 10.1177/030631282012004006.

Clegg, Stewart. 1989. *Frameworks of Power*. London: SAGE.

Costello, Amy. 2006. "PlayPump Project Receives Major U.S. Funding," accessed 17/7/2016. http://www.pbs.org/frontlineworld/blog/2006/09/playpump_projec.html.

Degelsegger, Alexander, and Alexander Kesselring. 2012. "Do Non-Humans Make a Difference? The Actor-Network-Theory and the Social Innovation Paradigm." In *Challenge Social Innovation: Potentials for Business, Social Entrepreneurship, Welfare and Civil Society*, edited by Hans-Werner Franz, Josef Hochgerner, and Jürgen Howaldt, 57–72. Berlin: Springer.

Dewey, John. 1927. *The Public and Its Problems*. London: Allen & Unwin.

Edson, Gary. 2009. "Letter released on PPI website," 21/09/09.

Franz, Hans-Werner, Josef Hochgerner, and Jürgen Howaldt, eds. 2012. *Challenge Social Innovation: Potentials for Business, Social Entrepreneurship, Welfare and Civil Society*. 1st ed. Berlin: Springer.

Frontline. 2005. "South Africa: The Play Pump," accessed 17/7/16. http://www.pbs.org/frontlineworld/rough/2005/10/south_africa_th.html.

Frontline. n.d. "Troubled Water: Timeline: The PlayPump Trail," accessed 17/7/2016. http://www.pbs.org/frontlineworld/stories/southernafrica904/timeline_tw.html.

Giddens, Anthony. 1984. *The Constitution of Society: Outline of the Theory of Structuration*. Berkley, CA: University of California Press.

Hobbes, Michael. 2014. "How to Save the World." *The New Republic* 245 (19):52.

Howaldt, Jürgen, and Michael Schwarz. 2010. "Social Innovation: Concepts, Research Fields and International Trends." In *Studies for Innovation in a Modern Working Environment—International Monitoring*, edited by Klaus Henning and Frank Hees. Aachen: IMA/ZLW.

Latour, Bruno. 1987. *Science in Action: How to Follow Scientists and Engineers through Society*. Cambridge, MA: Harvard University Press.

Latour, Bruno. 1988. "The Prince for Machines as well as for Machinations." In *Technology and Social Change*, edited by Brian Elliott, 20–43. Edinburgh: Edinburgh University Press

Latour, Bruno. 1996. "On Actor-Network Theory—A Few Clarifications." *Soziale Welt-Zeitschrift Fur Sozialwissenschaftliche Forschung Und Praxis* 47 (4):369.

Latour, Bruno. 2004. "Why Has Critique Run Out of Steam? From Matters of Fact to Matters of Concern." *Critical Inquiry* 30 (2):225–248.

Latour, Bruno. 2005. *Reassembling the Social An Introduction to Actor-Network-Theory, Clarendon Lectures in Management Studies*. Oxford: Oxford University Press.

Latour, Bruno. 2008. *What Is the Style of Matters of Concern?* Amsterdam: Van Gorcum.

Latour, Bruno. 2009. A Cautious Prometheus ? A Few Steps toward a Philosophy of Design (With Special Attention to Peter Sloterdijk). In *Proceedings of the 2008 Annual International Conference of the Design History Society*, 2–10.

Latour, Bruno. 2010. *Networks, Societies, Spheres: Reflections of an Actor-Network Theorist*. International Seminar On Network Theory: Network Multidimensionality In The Digital Age, Los Angeles: Annenberg School for Communication and Journalism.

Law, John. 2007. Actor Network Theory and Material Semiotics. Draft Paper. *HeterogeneitiesDOTnet*. Retrieved from http://www. heterogeneities. net/publications/Law2007ANTandMaterialSemiotics.

Obiols, Ana Lucia, and Karl Erpf. 2008. *Mission Report on the Evaluation of the PlayPumps installed in Mozambique*. St. Gallen, Switzerland: Swiss Resource Centre and Consultancies for Development (SKAT).

Owen. 2009a. "The Playpump." *Owen in Malawi*, accessed 17/7/16. http://thoughtsfrommalawi.blogspot.com.au/2009/08/playpump.html.

Owen. 2009b. "The Playpump II." *Owen in Malawi*, accessed 17/7/16. http://thoughtsfrommalawi.blogspot.com.au/2009/10/playpump-ii.html.

Owen. 2009c. "The Playpump III—'The Challenge of Good Inquiry'." *Owen in Malawi*, accessed 17/7/16. http://thoughtsfrommalawi.blogspot.com.au/2009/11/playpump-iii-challenge-of-taking-photos.html.

Palmås, Karl, and Otto von Busch. 2015. "Quasi-Quisling: Co-Design and the Assembly of Collaborateurs." *CoDesign* 11 (3–4):236–249. doi: 10.1080/15710882.2015. 1081247.

Shotter, John. 2009. "Perplexity: Preparing for the Happenings of Change." In *Managing in Changing Times*, edited by Sid Lowe, 137–178. New Delhi: SAGE.

Stacey, Ralph. 2001. "What Can It Mean to Say That the Individual Is Social through and through?" *Group Analysis* 34 (4):457.

Stern, Ken. 2013. *With Charity for All: Why Charities Are Failing and a Better Way to Give*. New York: Doubleday.

Stones, Rob. 2005. *Structuration Theory*. Basingstoke: Palgrave Macmillan.

Storni, Cristiano. 2012. "Unpacking Design Practices: The Notion of Thing in the Making of Artifacts." *Science, Technology & Human Values* 37 (1):88–123. doi: 10.1177/0162243910392795.

Storni, Cristiano. 2015. "Notes on ANT for Designers: Ontological, Methodological and Epistemological Turn in Collaborative Design." *CoDesign* 11 (3–4):166–178. doi: 10.1080/15710882.2015.1081242.

UNICEF. 2007. "An Evaluation of the PlayPump® Water System as an Appropriate Technology for Water, Sanitation and Hygiene Programmes." Retrieved from http://www-tc.pbs.org/frontlineworld/stories/southernafrica904/flash/pdf/uni cef_pp_report.pdf.

Venturini, Tommaso. 2012. "Building on Faults: How to Represent Controversies with Digital Methods." *Public Understanding of Science* 21 (7):796–812. doi: 10.1177/0963662510387558.

Whittle, A., and A. Spicer. 2008. "Is Actor Network Theory Critique?" *Organization Studies* 29 (4):611–629. doi: 10.1177/0170840607082223.

Willmott, Hugh. 2003. "Renewing Strength: Corporate Culture Revisited." *M@n@gement* 6 (3):73–87.

Wittgenstein, Ludwig. 1953. *Philosophical Investigations*. Translated by G. E. M. Anscombe. Oxford: Blackwell.

5 Reflexivity and Evaluation

We have not as yet addressed the process of mutual learning that lies at the heart of social innovation, the process by which we come into relationship with an issue and with other participants and through which we produce new proposals. Fundamentally, this involves developing an understanding of how we inform ourselves and what questions we ask about the reality we are examining. At the outset, it is vital to establish that we are not focusing "merely" on the abstract discussion and argument that might precede action. At least in this context, "abstract" contributions are as capable of influencing the process as physical action; and they are always developed with the possibility of action in mind and in relation to that possibility. The understanding is similar to that of Dewey, who: ". . . defined an idea as being the anticipation of an outcome of some action. He saw ideas having different stages. First, there is a suggestion, a vague possibility of what might occur. Then, such a suggestion might form the stimulus to action. Dewey argued that this process only creates an idea when it is examined and evaluated against some measure of functional success" (Ramsey 2011, 5) Suggestions are provocative, "what would happen if" questions, an invitation to explore without the proposer being committed to supporting them. Every suggestion is prone to being improved upon or superseded by a better one, so they have instrumental value as well as any inherent "validity" they may possess: "ideas are not things waiting out there to be discovered but rather tools that people devise to cope with the world as they find it (Menand 1997)" (Mulgan 2015, xii). They may reveal connections between actors that were not visible; they may lead to further suggestions, either as extensions or in opposition; they may challenge the purpose of the discussion. They only become ideas when they generate some level of commitment, an agreement that this could be carried forward, from at least some of the participants. All of them tangle together the interests, assumptions, prejudices, knowledge and ignorance of those who advance them and who respond to them, and so also serve to reveal them. Even though it is obvious that actions in the physical world cannot be reversed, and that they signal the highest level of commitment, it is also true that suggestions and ideas, once made, affect the *thing* that is considering them, and so also irreversibly affect the way interactions proceed, opening up some possibilities for suggestions, ideas or actions that would not have been possible before; but they might also close down possibilities that existed previously. Hence, ideas, suggestions and actions are all forms of solutions with more or less irreversible effects, but at the same time more or less provisional: they are different types of what we will call "proto-solutions".

Proto-solutions are instrumental, but are only interpretable when their implications are teased out and placed against some notion of desirable or undesirable outcomes related to the purpose the discussion is aiming to achieve, Dewey's "measure of functional success". In other words, the development of suggestions, ideas and actions is accomplished by placing them alongside our beliefs about how they would work and what they would lead to. I will call this our "theory of change", the articulation of our expectations about how something we are examining would impact on the situation and the results it would bring about. These are not "theories" in the formal sense; their purpose is not to explain reality, to provide an abstracted distillation of what matters. Instead, they share some aspects of both heuristics and hypotheses; more explicit versions of the former, but more instrumental than the latter. They are the tools with which we inspect reality, the scales, measures, templates and instruments with which we evaluate proto-solutions. When a suggestion is advanced, it can be seen as a "quasi-object", which we then start to imagine in use: we start to make sense of it by developing theories of change, which in ANT terms can also be seen as imagining the associations that might be produced by the quasi-object. If we believe those associations should be made, a certain level of commitment is developed; in Dewey's terms, an "idea" has been formed. When we start to perform as if those associations were in place, action has been taken: the associations are considered made. Hence, we might see the difference between suggestions, ideas and actions as a difference of degree; the degree to which the actors they connect are willing to accept the associations they might provoke. Our ability to "do" social innovation, and the direction in which we take it both before and after we take action in the world, depends then not only on what we "know" about the situation and how we interrogate it, our beliefs and assumptions about how the world works, but also on our imaginations about how our actions might affect the world. After we take action, our theory of change, to the extent that it is articulated, provides a point of reference by which we can not only see whether our expectations are being met, but also confirm or disallow our assumptions. Hence, while explicitly recognizing theories of change in social innovation will suggest strategies for evaluating programs or projects in implementation, it can also play an instrumental role in revealing unrecognized or hidden knowledge, desires or prejudices, and in challenging participants to consider what they are trying to achieve. Theories of change might then be seen as contributing to "making design *things* public", a process that we have proposed as underlying social innovation.

Applying Theories of Change

There is already a well-recognized group of "theory-based" approaches that apply theories of change to assist in evaluation of programs or projects, going under a variety of names including "intervention logic" or "program logic" (Baehler 2007). All involve the development of "an explicit theory or model of how the program causes the intended or observed outcomes and an evaluation that is at least partly guided by this model" (Rogers *et al.* 2000, 5). Their intention is not to produce fully specified explanations, but to surface aspects of a program that might be crucial to its success, in ways that make them amenable to testing or monitoring as development and implementation proceeds. This approach contrasts quite starkly with other ways of evaluating projects or programs, which are less interesting in the social innovation context: ". . . exercises in constructing clear and specific goals, finding and adopting 'proven' implementation models, and striving toward predefined measurable outcomes, while not totally ignored, are less important to social innovators than realizing the grander vision of enacting positive social change" (M. Q. Patton cited in Lam and Shulha 2015, 359). At the level of practice, theory-based approaches allow for the progressive verification of hypotheses and assumptions and the identification of unexpected influences or relevant changes in the environment so that appropriate adjustments can be made.

The starting point, then, is agreement on intention or purpose, and a description of how it is expected to be achieved by the actions proposed, in a series of connected intermediate causal links, that are then open to testing and verification. A critical review of the proposed theory of change, then, allows the identification of assumptions that may have previously been hidden, and suggests what key points might be monitored to determine whether the theory is valid. Using theory-based approaches encourages proponents of social programs to be explicit about their assumptions on what the issues are, what a desirable outcome looks like and how their proposed interventions are expected to produce outcomes. Although explicitly stated, these are, of course, provisional portrayals. No attempt can be made to present them as exhaustive or efficient—the possibility must be recognized that there were unexpected or unknown influences at the time of their elaboration, or that exogenous change might render them invalid, as well as the possibility that experience as it unfolds will cause a redefinition of the purpose itself. Indeed, this openness and contingency is part of the value of these approaches, since the theory of change becomes a reference point that can be used to detect such changes or unforeseen factors. Theory-based approaches can be seen as enabling reflexivity in the development and implementation of social innovation programs or projects: "an evaluation progressing in 'real time' contemporaneously with the intervention itself" (Ling 2012, 79).

Family by Family

In practice, these approaches are not about developing a dry theory and associating a measurement system with it. Rather, they can be seen as a process of open-ended mutual enquiry and the establishment of common understanding about the key points that participants believe will produce desirable outcomes. The Family by Family program, developed in South Australia, provides an interesting example of the integration of co-design and theories of change in social innovation.

Family by Family started with a general conception of a problem area— a recognition of the value of keeping children out of the child protection system, rather than dealing with them only when their lives degenerated to the point of crisis—and a commitment to the principles of co-design, which might be seen as, the initial theory of change of The Australian Centre for Social Innovation (TACSI), the organization that initiated the program. The starting point for its development was the formation of a team around a senior manager seconded from the relevant government department, who was to "provide insight into the existing system and learn a new way of working", as well as a service designer and a sociologist, who had developed a methodology combining design methods and social science in the United Kingdom (Schulman, Curtis, and Vanstone 2011, 33). Following this model, the program developers started by conducting ethnographic research with thirty-five families, which clarified "thriving as the primary outcome measure", and which crucially determined that the program should aim at addressing the family context of the child, rather than focusing on the child in isolation. Ideas about how to create opportunities to thrive were developed and used as the base for "co-design work with 30 families . . . [to] test how to enable families to adopt thriving behaviours and build the necessary support networks" (25). A prototype was tested on a small scale with twenty families for twelve weeks, before metrics and materials and the initial model for larger scale operations were put in place (34). The model has since gone through further iterations as the program has been extended and adjustments are made to local conditions. These adaptations involve going back to the ethnographic stage with each new community (TACSI 2013b). Where the approach appears to bring unexpected results, an adaptation is signaled, as occurred when, during implementation of Family by Family, it was noted that the needs and responses to the program amongst Indigenous families seemed to be different, and a separate design process was established to better tailor a specific approach for those families (TACSI 2013a).

The Family by Family program, then, was designed through a series of rich interactions with intended participants, both in development and after implementation, during which the purposes of the program were clarified and the details of how it would operate to bring about the desired result were defined. This provides a good example of a theory of change evolving and being elaborated together with the planned intervention, as a co-creation of participants in the process, including designers and beneficiaries. Co-design was a general form of process applied to different aspects of the development: "Family by Family has been co-designed at a conceptual and an interaction level. Where the conceptual level outlines the outcomes (e.g. thriving) and the activities . . ., the interaction level looks at how families engage with each component of the activities: the materials, the offer, the roles, the training, the tools, etc." (Schulman, Curtis, and Vanstone 2011, 26). The materials, roles and tools have, therefore, evolved differently in the different regions in which the program is being conducted, being adapted to the demographics, needs and concerns of users in each. Implicit in this is a model of expansion that is not about "scaling up" or replication, but rather of a general form of co-design guiding the development and adaptation of a conceptual model to ensure it meets the needs of each new community it is introduced to. This ensures that the program is as relevant as possible to each community, and also strengthens its attractiveness and engagement with participants—it is not just "another referral" (27) that is proposed by services in order to address issues that someone else sees as important.

One of the core concepts of the program is that each family that participates should choose their own goals for the engagement, around the open direction of "whatever the family feels it needs to thrive". These are explicitly recognized as not having to conform to what professionals think would be best (TACSI 2012, 19). Families are also able to choose the professionals who support them in a "coaching" relationship. This represents a fundamental repositioning of the families with respect to power, and contrasts sharply with the coercive tools used in the statutory child protection services (24). Family goals are set using "bubbles and stickers" that ". . . [document] the families' plan—the change they want to achieve, how they'll go about it, and how they'll know if they're getting there" (Community Matters Pty Ltd 2012, 9), explicitly articulating a theory of change at the family level. Depending on how the family progresses, perhaps achieving the goals originally set or deciding that others have become more relevant or desirable, the goals can be changed as the engagement proceeds (18), so explicitly restating the theory of change. In a very real sense, then, each engagement is tailor-made for the families involved and they retain ownership of where it goes: the delivery of the program can be seen as both co-designed and co-produced (a distinction that is very hard to make in this case, and which probably has more to do with the perspective of the observer than revealing any objective difference). The bubble and sticker charts developed by each participating family are entered into a database and categorized by staff (based on themes emerging from the bubbles, not on an external classification), with a view to measuring the levels of family success at the program level (9), where another theory of change has been developed that is appropriate to that perspective (14, also Appendix 1). From the ANT point of view, it is interesting to see here how the non-human actors, bubbles and stickers (what might be called artifacts in other traditions), serve to connect the family and the program level actor-networks, enabling and channeling agency at the family level, but also representing the family in the program level actor-network.

The tight integration of explicitly recognized theories of change in the Family by Family program thus enables a reflexive, evolving and forward-looking process that enacts and adapts the program in the same move. It is not in any sense the design, then "implementation", of a program as a "model" imposed by a "higher" level on the family, but rather the establishment of an actor-network or co-design process around each family's matter of concern, embedded in a broader web of formally similar processes that each respond to different but interrelated matters of concern forming around the ideal of "thriving".

Because Family by Family established explicit theories of change at the program level, it was also possible to construct evaluation approaches that guided the program in its further evolution and adaptation. However, this demanded a shift away from more traditional "summative" concepts of evaluation, towards theory-based ones that were able to inform the development and activity of the program as it occurred, specifically identified as Realist Evaluation and Developmental Evaluation (7–8). These approaches challenge the assumptions that the outcomes of a program can be separated from the particularities of its context and its specific participants, because they are active rather than passive subjects on whom the program operates. They recognize that the program will act differently on different people, and that it is not only inevitable but desirable that it should continue to evolve and adapt as the context changes and as learning accumulates from actions.

> Realist evaluation assumes that interventions 'do not work, it is the interpretation of their subjects that produce results' (Pawson, 2013, 34). Thus there is an immediate focus on the logic(s) of those responding to the intervention. It further assumes that these responses will be partly conditioned by specific contextual features, so that the same intervention will not work in identical ways in different places or times, or with different audiences. It emphasises the importance of digging out and analysing the theory underlying the programme, and then testing, empirically, whether and when this theory actually plays out when the intervention is implemented. It is alert to the fact that 'programmes [sic] not only work to change behaviour but they may also change the conditions that make the programme work in the first place . . . (Pawson 2013, 92–94).
>
> (Pollitt 2013, 357)

In both Developmental and Realist Evaluation, the focus is not on developing a "model", but on developing and adapting a program, "provid[ing] evaluative information and feedback to social innovators to inform adaptive development in complex dynamic environments" (Patton 2016, 253). In this way, evaluation ". . . becomes part of the change process itself, part of the intervention. It happens like this: In inquiring into the meaning of innovation within a context and particular change-focused initiative, and providing feedback about what is learned as well as further questions generated, Developmental Evaluation affects and alters the innovation process and outcomes" (255).

The Family by Family case, then, illustrates several ways that explicitly recognizing theories of change can impact on social innovation, and points towards specific approaches to evaluation that are generative rather than limiting the innovation to a fixed form, pinning it to a board so it can be measured. The proposal, in broad terms, is to simultaneously attempt to articulate and seek feedback against a theory of change at all stages of the process, allowing "evaluation" to effectively act as sensory data that the *thing* takes into account in its further activity, whether in design or implementation. By orienting interactions around such a framework, it becomes easier both to disentangle possible confusions around issues and to ensure testing of a proto-solution is monitored in a targeted and useable fashion, since it is linked directly back to key beliefs about how the model is to work. Theory of change approaches also assist in identifying if there are any actors who are critical to the success of a solution but are not involved in its preparation, and so form a basis for determining if new participants should be invited into the process (Baehler 2007, 165). It is even possible to consider a theory of change against what can be termed its "opposition logic", the causal chain by which some participants might see the proto-solution creating a worst-case result (Baehler 2007, 164). This can assist in identifying risks.

By orienting participants to generate data that is relevant to the on-going deliberation of the *thing*, allowing theory of change approaches to guide the way we interrogate the world offers potential to bring together and make commensurable the concerns of divergent stakeholders. In this, the theories of change seem to act as boundary objects: ". . . both plastic enough to adapt to local needs and the constraints of the several parties employing them, yet robust enough to maintain a common identity across sites. They are weakly structured in common use, and become strongly structured in individual-site use. . . . They have different meanings in different social worlds but their structure is common enough to more than one world to make them recognizable, a means of translation" (Star and Griesemer 1989, 393). However, the value of theory-based approaches rests mainly in their ability to provoke insight, challenge assumptions and so stimulate the innovation which is the purpose of the process.

Mutual Learning

The availability of information, particularly when compared to theories of change, will support or discourage certain ways forward. From any starting point, the information available will, in part, be a contextual factor, the result of our or others' past decisions about what to collect and make available, and in part be determined by the questions we ask as we seek to integrate what we know into our deliberations. We proceed by learning together, continuously developing possible theories of change alongside our data, by which standard we determine what is likely to be relevant or not. As we proceed, what we know becomes more and more dependent on our questioning, our decisions on what to select from reality so that we can elaborate or challenge our emerging imagination of what action will look like and what it will bring about. Our "questions" may also take many forms; they need not be limited to verbal interrogations. Making a suggestion, proposing an idea, building a prototype: all of these challenge our current view of a situation and can be seen as a form of question. We may inform ourselves by action.

Questioning is driven and constrained by our ideas about what rules constitute valid ways of coming to conclusions; by our views of rationality (not always consistent or shared). But what sorts of logic are appropriate for an open-ended, generative process of discovery? How can we be rational when our enquiry is shaped by apparently exogenous constraints on what we can know, by chance events as much by the consequences of our experimental actions, by the exigencies of working in community to produce some solution, even if it is not what we personally might consider best? We are talking not only about selecting and evaluating "proto-solutions", but also about generating new ones, which suggests that the two forms of ampliative logic, induction and abduction, are likely to be most appropriately employed: although they do not offer certainty, they are means to generate new possibilities. Schurz distinguishes between the two on the basis that induction is interested in predicting future events (which is not our purpose), while abduction seeks to generate ideas about causes or explanations, "which [are] of central importance for manipulating the course of events, that is, adapting the course of events to our wishes" (2008, 202). This is consistent with Pierce's view of abductive reasoning as being less concerned with establishing the validity of any particular hypothesis than with the generation of explanations that form the base for further development, either by testing for confirmation or for falsification.

Schurz distinguishes between types of abduction that aim to select the best explanation from amongst those available and types that aim to generate new concepts or models, which he describes as "creative". For our purposes, both can be seen as potentially relevant to the process of developing innovations, with the important observation that "the crucial function of a pattern of abduction . . . consists in its function as a search strategy which leads us, for a given kind of scenario, in a reasonable time to a most promising explanatory conjecture which is then subject to further test" (205). Hence, the innovation process reflects the application of abductive reasoning to develop, support or refute proto-solutions and render them accessible to testing through action, which generates new knowledge about possible ways forward. As for the role of evaluation, instead of being focused on a backward-looking determination of whether an intervention, innovation or program has been effective, this perspective suggests we should remain focused on informing the intended use of an intervention by its intended users (Patton 1994, 317). This sort of evaluation is "purpose-and-relationship-driven not methods-driven" (Patton 2011, 288), so it must be able to deal with changes of both context and even purpose, which may evolve as programs proceed. Patton sees this as one of the features of developmental evaluation, as ". . . a way of being useful in innovative settings where goals are emergent and changing rather than predetermined and fixed, time periods are fluid and forward-looking rather than artificially imposed by external deadlines, and purpose is learning, innovation, and change rather than external accountability (summative evaluation) or getting ready for external accountability (formative evaluation)" (Patton 1994, 318). Instead of seeking certainty, the role is to support a productive search and discovery strategy, and to shift the position of the evaluator from being an outside authority pronouncing on the program to one where the evaluator is an integral part of the program: indeed, one where they are an active participant in generating mutual learning.

As a tool for exploring "proto-solutions", this is an engaged, practical rationality that emphasizes sensitivity to reality, adaptation and the imagination of new ways forward, as well as pointing to productive forms of evaluation. Together with our theories of change, it allows us to make sense of a proto-solution in terms of its practical significance, at the same time acting as a way to surface our assumptions and interrogate our purpose, and identify what is not known about a context or problem. By challenging different assumptions about what underlies actions, and clarifying how they are believed to connect to a possible outcome, it becomes possible to specify new possibilities that may share similar purposes and relate them to the proposals under investigation. It may also be possible to agree that an action is acceptable to different parties, even if its expected outcome is different, allowing limited progress to be made.

We then propose to establish measurement and evaluation at the heart of the development of the proto-solution, through all its different levels of "completeness", not merely as something to be applied when the solution is "implemented". In any case, put in the context of our proposal that the results of the innovation process are always provisional and form the base for further development, there appears to be no reason to distinguish between these moments of application, since development always continues. The key concerns for an evaluation process are to assist in revealing the unexpected, providing a base to deepen understanding of how the solution might operate in the future and of what its effects will be on key groups of importance to participants. Establishing standards and seeing whether they have been achieved, or measuring a high-level Key Performance Indicator (KPI) that equates to the purpose of the solution is insufficient, if not irrelevant, to the process of innovation itself, although both these approaches might be useful for others' purposes. This view seems to contrast markedly with approaches to evaluation commonly discussed in the social innovation literature. Murray *et al.* propose twenty-four different types of measures (under the heading "Metrics to show what works and what deserves to be grown") in their compendium of methods and tools for social innovation (2010, 101–105). Although it is possible that some of the categories might be applied to encompass theory-based approaches, there is certainly no indication that this is intended. More importantly though, as Murray *et al.* observe, almost all of the methods noted are intended for external use by funders, rather than being intended for use by innovators themselves in the way we have proposed, to assist in creating, guiding and adapting innovation, or looking at the impact of social innovation processes over time. Of course, it is understandable that innovators should be concerned about generating the sort of data required to get funding for their projects, even if this comes at a cost in terms of additional data collection. However, it also seems to illustrate the risk identified in chapter 3, that the focus on funding and the institutional context of social innovation might distract from the process of innovation itself or, worse, distort or impede it. We see the development of the sorts of approaches we have sketched out here, tailored to the process of social innovation, as offering significant potential to redress this balance.

We cannot leave this topic, however, without specifically addressing the emerging push, already mentioned, to apply experimental methods and Randomized Control Trials (RCTs) to social innovation, which has been the subject of significant controversy in the field of international development aid (Picciotto 2012). Against these methods' claims of "scientific" certainty, the provisional and, by definition, possibly false "theories" that are produced by an abductive process of disputed mutual learning appear to be decidedly at a disadvantage.

Of course, it is crucial to recall that the purpose of these theories is fundamentally different: the theory of change is put forward to act as a reference point against which we can surface or check assumptions, recognize if the unexpected is happening or identify if there are things we need to explore more. Predictive certainty is not necessary; the emphasis is on utility to the process. We express ideas about what we think is likely to happen in the future, based on our current context and our beliefs about how things work. We know full well that if the future resembles what we expected, our "theory" has not necessarily been validated; it just remains plausible. If the future does not eventuate the way we expected, we will search for plausible alternative explanations. In either case, the context will probably have changed, perhaps precisely because of what we tried. We continue to experiment and move closer to confidence in our beliefs, perhaps even approaching something of the form that Mohr (1982) calls "process theory": if "b" then "a", where "a" and "b" are ordered events, describing conditions that are necessary but not sufficient for an outcome to occur, "the *unobserved causes* or *explanatory reasons* of the observed events" (Schurz 2008, 202, emphasis in original). There will always be many candidates for "a", too many to test for in reality, and certainly not in "controlled" conditions, so that the process of testing becomes one of seeking progressively better, but never final, theories about what causes things to occur in the (always changing) context in question. Not only does this process lead to a better understanding of the world we are operating in, it is flexible and allows us to progress even when we know we do not understand everything. Perhaps as importantly, though, this process of mutual learning, the exploring, imagining, questioning and challenging that we have described, is valuable in itself, building the capacity of the people individually and collectively involved. Theory that offers predictive certainty, if "a" then "b", which Mohr calls "variance theory", makes such a process irrelevant—the people enacting the new social practice will perform as expected, so there is no need to seek insight or develop relationships. The two forms of theory are both formally incommensurable and achieve different things.

With this in mind, it might seem possible to allow both types of theory their proper domain and seek only to apply the one that is appropriate to the question at hand. However, developing evidence that can be considered "scientific" is extremely attractive, particularly to funders, and so tends to displace other approaches, even where they may be more appropriate, so the way RCTs are used deserves some closer exploration. It is useful to look at a specific case, to clarify the limits and applications of both types of theory. In 2011, Pascaline Dupas, co-chair of the Health Sector at the Abdul Latif Jameel Poverty Action Lab (J-Pal), one of the main proponents of the use of RCTs in informing public policy, published a paper examining the relative effectiveness of providing Kenyan teenagers with information on the elevated risk of contracting HIV from older partners, compared with promoting (officially sanctioned) abstinence-only material (Dupas 2011). The study took the form of a "randomized field experiment" in 328 primary schools, and provided evidence "that the behavioral choices of teenagers are not responsive to risk avoidance messages, but are responsive to information on the relative riskiness of potential partners. Overall, the relative risk information led to an increase in reported sexual activity, but to a decrease in unsafe sex" (3). It also provides concluding remarks suggesting the relevance of the study more generally to public health prevention programs, as speaking to the value of providing information on risk reduction (the "intensive margin") as compared to seeking avoidance of the behavior in question (the "extensive margin"), since the data it presents show, at least with regard to sexual behavior, that behavior is much more elastic on the former than the latter (29).

Although these latter remarks are clearly more a reflection on possible implications of the study, and take no definitive position, they do raise the question of the level of external validity of studies of this kind (Ravallion 2009). Can the conclusions of this study be extended from the partner selection decisions of teenage girls to sexual behavior more generally, or to partner selection decisions amongst other cohorts? How firm a base would the study provide for extension into similar risk reduction/avoidance decisions in other domains of behavior? On any of these levels, can the conclusions of this research be applied outside the two districts of Western Kenya in which it was conducted? What effects might cultural or religious differences have on the conclusions, particularly in contexts where the status of women and girls differs from the study context? Although it is quite possible that the study provides a useful base case, or initial hypothesis, for anyone planning a campaign in other regions or health domains, it would seem advisable to proceed with some caution on these points. But there are other issues that must also be considered. The two educational methods that were compared in this study were 1) supporting the dissemination of the official government HIV/AIDS curriculum by enhancing teacher training, and 2) the direct provision of risk information by a project officer, including a ten-minute video on the risks of cross-generational sex. Are either of these approaches the best possible implementation of their respective strategies? Could a more effective campaign, perhaps reaching beyond the school curriculum into the broader community, reduce rates of sexual activity to the extent that better results are achieved than through risk reduction? Could the risk reduction strategy be made more effective through similar modifications, and what would the marginal effect be of increasing resources allocated to, say, the quality of the material or the frequency of the project officer visits? What would the relative effectiveness be of instituting legal or social sanctions on the behavior of the older males, such as mandated child support obligations? All these questions, without in any way casting doubt on the conclusions of the research as far as they go, draw attention to the process within which it is conducted and considered relevant. Attempting to apply the conclusions of this research by, for instance, funding extension of the risk reduction "solution" on a larger geographical scale based on the "scientifically proven" validity of these results, to the exclusion of broader engagement that might produce more effective solutions, could not in any way be seen as ensuring that the best results were achieved for the money, even if it were still to hold true that we could be sure the program works.

We find ourselves drawn back to the tension between applying solutions developed elsewhere and discovering them in context. In the process of innovation developed thus far, we lean towards the latter end of the continuum. Under this scenario, the process would start by examining the issue of HIV/AIDS transmission with local communities, providing not only the information being given to the teenagers in this case and the knowledge that informing students puts them less at risk, but also relevant data about the broader situation. It would also mean taking into the discussion the information, experience and concerns that the community expressed, then working with them to design actions that might bring about change. These might include a focus on informing students, but they might also include a range of other community supports. By agreeing on a "theory of change" with the community that they found convincing, and identifying points that might need verifying, not only might a more fully featured solution be developed, but much broader support for the initiative might also be garnered. To propose that this study on its own provides certainty for funders to determine what programs should or should not be supported completely removes the people it is intended to benefit from the actor-network, consigning them to the status of "intermediaries" or subjects. Furthermore, it provides no indications on where to go from here—what is the best way to follow up such a campaign? Where does the next "solution" come from? Our focus on investing scientific invincibility into the solution, which inevitably depersonalizes and decontextualizes it, may be relevant for funders to make a decision between alternative possible uses for their money, but it has little to do with sparking long-term, robust processes of social innovation in a target community: "Qualitative methods guided by theories of change examine what has actually happened and why. They are better equipped to determine the reasons for success or failure of achieving intended effects (and the extent and nature of unintended effects). In particular, they help to discriminate between design issues and implementation problems. Whereas experimental methods are shaped by data, qualitative, theory-based approaches are shaped by the questions of interest to stakeholders and the assumptions embedded in programme and project interventions (Bamberger, Rao, and Woolcock 2009)" (Picciotto 2012).

This is not to suggest that there is no use for RCTs in social innovation. The point is to be clear about what they are being mobilized to achieve. RCTs appear to be an extremely useful option to consider, assuming that they are ethical and not too costly, to test some aspect of a theory of change, or determine whether a program has made an impact over a period. However, when used to "validate a solution", even if they can credibly be said to have done so, they may tend to distract attention from the actual issue as it is being experienced in the community and militate against making adaptations that might be seen to make the research inapplicable. They may also discourage the sort of enquiry required to understand the systemic context in which a "solution" is to be applied, so disregarding the question of whether other, better or more appropriate, ways of proceeding might be developed, and also disregarding the possibility of unintended consequences. Used in this way, RCTs (and many other of the "scientific" methods) seem to exhibit many of the features of the Western PlayPump actor-network, but most particularly its focus on staging a performance for the benefit of a set of actors that has little to do with the purported purpose of the intervention. "Abandoning the search for 'incredible certitude' (Manski 2007), and embracing the idea that an evaluation should aim to reduce key uncertainties, leads us to an approach which takes place in real time, is formative in nature, and aims to produce findings that are explicitly contingent. Being explicitly contingent, providing these contingent factors are adequately explained, prevents universal conclusions being drawn, but they do allow lessons to be drawn and applied elsewhere" (Ling 2012, 89).

The problem appears to be exacerbated by the predilection that some funders and promoters of social innovation display for applying measures of this kind at the individual project level. The assumption appears to be that the way to maximize the efficiency of funding is to ensure that every project performs as efficiently as possible. This is akin to insisting that every product group or innovation in a growing company must achieve a minimum growth rate. It ignores the potential of working across a number of projects that may have different time-lines, risk profiles and may support each other. Not only does this encourage risk aversion, but more importantly it fails to allow for the fact that some initiatives may make it possible for others to succeed, even though they may not appear to meet standards at the project level. This sort of rigid approach to measurement at the micro-level seems likely to produce the most damaging effects on genuinely participative design and innovation, as measures effectively become controls to discipline individual implementations of an externally developed model. Of course, there are many evaluation approaches that do allow theory of change approaches (such as those used by TACSI in the Family by Family case). Of particular interest are examples of these that take advantage of technology. For example, Acumen's "Lean Data" seems to be specifically intended to allow adaptation to measurement of different key indicators in a theory of change (Adams, Gawande, and Overdyke n.d., 8). These are welcome developments, but the risk is that, precisely because of their novelty and the way such tools support a narrative of "marvelous new tools from very clever innovators", they draw attention away from what is actually being measured, which is where social innovation is taking place. We have proposed that measurement and evaluation should be seen as integral to social innovation: however, this does not mean measurement *is* social innovation. Once its focus shifts from nourishing the process at the local level, measurement becomes a control device, or a way by which an external party meets its needs. This is also true of the insistence on always measuring against a "counterfactual", which is scarcely, if ever, likely to be a concern for those who are actually enacting social innovation, since their action effectively removes the alternative from the picture.

References

Adams, Tom, Rohit Gawande, and Scott Overdyke. n.d. *Innovations in Impact Measurement.* Acumen/Root Capital. Retrieved from http://acumen.org/wp-content/uploads/2015/11/Innovations-in-Impact-Measurement-Report.pdf

Baehler, Karen. 2007. "Intervention Logic/ Program Logic: Toward Good Practice." In *Improving Implementation—Organisational Change and Project Management*, edited by John Wanna, 157–175. Canberra: ANU E Press.

Bamberger, Michael, Vijayendra Rao, and Michael Woolcock. 2009. Using Mixed Methods in Monitoring and Evaluation: Experiences from International Development. *BWPI Working Paper 107*. Manchester UK: Brookes World Poverty Institute.

Community Matters Pty Ltd. 2012. Family by Family Evaluation Report 2011–2012. Retrieved from http://www.tacsi.org.au/wp-content/uploads/2014/08/TACSI-FbyF-Evaluation-Report-2012.pdf

Dupas, Pascaline. 2011. "Do Teenagers Respond to HIV Risk Information? Evidence from a Field Experiment in Kenya." *American Economic Journal: Applied Economics* 3 (1):1–34. doi: http://dx.doi.org/10.1257/app.3.1.1.

Lam, C. Y., and L. M. Shulha. 2015. "Insights on Using Developmental Evaluation for Innovating: A Case Study on the Co-Creation of an Innovative Program." *American Journal of Evaluation* 36 (3):358–374. doi: 10.1177/1098214014542100.

Ling, T. 2012. "Evaluating Complex and Unfolding Interventions in Real Time." *Evaluation* 18 (1):79–91. doi: 10.1177/1356389011429629.

Manski C (2007) Identification for Prediction and Decision. Cambridge, MA: Harvard University Press, 7–8. Quoted in Manski C (2011) Policy analysis with incredible certitude. Paper presented at the Institute for Fiscal Studies, February 2011.

Menand, Louis. 1997. "The Return of Pragmatism." *American Heritage*, October, 48–63.

Mohr, Lawrence B. 1982. *Explaining Organizational Behavior*. 1st ed. San Francisco, CA: Jossey-Bass.

Mulgan, Geoff. 2015. "Foreword: The Study of Social Innovation—Theory, Practice and Progress." In *New Frontiers in Social Innovation Research*, edited by Alex Nicholls, Julie Simon, and Madeleine Gabriel, x–xx. Basingstoke: Palgrave Macmillan.

Murray, Robin, Julie Caulier-Grice, and Geoff Mulgan. 2010. *The Open Book of Social Innovation*. London: NESTA.

Patton, Michael Quinn. 1994. "Developmental Evaluation." *Evaluation Practice* 15 (3):311–319.

Patton, Michael Quinn. 2011. *Developmental Evaluation: Applying Complexity Concepts to Enhance Innovation and Use*. New York: Guilford Press.

Patton, Michael Quinn. 2016. "What Is Essential in Developmental Evaluation? On Integrity, Fidelity, Adultery, Abstinence, Impotence, Long-Term Commitment, Integrity, and Sensitivity in Implementing Evaluation Models." *American Journal of Evaluation* 37 (2):250–265. doi: 10.1177/1098214015626295.

Pawson, Ray. 2013. *The Science of Evaluation: A Realist Manifesto*. London: SAGE.

Picciotto, Robert. 2012. "Experimentalism and Development Evaluation: Will the Bubble Burst?" *Evaluation* 18 (2):213–229. doi: 10.1177/1356389012440915.

Pollitt, C. 2013. "The Logics of Performance Management." *Evaluation* 19 (4):346–363. doi: 10.1177/1356389013505040.

Ramsey, Caroline. 2011. "Provocative Theory and a Scholarship of Practice." *Management Learning* 42 (5):469–483. doi: 10.1177/1350507610394410.

Ravallion, Martin. 2009. "Evaluation in the Practice of Development." *The World Bank Research Observer* 24 (1):29–53. doi: 10.1093/wbro/lkp002.

Rogers, Patricia J., Anthony Petrosino, Tracy A. Huebner, and Timothy A. Hacsi. 2000. "Program Theory Evaluation: Practice, Promise, and Problems." *New Directions for Evaluation* 2000 (87):5–13. doi: 10.1002/ev.1177.

Schulman, Sarah, Carolyn Curtis, and Chris Vanstone. 2011. "Family by Family: A Co-Designed & Co-Produced Family Support Model." In *Building Integrated Connections for Children Their Families and Communities*, edited by Karl Brettig and Margaret Sims, 23–41. Newcastle upon Tyne: Cambridge Scholars Publishing.

Schurz, G. 2008. "Patterns of Abduction." *Synthese* 164 (2):201–234. doi: 10.1007/s11229-007-9223-4.

Star, Susan Leigh, and James R. Griesemer. 1989. "Institutional Ecology, 'Translations' and Boundary Objects: Amateurs and Professionals in Berkeley's Museum of Vertebrate Zoology, 1907–39." *Social Studies of Science* 19 (3):387–420. doi: 10.1177/030631289019003001.

TACSI. 2012. Family by Family Explained for Professionals. Retrieved from http://familybyfamily.org.au/wp-content/uploads/2012/10/SV001-Pages1.pdf

TACSI. 2013a. "Family by Family: Enabling change with Aboriginal Families and Services," accessed 14/9/2016. http://familybyfamily.org.au/2013/08/enabling-change-with-aboriginal-families-and-services/.

TACSI. 2013b. *Family by Family: Mount Druitt Scoping and Start-up Report*. Emerton, Australia: The Australian Centre for Social Innovation.

6 Impact, Governance and Ethics

Making an Impact

We have now developed a view on the nature of the social innovation process, and on the general form it takes. The conceptualization that has emerged is essentially a micro-level one: in the absence of "the social", interaction is inherently local, or multi-local. The content of local interactions is not only able, but expected, to differ from one site to another. The ambitious "top-down" views of social innovation that promise the development of comprehensive "high-level" models that revolutionize society and solve its problems with a determined push to implement "at scale" are seen as not only potentially obstructive to the mobilization of local actors in developing their own solutions, but also at a high risk of failure, due to the likelihood that they neither anticipate and adjust to local concerns nor generate the necessary interest and support from the local actors required to bring them into being on the ground. The quest to find these cross-cutting, powerful solutions risks smothering local initiatives and hijacking the resources and attention they need to develop and flourish.

Does this mean that large-scale impact of social innovation is a delusion? Can widespread transformational change be achieved, or must we resign ourselves to incremental small steps? We will propose that this apparent compromise is not necessary, and only appears to be so if we assume that large-scale change must be planned and controlled, an approach that in fact is only capable of delivering incremental change, if any change at all. We will assert that large-scale change is indeed possible, if we are willing to abandon the illusion of control and allow it to emerge from a ground-swell of local activity, creatively adapted, connected and amplified across new sites. We will explore how this sort of innovation might produce not only a response to immediate concerns, but also contribute to the establishment of infrastructure, or social capital, that can be exploited in future innovation challenges. We will conclude by exploring what sort of a role exists for the designer, and explore how this role can be ethically fulfilled.

Revisiting Scaling

In chapter 3, we introduced the proposal of Iversen and Dindler (2014) that there are three ways for a social innovation to develop over time, in addition to scaling: maintaining, replicating and evolving. Of these, scaling and replicating share the ambition of extending the innovation beyond its initial site; evolution might also lead to larger scale, but is first concerned with achieving adaptation to changing conditions; whereas maintaining is satisfied with the on-going production of the innovation at its original site and scale. All except evolution treat the innovation as in some sense finalized, the product of a pre-occurring development process or project. This seems to effectively exclude new participants in new locations from participating further in its design, imposing a pre-established model across new contexts. Maintenance, on the other hand, appears to attempt to hold the model in a fixed state, which sounds unambitious but may actually be quite a feat. Hence, this notion of finalization, particularly as it is imposed by the delineation of boundaries around projects, appears to be intimately connected with the issue of scaling.

Projects, at least in the way that they are usually defined and funded, are bounded, both temporally and in terms of participation: they are structures that do not encourage open-ended negotiation of purpose or easily accept emergent outcomes on uncertain time-scales. However, it is possible to see this apparent conflict as a question of the level at which the conceptualization is applied. If we take the project level as a design process, but as one that is embedded in or entangled with others, just one exercise in a continuing stream of work around one or more matters of concern, it is much easier to reconcile with the model being developed here. The suggestion seems to be that we need to consider projects as transitory efforts that form part of a larger stream of work that is itself truly open. This would mean paying attention to these specific activities as moves within the broader collaboration, but also considering the conditions, structures and influences within which they occur and which over time they modify—how they relate to each other and the whole. Of course, the decision on how to frame specific projects, and who to involve or exclude from them, potentially has tactical impact and, because of path-dependency, may thus close off or open up possibilities in the future, having a lasting impact on outcomes.

Contextualizing the project in this way can also be seen as an interaction between temporal perspectives, with the project representing the located present, its possible evolutions and connections constituting a future that it is involved in producing; and its past, its origins, causes and meaningful events constituting a foundation or justification for how it is now being approached. Each of these perspectives is suggestive of both possibilities and constraints. Three different ways of orienting ourselves to these different temporal perspectives can be discerned (Britton and Bonser 2014):

- Foreshadowing: the imagination of the future;
- Back-shadowing: the focus on evidence, "reality" and narrative logic; and

- Side-shadowing, in which there is a recognition that there are a range of possibilities that might have come into being, many more than are realized. It is an orientation towards the possibility that ". . . things could have been different from the way they were, there were real alternatives to the present we know, and the future admits of various paths" (Morson 1996, 4).

The process of developing proto-solutions, expressions of a design *thing*, draws on each of these understandings. Proto-solutions take their aura of plausibility from their connection to what is "known" to be real; they challenge the present by contrast with alternatives that might have existed and that suggest different ways forward, and they offer imaginations of alternative futures that can be compared with each other and the present. As each proposal is put forward, it provokes reactions, critiques or support and becomes subject to further modification, in an attempt to better integrate what is known or define a future that is more attractive. This occurs in a reflective space somewhere within the tension between agency and structure; the interpretations and reflections provoked by the experience of the proto-solution themselves become part of the matter for concern around which the group has coalesced, as it collaborates (agonistically) to make sense of the new reality it is creating.

Once we accept that no proto-solution exists in isolation, either from its past, its unrealized alternative presents or its possible futures, it becomes possible to see the outcome of a local design *thing* becoming a quasi-object with which a new design *thing* may occupy itself. The process of "scaling", or using a proto-solution to bring about action in a different context, is not about "transferring a model" from one context to another, but about connecting it to new contexts, as a catalyst for local work. The proto-solution is not used as a ready answer, but as a generative, provocative actor around which matters of concern may be developed. The same thing may occur when new people are introduced to the *thing*; indeed, this is formally identical in ANT terms, since objects, quasi-objects and individuals are all actants to be handled consistent with the principle of general symmetry. The connection opens up the possibility that the proto-solution might be modified by the new design *thing*, but it may also lead to further modifications in the original *thing*, as new perspectives open up possibilities, or reveal concerns, that were not taken into the initial deliberations. Hence, the process of scaling an innovation is not akin to the shift from a design phase to a production phase; it is the extension of the same process over time and across new publics, during which it opens the innovation up to further change, to failure or to the development of unforeseen new alternatives. The feature of interest is not the place of the work in a sequence, but how the work evolves over time, and on its various sites.

This is the same dynamic that has been observed in the discussion of co-design in chapter 2. New "users" may take the proto-solution in a new direction, one unforeseen during its initial development, making it impossible to distinguish between co-design and co-production as qualitatively distinct phases. In ANT terms, the proto-solution is an actor representing the earlier design *things*. Ehn (2008) raises the question of whether, in the same way that the design object represents the past to the future in design after design, it is then possible to represent the future in use before use: to "design for design", in anticipation and facilitation of future modifications to be made to the design object. This would be a "metadesign" approach, where "both professional designers and potential users are seen as designers, much as in Participatory Design, but they are not participating in synchronous entangled design-games, but in design-games separated in time and space" (96). Design for design then becomes ". . . a chain of one design-game after another" (Ehn 2008). Ehn proposes that the designed object performs a mediating function, being present as both a "representative of the objects of design and, as boundary objects, also socio-material public things". He then identifies this mediation as "infrastructuring", where the infrastructure becomes " 'sunk into' other socio-material structures and [is] only accessible by membership in a specific community-of-practice. Infrastructure or rather *infrastructuring* is a socio-material public thing, it is relational and becomes infrastructure in relation to design-games at project time and (multiple potentially conflictious) design-games in use" (Ehn 2008, emphasis in original). Ehn treats this question from the point of view of the designer, and proposes strategies for deliberately "infrastructuring" to be "enacted as design at project time", focusing initially on features of the designed object, such as the development of protocols within which it is embedded. In our context, these seem analogous to looking at possible forms that proto-solutions might take, such as the general construct of a theory of change, which might be seen as acting as a protocol through which future *things* might be able to re-engage in design at use time. However, the relational connections established during design project time are themselves resources that enable future action on different design objects, and must also be seen as a form of infrastructuring, one that transgresses the boundary of a specific project and potentiates engagement with new matters of concern.

This discussion, then, further develops the point made about the nonviability of fixing project boundaries, except as matters of convenience or tactics within a broader process, to specify that this is as true for temporal boundaries as it is for structural and organizational boundaries. The "leakage" that occurs across any such imagined boundaries occurs through the means of proto-solutions, acting as boundary objects that are able to spark new *things*, either in a different place or at a different time. These boundary objects may themselves be protocols that carry some of the original design concerns into the new *thing*, so offering the potential for "design for design", the anticipation of future modifications, to be incorporated into initial design of the proto-solution. This does not represent a means to "control" the design process into the future, even if that were the intention, as every *thing* is free to choose what it makes of the proto-solution it is examining. However, it does suggest that social innovation can and should be looked at in its fuller context, both at a specific time and as it develops over time. Our tendency to speak of "social innovations" as an ever-growing inventory of unitary "solutions", and the associated organizational convenience of adopting a project perspective, should be complemented by a sensitivity to detecting connections between local *things*, and perhaps even promoting them.

It is important to note that we have been talking here about the extension of innovations beyond their original context in space or time, in which case they are effectively reinvented. "Maintenance" represents quite a different set of challenges. Based on the ideas being developed here, maintenance would involve repeating the same social practices in the same context. As was pointed out earlier, this would appear to be a significant accomplishment in its own right if social practices are seen as being reenacted each time they occur, if only due to the likelihood of micro-variations. There is also an issue around the stability of the context: to what extent is a social setting able to remain effectively unchanged over time? These questions serve to underline the value of clearly articulating a theory of change, as discussed in chapter 5, and continuing to use it as a reference point, even after project time. In this way, on-going evaluation serves to alert us if unexpected variation is occurring, or if conditions appear to have changed, in which case it may be necessary to consider how to adapt the innovation. Variation may be suppressed or amplified. Depending on the way the proto-solution has been structured, maintenance may also involve collecting data to justify funding from external bodies, using measurements adapted to their needs.

The foregoing represents a significant challenge to assumptions that "small" should be regarded as inherently preliminary, and that an innovation only becomes worthwhile when "it" is somehow transformed to a larger version of itself. It is reminiscent of what Ostrom and Cox call the "panacea problem", which occurs "whenever a single presumed solution is applied to a wide range of problems" (2010, 452), which may arise either because "a theory is too precise to be flexibly adapted to the range of cases to which it is applied" or, conversely, when it is too vague to suggest meaningful solutions (such as the debate over private or public ownership in environmental conservation). The risk with taking a solution and either "replicating" it or "scaling" it is either that insufficient attention will be paid to the local realities of the focus problem, the resources and institutions available to implement the solution, or that the proposed "solution" is simply irrelevant in the new context. The challenge to the ideal of the "scalable solution" is, therefore, at multiple levels: the possibility of declaring that "completion" has been achieved; the idea that the design object must remain inviolate as it is scaled or replicated (even if that were possible, given the unique context of each implementation); and the possibility of "planning" or predicting the results of scaling, as distinct from facilitating the possible emergence of new objects in design after design phase. It suggests that, rather than being preoccupied with how to scale innovations, we might be better served by turning our attention to influencing and facilitating the process by which local innovation connects to local innovation, both synchronously and asynchronously. As Manzini says, "[S]mall is not small . . . local is not local" (2010, 10–11). If we see the link between small projects and large changes as "participatory design as an open participated process", and focus our efforts on that process, each becomes a manifestation of the other. Moreover, the structures within which this translation occurs, and the connections that are made in linking the local, become a resource for new issues to be addressed—an infrastructure for innovation.

Starting with a local focus that brings matters of concern to life in a specific context and demonstrates the viability of small-scale action may also be preferable to attempting to challenge large issues at the systemic level. This is exemplified in the "eco-acupuncture" approach that has been adopted at the University of Melbourne's Victorian Eco Innovation Lab (VEIL) and elsewhere. This brings issues of sustainability to life in specific communities through a series of projects that are small enough to be affordable for the community concerned (and not create major issues if they fail), but large enough to demonstrate that different ways of living are possible. Ryan observes that this approach "overcomes a sense within the community that the change beyond a small variation of business-as-usual is simply not possible . . . if we can move in to situations where we're able to say 'The future can change. It can change quite quickly and here're some ways in which the future might be very different than the present' and do that in a way that people, communities, businesses, service companies, built environment companies and so on can get ideas about alternative futures, then I think we can achieve a lot in terms of speeding up the change" (quoted in Gaziulusoy 2014). The desired result is described as "new projects 'on-the-ground' that can release new community energy and support for a new trajectory of development" (VEIL n.d.).

In one particular project using the eco-acupuncture approach, VEIL specifically identifies six themes of activity. The first, "Encounter", involves the development of ways for the community to directly experience a possibility that might otherwise not be considered possible. This theme of presenting something "concrete" for the community to engage with is echoed in two other themes, "Regenerate", which brings "old" things back to the attention of the community in ways that may allow them to become relevant in the future; and "Make Transparent", by which hidden things, such as the "pathways of production and consumption", are made visible. In all three cases, this might be seen as the provocative presentation of "proto-solutions" in order to spark the engagement of the community in developing (or supporting the development of) futures that have been made possible. These design objects might also arise from, or be extended into, new contexts, through "replication" (perhaps, given our discussion, adaptation) in a new context; "amplification" (designing something existing to be bigger); or "simplification" (focusing on the essential to allow "imaginative action and local innovation"). This approach treats the innovation as a metaphorical catalyst, by which action on a larger scale may be stimulated or enabled.

The phenomenon of relatively small events potentially having far-reaching effects (or large ones having very little effect) is reminiscent of complexity theory, and particularly the concepts of systems being far from equilibrium, allowing the emergence of starkly different patterns in the system to arise from relatively minor actions or because of sensitivity to initial conditions (the so-called "butterfly effect"). Differing notions of complexity theory are widespread amongst social innovation practitioners. As Mulgan points out, ". . . it offers frames and metaphors that fit their experience of engaging with the world at multiple levels; it can combine the subjective and objective, the roles of culture and psychology as well as economics; and it points to the importance of non-linear as well as linear changes. The social innovation field is instinctively at home with organic development, trial and error; dispersed power, and with the ideas associated with the open source and open data movements which emphasise self-organising systems which use multiple horizontal links and complexity to solve problems" (2012, 28).

It is interesting that we have come to this resonance by examining the dynamics of co-design in its local enactments, based on a theoretical approach that eschews the "top-down" views of society that might be taken as the perspective of complexity theory. This apparent contradiction, however, depends on the notion that complexity theory requires that the systems of which it speaks are in some sense objective realities that can be viewed from outside, which would erect the sort of realm of the social rejected by ANT. However, this is unnecessary if we see "systems" as relational traces, with very much the same status as the networks of actor-network theory: "A network is not a thing, but the recorded movement of a thing" (Latour 1996, 378). In an extended body of work, Stacey and colleagues have addressed the same issue, through a critique of some streams of complexity and systems thinking that theorize systems, or complex adaptive systems, as existing "outside" or separate from the individual and interaction (see, for example, Stacey 2001b, 2007, Stacey, Griffin, and Shaw 2000). Building on Mead (1967), they propose that we should instead consider "complex relational processes", where the self and the collective mutually constitute each other in self-organizing processes of relating (Luoma 2007). This corresponds to a "transformative teleology", in which the future "express[es] continuity and transformation of individual and collective identity and difference at the same time" (Stacey, Griffin, and Shaw 2000, 37), where small differences in the very process of re-constructing identity can lead to "transformative shifts" (Stacey 2003). Eppel speaks of "the system 'whole', [t]he ongoing, iterative, interaction of human actors . . . featur[ing] many interacting parts, with interdependent dynamism between them, such that the whole cannot be understood as the sum of its parts, or reduced to its parts to assist understanding (Kauffman 1995, Prigogine 1987, Waldrop 1992)" (2012, 887). In fact, the notion of "parts" is itself challenged by this ontology ". . . in which individuals form while being formed by the social at the same time. Individual minds and the social are then the same processes of communicative interaction, in which the social is not outside the interaction . . ." (Stacey 2001b, 470). The very idea of scale is challenged, in a fashion that is very similar to the way that Latour frames the apparent paradox of an action whose "universality is fully local" (Latour 2010, 7).

The problem with the notion of scaling appears, then, not only to be that it challenges the agency of people who are expected to enact new social practices; it seems also to favor a view in which we distance ourselves from the very interactions by which we bring the social into existence, choosing instead to construct a "system" somewhere out there that limits and directs us. As discussed in chapter 4, this is not to deny the existence of constraints, institutions or power relations. Rather, it encourages us to understand them as constantly reproduced and therefore constantly open to modification, subversion or mutation, even if only in small ways. However, in following this line, we are also brought to the point where we have to investigate what we mean by "local". If there is no "scale", what does focusing on the local level mean? The term is clearly a geographical metaphor, but technology has now made it possible for us to treat even widely dispersed groups as "local" for the purposes of our interactions. What matters is the ability to interact directly, and bring something into being through that interaction— we are back to the centrality of connections. ". . . [I]nstead of having to choose between the local and the global view, the notion of network allows us to think of a global entity—a highly connected one—which nevertheless remains continuously local" (Latour 1996, 372). The question to be answered is not whether we are operating at "higher" or "lower" scale, but what connections are being made, around what matters of concern.

Hassan proposes that ". . . the social realm is scale-free by nature. A social lab can be designed to operate at any scale, depending on the intentions of the people in it. It will grow in whatever direction and way is needed and doesn't necessarily require central planning. . . . If successful, a social lab will produce direct results addressing the challenge at the scale it's designed for, be that a community or a country" (2014, 22). The decision to address the supply of water in Africa can be as "local" as the decision to focus on the water supply of a small village in remote Zambia. Both are achieved in the same way, by connecting actors, tracing associations, achieving translations: both may have effects that participants see as positive or negative. However, we are not reinstating the idea of scale in saying this: we are merely pointing out that activity can take place between different actors around different matters of concern. The mistake would be to imagine that the work of the small village in Zambia was embedded, formed part of or was subject to the African water supply actor-network. If connections are made between the two, they may influence each other, but we cannot subsume the former into the latter and forget about it (black box it), at least without doing the work to connect the actor-networks to achieve that. We might be better served to accept that these are different *things* and that, rather than trying to subordinate one into the other as part of a grand plan to extend our "impact" as far as possible, it might be better to work out how to make connections that will support the work of the small village *thing* in the most effective way. A useful notion here might be that of "cross-scale interactions", advanced by Westley and colleagues (Westley and Antadze 2010, Westley *et al.* 2014) as a way of understanding how some social innovations achieve high impact. Although this might seem to contradict the points we have just made about the problems of "scale", the five configurations of five key analytical categories that they propose are metaphorical, and so might be taken more as sensitizing concepts, as ways of imagining how the process of making connections might proceed between actor-networks that we perceive as operating at different "levels". Of particular interest is the distinction Westley *et al.* draw between "scaling out", which involves engaging more people over a larger area, and "scaling up", which aims to address the institutional causes of a problem and so impact on it for all who are affected[1] (2014, 237). Westley and Antadze specifically frame "scaling up" in terms of making connections, and also point to the demands that the "institutional entrepreneurship" required to achieve it make on both the proto-solutions and the people (individually and collectively) engaged in enacting them, "involv[ing] a set of skills including pattern recognition, resource mobilization, sense making, and connecting (Dorado 2005). It involves a deliberate focus on '*up-down*' strategies of *reflecting on* and *connecting to* decision makers and opinion leaders in policy, economic, and cultural arenas, engaging and questioning the strategic context of their decisions. It also involves recognizing local and 'front line' innovations that promise institutional disruption, and selling these to the decision makers/ opinion leaders when windows of opportunity open (Burgelman 1983)" (2010, 14, emphasis in original).

We then see both ANT and complexity thinking pointing in the same direction with regard to scaling; away from attempts to encompass everything in a hierarchy of embedded systems and sub-systems that give us access to a few levers so that we may bring about a desired change across the broadest extent possible, towards a focus on making connections across interlocking, non-hierarchical and self-determining groups of people working "locally" on what matters to them. This has less to do with engineering solutions than it has to do with seeing and grasping opportunities, adapting and promoting, inquiring and supporting people in what they seek to achieve. It reminds us that social innovation is not something that we can pin down to a repertoire of procedures to be followed, a methodology that can be reliably implemented for results; it is fundamentally emergent, opportunist and requires agility and non-conformism as well as discipline and professionalism.

From Project to Framework

We have seen that social innovation offers benefits both in regards to a specific problem or concern and in terms of longer term potential for action. This comes about when action around a particular concern also generates infrastructure that might enable future work around other concerns—residual features and structures that survive an engagement in one context that may be used in another. This follows the general form of capital defined as "the creation of assets by allocating resources that could be used up in immediate consumption to create assets that generate a potential flow of benefits over a future time horizon" (Ostrom and Ahn 2009, 19), and so supports the connection made in chapter 2 between "infrastructuring" and social capital. We take both to refer to capabilities, knowledge or relationships, whether formalized, as in the sense of institutions, rules, rituals, etc., or informal, as in networks, social groups or bonds, that increase the capacity of groups to respond collectively to problems in the future. Hence, social capital and infrastructuring can be expressed as a potential for collective action. Ostrom, in works over many years, has developed an approach to understanding how collective action is achieved by groups when there is a potential or actual conflict between the interests of at least some of the members of the group and the group as a whole, as in the *thing* we invoke around a matter of concern. Collective action may be for good or evil; the nature of the reconciliation of individual and group interests may be more or less repressive; and the assertion of the group's interests may be for either the good or to the detriment of the broader society within which the group is embedded, so social capital is not inherently positive. Nevertheless, "[t]he economic and political performances of societies, from villages to international communities, depend critically on how the members of a community solve the problem of collective action" (Ostrom and Ahn 2009, 19). In exploring the factors that enable collective action, Ostrom and Anh abandon the notion of "atomized, selfish and fully rational individuals" (21), recognizing that the existence of multiple types of individuals, and therefore interests and values, is a necessary pre-requisite to the explanation of collective action. They call for us to "recognize genuine trustworthiness, defined in terms of preferences that are consistent with conditional cooperation, as independent and non-reducible reasons why some communities achieve collective action while others fail" (22), and propose that trust, which allows collective action to occur, is the result of beliefs about the ". . . trustworthiness of people, networks and institutions". These beliefs may arise from either repetitive interactions that establish confidence in reciprocity; beliefs about the expected "pro-social" nature of behavior within the group (Torsvik 2000); or from beliefs about the intrinsic values of an individual. They may be an expression of "bonding" capital, which arises from "dense horizontal networks" (Ostrom and Ahn 2009, 24) and creates incentives and sanctions that give confidence in trustworthiness. They may also arise because recognized institutions exist that seem to promote trustworthiness: these are formal or informal rules and structures that members of society believe will regulate behavior. In addition, in order to solve "big problems", it is necessary to have "bridging capital": "[t]he possibility of sustaining cooperation via reputation in widespread networks connecting individuals who do not live in the same community" (Ostrom and Ahn 2009, 24).

If we take the problem faced by a *thing* as being how to enable collective action, in the form of generating a "proto-solution", when individual interests and perspectives are potentially widely divergent, we are able to then open up the question of how to establish a sense of trust between the assembled participants. Of course, trust is not absolute, least of all in this context, but is rather concerned with beliefs that another party will act in a certain way, despite having no guarantee or ability to enforce that action. The juxtaposition with Ostrom's work suggests that, within a specific *thing*, this belief will depend on the level of bonding capital established, and whether this is supported or not by confidence in an institutional structure to which all may refer. However, it also suggests that the *thing* will most likely be able to bring about significant action if it has strong bridging capital, in the form of a diversity of connections to external actors, and a reputation that allows actors to be trusted by and trust those external players. To the extent that the *thing* is able to produce a proto-solution in a way that demonstrates its trustworthiness both internally and externally, promotes the densification of internal networks, and the multiplication of external connections, social capital may be seen to have been established.

However, the *thing* is not necessarily durable, and its central values of agonistic, democratic voice and openness do not seem to lend themselves to the sort of structuring or organization that would promote longevity. Social capital, then, to the extent that it is to be preserved beyond a specific site, cannot be a property of the *thing*, but rather of the connections that have been made and that can be reactivated in a new context. If we are to understand infrastructuring, we need to look at the context of the *thing*, at how it connects with other actor-networks. Manzini outlines the possibility of small "human scale" systems that "can be (and have to be)" connected so as to interact with people and ideas more broadly, encapsulating this in the phrase "cosmopolitan localism" (2010, 10). Manzini and Rizzo take this one step further when they propose that this model might apply to "constellations of interrelated small-scale, short-term . . . *local projects*, co-ordinated, synergised and amplified by larger initiatives . . . call[ed] *framework projects*; their overall outcomes are large-scale transformation processes" (2011, 199–200, emphasis in original). In ANT terms, the framework project might be seen as a translation, which allows the local project to co-exist with an actor-network that occupies itself with matters of concern on a broader horizon. It might also be seen as a form that allows for the preservation of social capital. Manzini and Rizzo exemplify this approach by reference to five framework projects that each consist of several local projects aimed at achieving different outcomes. In the UK, "Designs of the Time" focused on building awareness of design and stimulating innovation within North East England. It was implemented by a collaboration between the Design Council and the regional development agency, and engaged with the community in "five crucial everyday contexts: mobility, health, food, school and energy" (203), using multiple different forms of event and design tools. In Italy, the "Feeding Milan" program implemented multiple projects to explore with the community how to "foster the relationship between the city and the productive country-side through de-mediation of the agri-food chain" (204). In China, the "Chongming Sustainable Community" project aimed to "design and promot[e] new economies based on local resources and the proximity to a huge metropolitan area [Shanghai]" (205). In New York, the Amplify project aimed to identify examples of local innovation that were not visible to the broader community and bring them to its attention, with the aim of "supporting people's participation in the process of diffusion and amplification of social innovation and at triggering new social innovation initiatives" (207). Finally, in Malmö, Sweden, three Living Labs were established with different foci, ranging from urban spaces and services, cultural production and media, to the support of early stage innovation.

Although Manzini and Rizzo do not explicitly discuss this in their 2011 paper, all five of these projects also connect to a larger network of activity animated by DESIS (Design and Social Innovation for Sustainability), "a network of schools of design and other institutions, companies and non-profit organizations interested in promoting and supporting design for social innovation and sustainability" (DESIS n.d.). DESIS is described as "a light, non-profit organization, conceived as a network of partners collaborating in a peer-to-peer spirit". It identifies the possibility for design schools to act as "a major driver for [social innovation's] application and diffusion" (DESIS 2016), generating new visions, defining and testing new tools, and starting and supporting new projects. Members are higher education institutions or universities with design disciplines, each of which are subject to their own governance processes, but which agree to establish and maintain a "design lab" where academics and students participate in social innovation projects. An annual assembly approves an annual program, which is implemented by an International Coordinator and committee: however, all expenses are born by members and DESIS has no common costs or remunerated positions. At the time of writing, forty-one members are listed on the DESIS website.

Manzini describes DESIS as "a free-choice platform that can help different design teams (the DESIS Labs) to align ongoing activities, create arenas for discussing their projects, and compare tools and results, as well as a place where new joint initiatives can be started" (Manzini 2015, loc 1727). It also maintains "Thematic Clusters", which allow design teams who are "working on similar topics in a similar way" (loc 1747) to collaborate. In this way, more or less explicitly, DESIS provides a framework that enables connections, in the form of partnerships and the exchange of experience, information and resources, between members, and which is engaged in developing a shared view of the nature, direction and appropriate ways of doing social innovation. Likewise, each of the five framework projects perform similar roles for the multiple activities occurring on their specific sites. This is not a hierarchical structure, but one that provides multiple points where beliefs about trustworthiness, built on shared experience and reciprocity and expectations of shared values, as well as specific relationships that extend beyond specific sites, can accumulate. To the extent that it functions in this way, it therefore seems to meet the requirements for enabling collective action or, in an alternative formulation, to accumulate social capital. It seems to exemplify the possibility of establishing loose organizational forms that support and connect, but do not attempt to direct, the actual work of social innovation. It might even be seen as a minimal form of governance, one concerned with establishing a sort of reflexivity at the level of the of social innovation system, where fundamental values such as enabling voice and transparency might be promoted, and the opportunistic connection of actors that might generate new initiatives enabled.

Of course, DESIS is not unique in this sense: many other networks exist that connect projects and promoters of social innovation, none the least the global SIX Social Innovation Exchange network, and the European Network of Living Labs (ENoLL—http://openlivinglabs.eu/). The membership of these networks overlap, as do their approaches to social innovation, demonstrating both common interests and differences, some of them giving rise to tension: "There is no consensus on how to define a living lab (Følstad 2008; Stålbröst 2008), but usually such a lab is described as a long-term environment for open innovation that supports experimentation with real users in real contexts (Følstad 2008). This fits very well with what we see as essential in a platform that could facilitate social innovation. However, most living labs are strongly driven by industry and commercial interests, and that has consequences for how open 'open innovation' can be (Kommonen and Botero 2013) and for what is regarded as innovation (Björgvinsson, Ehn, and Hillgren 2010, 2012)" (Emilson, Hillgren, and Seravalli 2014, 35).

To the extent that we can use the term governance, the sort of arrangements we have described here seem to approximate the form defined by Ostrom as "polycentric", in contrast to both formal top-down hierarchy and chaos arising from lack of coordination. "No governance system is perfect, but polycentric systems have considerable advantages given their mechanisms for mutual monitoring, learning, and adaptation of better strategies over time" (Ostrom 2010, 552). Of course, this is a very different form of governance than the structured institutions and processes that govern private and public sector bodies. In a formal sense, it appears to be close to conceptions of network governance. Using the classification proposed by Forrer, Edwin and Boyer (2014), the sort of network that seems to be in place could be described as either informational or developmental; focused on the exchange of information and possibly the development of ways to increase member capacity. Likewise, it seems appropriate for the networks to be considered as self-governing, with no single organization taking the lead, and no central administrative infrastructure. However, the parallel with network governance raises some interesting issues for social innovation networks, with regard to both their nature and eventual evolution. These turn on the question of whether the networks can be seen as "goal-directed" or rather "serendipitous" in nature. The former sort of network "exhibits purposive and adaptive movement towards an envisioned end state (van de Ven and Poole 1995, 516)" (Kilduff and Tsai 2003, 91–92), whereas the latter "capitalizes on an opportunity". According to network theorists, this distinction has potentially far-reaching effects on the way the network is likely to evolve and its likely effectiveness (Provan and Kenis 2008). In particular, it has been proposed that "goal-directed" network trajectories are likely to produce an "administrative entity" to broker plans and coordinate members (Kilduff and Tsai 2003, 89). This might take the form of either a "lead organization", one of the members of the network that determines it should take a leadership role, or an external entity. At present, there is little evidence of either such administrative entity emerging in DESIS, SIX or ENoLL, and if one were to arise it would potentially be in tension with the apparent current configuration of all of them as informational and developmental networks, with their aim being to promote the densification of horizontal linkages of independently governed members, rather than charting a course for what might become "the social innovation movement". However, to declare purposive development as outside the scope of the networks, and envisage them henceforth as serendipitous, would seem to deny the common purpose that already clearly exists at the heart of all of them: advancing the practice of social innovation. What role can usefully be performed by these networks that enhances rather than suppresses local innovation? I take this as a question of meta-design at the highest level, how to "infrastructure" social innovation practitioners to be able to carry forward and extend their practice in the most productive way.

It may be useful here to refer back to Ostrom's conditions for successful collective action; the development of trust through interactions and the development of shared values; expectations of reciprocity; the establishment of dense internal network ties and strong external bridging ties; as well as the establishment of some form of system of rules and sanctions that allows members to expect others to behave in the collective interest. As has already been observed, social capital cannot be taken as an inherent good. To the extent that it becomes exclusive and either internally oppressive or externally destructive, as in the case of the Mafia, or Manzini's "closed communities" from chapter 1, it may in fact exemplify "evil". It would seem that this ethical perspective turns on the purpose of the network, the nature of its shared values and its inclusiveness. In the context of the networks that might govern social innovation, it seems to me that there is an opportunity, as long as we are clear on these points, to promote and develop social innovation, but that these questions come down to establishing a sort of purpose with which the organizational world is unfamiliar and that may be very difficult to sustain over the long-term; the notion that the network is there to establish and elaborate a guiding framework of values within which social innovation is practiced freely, and which promotes and supports the development of knowledge around which members engage, both amongst themselves and with external networks, in a way that is open and seeks out difference. This allows for the establishment of a clear purpose, but one within which serendipity, in the form of useful connections to extend and provoke innovation, can be fostered. The concept seems to come close to what Adler offers as an alternative to both *Gemeinschaft* and *Gesellschaft* (see chapter 1): *Genossenschaft*, or a collaborative community,[2] which is:

> *in its norms, a synthesis of universalism and particularism: formalized procedures are used to ensure universal diffusion of best practices, and systematic ways of tailoring those procedures facilitate their adjustment to particular circumstances.
>
> *in its values, a synthesis of individualism and collectivism: the paramount value is the individual's ability to contribute creatively to the community's shared purpose.
>
> (Adler 2015, 452, emphasis in original)

The networks we have been discussing, where social capital is expressed in terms of the connections, resources and boundary objects available to their members, are very diverse, open and relatively unstructured. It is equally possible to envisage more formalized structures as sites for the accumulation of social capital. We might call these *platform organizations*; structures that are established to provide a context for *things*, preserving their autonomy, but offering connections, resources and boundary objects in a more tight-knit and probably more local form. We might see some of the "Labs" that exist around the world in this way. Many of them maintain portfolios of "projects" in which they are involved, and engage individuals over time in one or more of these, in the process building up expertise and maintaining a range of connections to specific communities that may generate further projects. Their longevity varies, but some, such as La 27e Région in France, MindLab in Denmark, TACSI in Australia and Social Innovation Generation (SiG) in Canada, to mention a few, appear to have established an enduring presence. Ashoka could also be seen in this way. In some cases, such organizations might develop within an academic institution as well; all the members of the Living Labs network and many of the members of DESIS could probably be seen in this way. These, and many other organizations that no doubt should be mentioned, all fit the general description of platform organizations: they provide an organizational structure within which *things* might be initiated and supported, and that might act as a site for the accumulation of expertise, relationships and boundary objects that could spark further action. We should not forget, either, the long list of bodies engaged primarily in teaching and researching social innovation, such as the Centre for Social Impact at Stanford Graduate School of Business, or the Skoll Centre at Saïd Business School at the University of Oxford. These perform a central role in both developing and connecting practitioners, and also potentially play a crucial role in establishing broadly held views on what constitutes good practice and articulating the values of the community of social innovation practice. Whether they can be seen as platform organizations or not depends on the extent to which they directly provide support for specific social innovation sites, but their influence on the broader system is very significant in any case.

The possibility of connecting "locally" based activity with other sites, both synchronously and across time, whether through framework projects, within platform organizations or as unstructured connections across networks that may have thematic groupings, allows us to envisage approaching truly complex issues in a way that respects their complexity. Poverty, water access or the rise of chronic health conditions are multi-faceted issues that exist within complex systems that defy exhaustive description. Their causes are multiple and usually interdependent, defying isolation and often only visible with the benefit of hindsight. They are intergenerational concerns, entangled with culture, politics and social structures that not only protect interests, but that are also often at the core of community, group or national identities. These are not issues that are amenable to "analyze-plan-implement" type actions, to "big solutions". To the extent that it makes sense to talk about "solving" them as problems, rather than treating them as symptoms and seeking to influence their systemic causes, our interventions will have to be multi-stranded, adaptable and, in some sense, opportunistic. Their impacts will often be unpredictable, or give rise to unintended consequences, and their context will change constantly because of external, usually unforeseeable, influences. We will need to "probe-sense-respond" in the way Snowden and Boone suggest operating in complex environments (2007), amplifying what works and suppressing what doesn't. We will need to string together multiple often small interventions on many dispersed sites, targeted at different concerns, working with different groups, responding to unexpected obstacles or opportunities, none of which were predictable in advance, and likely over time-scales that extend beyond the span of attention or operating life expectancy of many of the actors. Networks and framework projects are not just ways to deal with large problems if we admit that we have to allow agency at the level of the *thing*; they are ideally suited to this sort of issue. So are platform organizations, as long as they preserve the autonomy of the co-design work on the ground, and do not fall back into the planning trap.

We are beginning to see, then, a variety of forms of community, some very open and unstructured, some more tightly structured, many of them at the heart of their own networks, that connect social innovators and social innovation activity. Their approaches vary widely, but this eclecticism should be seen as an asset, rather than a liability, since differences in perspective and approach are precisely the source of new insight. Based on our discussion, the success of this network of networks in enabling social innovation is likely to depend significantly on the extent to which work that is being carried on at each specific site, each *thing*, is truly co-designing a way forward with all those impacted, rather than being forced to conform to models or procedures brought in from "outside". In the end, we must seek to enable mutual learning, not to stifle it with answers that we have found to other questions, no matter how clever they are.

The Ambiguous Role of the Designer

This chapter has examined social innovation beyond the local, and attempted to understand the nature by which it may spread and create major impact. Based on a fundamental understanding of *things* that undertake the actual work of social innovation, it has developed the notion that the impact of social innovation depends on processes of connection and reinvention, rather than of replication or "scaling". It has suggested that we therefore need to look at challenging the boundaries of projects and concepts of completion if we are to enable innovation to extend. This is a process that will always be largely emergent and opportunistic, at the same time as it will benefit from initial conditions that build in flexibility and openness to new contexts and adjustments, and see extension as a cross-scalar relationship, rather than a uni-directional transfer. On the one hand, this means that it is possible (but by no means guaranteed) that larger scale change can be set off by making small interventions that engage more people in supporting change. On the other hand, it suggests that "planning" approaches to scaling are at best likely to be unsuccessful; at worst, they may actively inhibit the spread of innovations by making them too rigid to adapt to new contexts or changing conditions. Lastly, it has been proposed that the networks that have grown up around the promotion of social innovation may provide platforms to enable scaling in unexpected fashions, by connecting local projects to other local projects across a broader horizon, stimulating further development without attempting to control or subordinate them to "higher level" goals.

These propositions call for us to further develop our ideas about the role of the "designer" in social innovation. Firstly, designers are no longer able to focus exclusively on the *thing* they are facilitating. As well as bringing their special skills to bear to maintain a delicate balance between allowing different perspectives, needs and interests to become visible in a potentially conflictual way, while at the same time assisting participants to agree on a common way forward, they must now also be conscious of, and perhaps assist in, building connections with other projects, contexts and groups. This might affect the design of the proto-solution itself, or it may involve "infrastructuring" the *thing* with connections that will be valuable for their future activities. This dual orientation adds to the ambiguity already present in the designer's role, and places significant demands on the designer, as noted earlier in this chapter (Westley and Antadze 2010, 14). On the one hand, the designer carries a measure of influence, even if only at the level of the process (or protocols) used to shape the *thing*; but we have proposed that her vital role is in making the "traces" of the work of the *thing* visible, seeking to reveal the unrevealed and give voice to the silent, in a sense subverting the very process she might be seen as leading. Now, in addition to that, we seem to be saying that the designer must also challenge the very boundaries of that process, in terms of both the scope of the "project" being undertaken and in terms of the temporal horizon over which participants are engaging, by actively reaching beyond it and connecting it to other networks. How is it possible to achieve this and still remain true to the fundamental underlying value we have designated for co-design, enabling the agency of the participants themselves? How can the designer's view of what would be "useful" at the broader level be reconciled with local self-determination? Even if cautious, Prometheus is still a titan, and determining the responsible use of the designer's particular powers without seeking to influence purpose presents both a technical and a moral challenge.

There can be no simple answer to this question, which has at least two aspects, one challenging the distinctiveness of the role of designer, the other a matter of ethics. The differentiation between the designer and other participants in a *thing* seems to be based on assumptions that may be irreconcilable. On the one hand, the designer is vested with voice in the process and influence on the choice of tools for the *thing*; on the other, he is expected to be neutral or agnostic about its purpose or direction, since it is his role to draw this from the beneficiaries. This implies a simultaneous deep engagement and total detachment. We have already proposed in chapter 4 that the role of the designer is operationalized by making "maps" of actor-networks publicly visible, and suggested that this may not be the exclusive preserve of any specific class of actor. The possibility is opened up that the role of designer might shift from one actor to another. We now also challenge the implied distinction between method and substance—the choice of "protocols" involved in shaping the work of the *thing* must be intimately entangled with its outcomes, predisposing towards some and away from others. We return to the proposal by Binder *et al.* (2015) to see design thinging as a "flickering" between "parliamentary" and "laboratory" practices, which reminds us of the role of the designer and the design in promoting speculation, provocation and experimentation. In the context of a fully developed understanding of social innovation as co-design, the designer can no longer be the professional, detached process expert: firstly, any participant might take this role and, secondly, detachment and the distinction between process and substance has become untenable. Instead, the designer is seen as proposing new connections, disrupting consensus, provoking disagreement by introducing or hinting at controversial "proto-solutions" around which the work of the *thing* can continue, but which will nevertheless influence the direction of that work. What might be added to this apparently spontaneous (and slightly anarchical) view is the necessity of establishing reflexivity at the level of the *thing*, the ability to collectively understand what has just happened and why it is of value (even if it engenders conflict and frustration). Instead of design being in the head of an individual or class of actors, we start to see it as the capacity for the *thing* to understand its work self-consciously, a sense of self-awareness that opens it up to challenging purpose.

Inevitably, there will be objections to such a conceptualization based on its apparent lack of direction and haphazardness, the likelihood that it will result in confused or no progress over time, the near-certainty that it will not be "efficient" in terms of either the time taken to get to a conclusion or the resources expended in doing so. The temptation will be strong to examine design processes in arrears and observe where "wrong turns" were taken, or where "red herrings" were set free. These concerns should elicit two responses: first, that the abandonment of an externally set purpose is only an issue if we see things in a modernist, instrumental paradigm, where agency must be limited, which would involve abandoning the very engine we have proposed for social innovation; and, second, that suppressing agency or making it "manageable" is necessarily at best a transitory convenience that temporarily screens from view the messiness of conflict and complexity in order to establish an illusion of control. Even if this sleight of hand is able to declare itself "successful" based on "results" it produces, it will produce unintended consequences and obstacles that will then have to be worked on—over the sweep of time and a broad horizon, there can be no evading dispute and compromise.

There is, however, a third objection that can be added to this, one which must be considered further. This has to do with the basis on which it is possible to make "good" decisions about what interventions to make, or to judge their outcomes—what ethical stance can be brought to bear in such a context? The approach that appears to offer the best fit with the framework and values that have been proposed here seems to be that of the pragmatists, and particularly John Dewey. This is not just because it makes a fundamental rejection of the notion that any single moral principle might be applied to work out what is the right decision in every situation; it is also because of the central role that Dewey placed on the value of imagination in moral deliberation. For Dewey, ethics is about ends: "what is most at stake is 'what kind of person we wish to become' and what kind of world one wishes to participate in making" (Fesmire 2015, 134). Dewey accepts that there are irreconcilable tensions between different principles by which moral decisions can be made, and that it will be impossible to make a perfect decision, but nevertheless proposes that we have an obligation to seek a "best" way, in terms of the impact decisions will have on the lives of those involved. In our context, this means finding ways to live together and move forward with regard to a matter of concern. Making these decisions is a creative task, attempting to build the best response from what is at hand, and doing so while "entering by imagination into the situation of others" (Dewey, cited in Fesmire 2015, 133). It is also a task that will never meet all the needs of the situation: "moral experience is unavoidably tragic, in the classical Greek sense" (Fesmire 2015, 129). This creative, imaginative work is not confined to moral decisions; indeed, Dewey does not see moral decisions as fundamentally different from other classes of decision, treating all of them as essentially practical concerns. This means it is not necessary to erect walls around the ethical "aspect" of the co-design work that would separate it from the proto-solutions that are being produced or the socio-material arrangements that constitute it. Rather, all are bound together: a "good" solution must take all into account. We experience our world through enquiry, which can be conducted by either overt or imaginative action (Martela 2015, 554), provisionally forming and reforming our understandings through abduction, with the aim of achieving "warranted assertability" (540). This involves a form of "experimental simulation": "An act overtly tried out is irrevocable, its consequences cannot be blotted out. . . . An act tried out in imagination is not final or fatal. It is retrievable" (Dewey, cited in Fesmire 2015, 134)—although, as argued earlier in the chapter, this does not mean it is without consequence!

All these features are compatible with the positions we have so far derived. Likewise, they were all developed with a deep commitment to democracy, not as an institutional feature of the state, but in the local living out of our experience, following the same route: "In line with Dewey's genuinely experimental attitude towards democracy, we may think of design collaborations as the making of things that explore forms of emerging publics, and thus enrich the current repertoire of democratic engagement and expression" (Binder *et al.* 2015, 153).

Notes

1 Note the very specific meaning applied to "scaling up" here, which is quite distinct from the way it has been used to this point.
2 Clearly, this term is not being proposed either here or by Adler in the more limited sense of the legal form that exists in Germany, which this term also denotes: rather, attention is drawn more to the etymological connections with enjoyment and mutuality.

References

Adler, Paul S. 2015. "Community and Innovation: From Tönnies to Marx." *Organization Studies* 36 (4):445–471. doi: 10.1177/0170840614561566.

Binder, Thomas, Eva Brandt, Pelle Ehn, and Joachim Halse. 2015. "Democratic Design Experiments: Between Parliament and Laboratory." *CoDesign* 11 (3–4):152–165. doi: 10.1080/15710882.2015.1081248.

Björgvinsson, Erling Bjarki, Pelle Ehn, and Per-Anders Hillgren. 2010. "Participatory Design and 'Democratizing Innovation'." Proceedings of the 11th Biennial Participatory Design Conference, Sydney, Australia.

Björgvinsson, Erling Bjarki, Pelle Ehn, and Per-Anders Hillgren. 2012. "Agonistic Participatory Design: Working with Marginalised Social Movements." *CoDesign* 8 (2–3):127–144. doi: 10.1080/15710882.2012.672577.

Britton, Garth M., and Phillip Bonser. 2014. "Co-Design as a Frame for Researcher/ Practitioner Collaboration." *IRSPM XVIII*, Ottawa, Canada, 9–11 April.

Burgelman, R. A. 1983. *Managing Innovating Systems: A Study of the Process of Internal Corporate Venturing*. Ann Arbor, MI: University Microfilms International.

DESIS. 2016. "About," accessed 19/9/16. http://www.desis-network.org/about/.

DESIS. n.d. "DESIS: DesignSocial Innovation for Sustainability," accessed 19/9/16. http://www.sustainableeverydayexplorations.net/desis/.

Dorado, Silvia. 2005. "Institutional Entrepreneurship, Partaking, and Convening." *Organization Studies* 26 (3):385–414. doi: 10.1177/0170840605050873.

Ehn, Pelle. 2008. "Participation in Design Things." Proceedings of the Tenth Anniversary Conference on Participatory Design 2008, Bloomington, IN.

Emilson, Anders, Per-Anders Hillgren, and Anna Seravalli. 2014. "Designing in the Neighborhood: Beyond (and in the Shadow of) Creative Communities." In *Making Futures: Marginal Notes on Innovation, Design, and Democracy*, edited by Pelle Ehn, Elisabet Nilsson, and Richard Topgaard, 35–62. Cambridge, MA: MIT Press.

Eppel, Elizabeth A. 2012. "What Does It Take to Make Surprises Less Surprising? The Contribution of Complexity Theory to Anticipation in Public Management." *Public Management Review* 14 (7):881–902. doi: 10.1080/14719037.2011.650055.

Fesmire, Steven. 2015. *Dewey*. Edited by Corporation Ebooks. London: Routledge.

Følstad, Asbjørn. 2008. "Living Labs for Innovation and Development of Information and Communication Technology: A Literature Review." *Electronic Journal for Virtual Organizations and Networks* 10 (7):99–131.

Forrer, John J., James Edwin, and Eric Boyer. 2014. "Governing Cross-Sector Collaboration." In *Network Governance*, edited by John J. Forrer, James Edwin, and Eric Boyer, 111–137. San Francisco, CA: Jossey-Bass.

Gaziulusoy, İdil. 2014. "Interview with Professor Chris Ryan: Part II: Victorian Eco-Innovation Lab." *System Innovation for Sustainability*, accessed 19/9/2016. https://systeminnovationforsustainability.com/tag/victorian-eco-innovation-lab/.

Hassan, Zaid. 2014. *The Social Labs Revolution: A New Approach to Solving Our Most Complex Challenges*. San Francisco, CA: Berrett-Koehler.

Iversen, Ole Sejer, and Christian Dindler. 2014. "Sustaining Participatory Design Initiatives." *CoDesign* 10 (3–4):153–170. doi: 10.1080/15710882.2014.963124.

Kauffman, Stuart A. 1995. *At Home in the Universe: The Search for the Laws of Self-Organization and Complexity*. New York: Oxford University Press.

Kilduff, Martin, and Wenpin Tsai. 2003. *Social Networks and Organizations*. London: SAGE.

Kommonen, K.-H., and Botero, A. (2013). "Are the Users Driving, and How Open is Open? Experiences from Living Lab and User Driven Innovation Projects 9 (3)." Available at: http://ci-journal.net/index.php/ciej/article/view/746/1026

Latour, Bruno. 1996. "On Actor-Network theory—A Few Clarifications." *Soziale Welt-Zeitschrift Fur Sozialwissenschaftliche Forschung Und Praxis* 47 (4):369.

Latour, Bruno. 2010. *Networks, Societies, Spheres: Reflections of an Actor-Network Theorist*. International Seminar On Network Theory: Network Multidimensionality In The Digital Age, Feb 2010, Los Angeles: Annenberg School for Communication and Journalism.

Luoma, Jukka. 2007. "Systems Thinking in Complex Responsive Processes and Systems Intelligence." In *Systems Intelligence in Leadership and Everyday Life*, edited by Raimo Hämäläinen and Esa Saarinen. Espoo: Systems Analysis Laboratory, Helsinki University of Technology.

Manzini, Ezio. 2010. "Small, Local, Open and Connected: Design Research Topics in the Age of Networks and Sustainability." *Journal of Design Strategies* 4 (1):8–11.

Manzini, Ezio. 2015. *Design, When Everybody Designs an Introduction to Design for Social Innovation*. Translated by Rachel Coad. Cambridge, MA: MIT Press.

Manzini, Ezio, and Francesca Rizzo. 2011. "Small Projects/Large Changes: Participatory Design as an Open Participated Process." *CoDesign* 7 (3):199–215. doi: 10.1080/15710882.2011.630472.

Martela, Frank. 2015. "Fallible Inquiry with Ethical Ends-in-View: A Pragmatist Philosophy of Science for Organizational Research." *Organization Studies* 36 (4):537–563. doi: 10.1177/0170840614559257.

Mead, George Herbert. 1967. *Mind, Self and Society, From the Standpoint of a Social Behaviorist*. Edited and with an introduction by Charles W. Morris. Chicago, IL: University of Chicago Press.

Morson, Gary Saul. 1996. *Narrative and Freedom: The Shadows of Time*. New Haven, CT: Yale University Press.

Mulgan, Geoff. 2012. "Social Innovation Theories: Can Theory Catch Up with Practice?" In *Challenge Social Innovation: Potentials for Business, Social Entrepreneurship, Welfare and Civil Society*, edited by Hans-Werner Franz, Josef Hochgerner, and Jürgen Howaldt, 19–42. Berlin: Springer.

Ostrom, E. 2010. "Polycentric Systems for Coping with Collective Action and Global Environmental Change." *Global Environmental Change-Human and Policy Dimensions* 20 (4):550–557. doi: 10.1016/j.gloenvcha.2010.07.004.

Ostrom, E., and T. K. Ahn. 2009. "The Meaning of Social Capital and Its Link to Collective Action." In *Handbook of Social Capital: The Troika of Sociology, Political Science and Economics*, edited by Gert Tinggaard Svendsen and Gunnar Lind Haase Svendsen, 17–35. Cheltenham: Edward Elgar Publishing Limited.

Ostrom, E., and M. Cox. 2010. "Moving Beyond Panaceas: A Multi-Tiered Diagnostic Approach for Social-Ecological Analysis." *Environmental Conservation* 37 (4):451–463. doi: 10.1017/s0376892910000834.

Prigogine, I. 1987. "Exploring Complexity." In *Systems Thinking*, edited by G. Midgley, 409–417. London: SAGE.

Provan, Keith G., and Patrick Kenis. 2008. "Modes of Network Governance: Structure, Management, and Effectiveness." *Journal of Public Administration Research and Theory* 18 (2):229–252. doi: 10.1093/jopart/mum015.

Snowden, David J., and Mary E. Boone. 2007. "A Leader's Framework for Decision Making." *Harvard Business Review* 85 (11):68–76

Stacey, Ralph D. 2001a. *Complex Responsive Processes in Organizations: Learning and Knowledge Creation*. London: Routledge.

Stacey, Ralph D. 2001b. "What Can It Mean to Say That the Individual Is Social through and Through?" *Group Analysis* 34 (4):457.

Stacey, Ralph D. 2003. "Learning as an Activity of Interdependent People." *The Learning Organization* 10 (6):325–331. doi: 10.1108/09696470310497159.

Stacey, Ralph D. 2007. *Strategic Management and Organisational Dynamics: The Challenge of Complexity to Ways of Thinking about Organisations.* 5th ed. Harlow: Financial Times Prentice Hall.

Stacey, R. D., D. Griffin, and P. Shaw. 2000. *Complexity and Management: Fad or Radical Challenge to Systems Thinking?* Abingdon: Routledge.

Stålbröst, Anna. 2008. Forming Future IT: The Living Lab Way of User Involvement. Doctoral thesis, Luleå University of Technology.

Torsvik, Gaute. 2000. "Social Capital and Economic Development: A Plea for the Mechanisms." *Rationality and Society* 12 (4):451–476. doi: 10.1177/104346300012004005.

van de Ven, Andrew H., and Marshall Scott Poole. 1995. "Explaining Development and Change in Organizations." *The Academy of Management Review* 20 (3):510–540. doi: 10.2307/258786.

VEIL. n.d. "What Is Eco-Acupuncture?" accessed 19/9/2016. http://www.ecoinnovationlab.com/project_content/what-is-eco-acupuncture/.

Waldrop, M. M. 1992. *The Emerging Science at the Edge of Order and Chaos.* New York: Simon and Schuster.

Westley, Frances, and Nino Antadze. 2010. "Making a Difference: Strategies for Scaling Social Innovation for Greater Impact." *Innovation Journal* 15 (2):1–19.

Westley, Frances, Nino Antadze, D. J. Riddell, K. Robinson, and S. Geobey. 2014. "Five Configurations for Scaling Up Social Innovation: Case Examples of Nonprofit Organizations from Canada." *Journal of Applied Behavioral Science* 50 (3):234–260. doi: 10.1177/0021886314532945.

Part 3

Implications and Questions

In Part 1 of this book, we examined how co-design relates to social innovation, with an emphasis on the claims that were being made for both. In the second part, we outlined some theoretical frameworks that seem to offer a way of explaining the connections between the two. In this third part, we will reassess the field and develop some ideas on the implications of the understanding that has emerged for the practice and study of social innovation.

7   Organizations and Networks

We started our journey by noting that social innovation displays the features of a "quasi-concept", identifying itself as much by the communities of practice that gather around it as by any common definitional core. We looked at social innovation through a design lens, and concluded that this empty space at the core of social innovation could be filled by people engaging with matters that concerned them, and that promoting social innovation would therefore fundamentally involve enabling people to connect, dispute and make agreements on how to move forward, even if those agreements were never final or complete. We then elaborated this idea, seeking to explore theoretical traditions that would shed light on what its implications might be and help assess whether it was credible. Along the way, we have abandoned the idea that there is an explicitly "social" domain, without being able to stop using social as an adjective, since if we cease using it we seem to be ignoring (or, worse, hiding) the relational nature of the process, and start to sound like we are describing precisely the depopulated world of techniques and machines (organizational or physical) that we are trying to escape. We have concluded that it is impossible to control or direct social innovation over any significant reach of time or population, and that successfully doing so on even a limited scale carries costs that may outweigh the benefits. What are the implications of the framework we have developed for both practice and research? Using what has been proposed up to this point, what can we contribute to the discussion about social innovation that would give us some hope of living up to the pragmatic standard outlined in the last chapter? How might it be reconciled with existing institutions and narratives?

It may first of all be useful to take our bearings in reference to the three narratives we dealt with in chapter 1. What has been proposed is not intended to stand as "the right", or even "a better" definition of social innovation that would allow us to critique these narratives against a firm standard. To the extent that it can be taken as a definition at all, it is only because it asserts some apparently fundamental aspects of social innovation and elaborates their implications across multiple levels. It makes no claim to exhaustively describe social innovation or to substitute for more useable shorthand expressions of what it is about, as long as these fundamentals are preserved in the action taken. However, at a general level, it is striking how the three narratives of social innovation seem to display quite different concerns from the conceptualization developed here. There is a heroism in the aspiration of the narratives that seems oddly out of place compared to the messy, controversial, emergent and fundamentally parochial focus that we have proposed for social innovation. This disconnect is not just a question of scale, which was discussed in the previous chapter: it has more to do with the perspective of the narrator, who seems to be placed at a great height, from where it is possible to see the forces that cause the problems we face, to detect the features of the landscape we must traverse and to tell us in what direction we must move to reach our destination, a direction that is hidden from those on the ground, who are lost without these instructions. Contrast this with the fine-grained attention to local purposes and factors that presents itself in the understanding of social innovation we have developed; the engagement with the specifics of reaching even a provisional agreement on purpose; and the attention paid to sensitizing the actor to what is occurring, rather than equipping her with a procedure. Any heroism in our scenario is the heroism of the everyday individual, doing the best he can, and getting on with things despite inevitable imperfections, unknowns and accidents.

This is not to say that the view from the eagle's aerie is wrong, or even irrelevant. It simply occupies itself with different matters. Indeed, in the sense of the *things* we have been using, this may be precisely at the root of the apparent disconnect: the grand narratives are the sound of different socio-material assemblies, gathered around different matters of concern than those where we have suggested the work of social innovation is actually taking place. Of course, there are connections between these different actor-networks, and these connections may be essential to enable, catalyze or challenge social innovation. However, it would seem to be vitally important, first, that we are clear that it is only through those connections, and to the extent that they function, that social innovation is likely to occur in relation to any of the grand narratives; and, second, that there is a risk that our tendency to seek the grandest view, the point from which we believe ourselves most powerful and capable of influence, might distract from or even smother the very work that we purportedly seek to enable.

The narratives seek to present social innovation, at least as it is now practiced, as a recent, or recently resurgent, phenomenon. Both the Philanthro-capitalistic and Reform narratives go further than this, to imply that social innovation responds to the opportunities and needs of our time in ways that are qualitatively different from what went before. They both foreground techniques and models that represent some form of advanced capabilities. In the first case, these techniques happen to validate a particular view of how society should operate; in the second, they represent an emerging body of expert practices, part of a professional "batterie de cuisine", whose impact depends on how the professional applies them; whether supporting a collaborative approach in favor of and conducted by the beneficiaries, or as a preconfigured intervention performed by a specialist expert. The standardization of methods and tools points in the direction of the accusation, noted earlier, that has been levelled against the Philanthrocapitalists: that they risk relegating those actually undertaking the work of social innovation to the role of implementers of some pre-conceived approach, builders executing a clever plan. However, the claims of these narratives to specialist expertise and knowledge also play a key role in attracting funding and resources, and developing the credibility that allows those involved to act as interlocutors in the development of social innovation policy and programs. Although such concerns are not those of practitioners of social innovation as it has been proposed, those using the narratives have the potential to generate enormous support for it, depending on how the resources they garner are deployed, and therefore play a significant if indirect role. Put another way, the Philanthrocapitalistic and the Reform narratives tend to direct attention to the institutional context of social innovation and a more or less systematized body of knowledge about it, which are perfectly valid, and indeed vital, fields of enquiry, but ones that need to at least be complemented by attention directed at the process of social innovation itself.

Its proponents may, with good reason, feel that these observations are less true of the Social Justice narrative. Certainly, this narrative points to almost precisely the values we have placed at the center of social innovation, voice, agency and democracy. Even with this in mind, though, there is at least a potential tension between the identified end-point of social justice and the concerns of the people who are actually doing the work, and those who are meant to benefit from it. A strong case could be made that the more abstract and idealistic portrayals of social justice should in fact be seen as nothing more than templates, or protocols, and particularly vague ones at that, for what is really being sought, which is the concrete working out of social justice on the ground by the people who bring it to life. Moreover, although the Social Justice narrative is much more interested in the act of innovation itself, rather than its institutional context, the work we have done suggests that even this narrative needs to be approached with a level of reserve, lest it should start to surround social innovation, as well as the actors engaged in it, with an aura of inherent goodness. We have already discussed the reasons that such evaluations need to be treated skeptically. Placing voice and agency at the center of social innovation might well be inherently ethical, but by the pragmatic standards we propose to adopt, evaluation should probably be suspended until outcomes can be assessed. This view also suggests that we should not become too deeply attached to specific organizations as entities that are valuable in themselves: the demise of an organization, association or gathering engaged in social innovation might be necessary if progress is to be made for its beneficiaries. This is not to say that existing associations or organizations should accept uncritically that every newcomer is entitled to bring about their downfall, in some sort of perversion of natural selection. Rather, if social innovation occurs as an on-going process of publics engaging with matters of concern that co-evolve within a changing context, the question is whether there should not also be an expectation that organizational actors who are attempting to promote social innovation should themselves evolve, and sometimes leave the scene, rather than insisting on a right to continue to exist based on the "good" that they have done in the past. The issue becomes how best to continue to develop the social capital that is built up, to maintain and preserve the infrastructure that has been developed by the work of social innovation. This may not always point to the preservation of a specific organizational entity.

The understanding of social innovation that we have developed renders two of the contentions discussed in chapter 1 simply nonsensical. It is not possible to achieve social innovation without enlisting the people who enact that innovation at the local level. Without engaging their agency, we are left with either coercion or maintenance of current arrangements. Moreover, it would be a denial of the nature of social innovation to depict it as achieving a stable end-state: it is quintessentially a process, and a radically incomplete one, that moves unpredictably from one matter of concern to another, as it does so engaging different actors and generating new patterns of activity. However, the approach that we have proposed also insists that social innovation be understood as taking place through, and consisting of, connections. Hence, proto-solutions developed on one site may influence, inspire or confront another. Actors, be they individuals, organizations or technologies, can therefore play a role in engendering change by engaging with new publics, around new concerns, bringing their own unique history, capability and perspective into a new context. They can no more claim any resulting "success" as theirs than any specific atom can be claimed to have caused a chain reaction, but nevertheless it is possible that without their (and everyone else's) intervention, things would not have worked out as they did. Those individuals or organizations who are taking an interest in promoting the connections that may enable social innovation, in this new way of looking, are drawn to monitoring what is occurring in different places, or what has occurred in the past that might be brought into the present, and imagining where that might lead, together with the people who would be affected. They must see, imagine, listen, enable; and, in the process, take risks, provoke, challenge and seek to generate the best outcome in the minds of those who will live with it. Their involvement, and their responsibility, does not cease when something is "implemented". It continues and extends the same process, taking form in multiple contexts and chains of consequence.

Of course, this also dissolves the contention between a problem or a systemic focus: neither can exist without the other, no action can be taken at one level without affecting the other. Here, the social innovator is seeking patterns that emerge on different horizons, that are propitious to the raising of new concerns. She looks not only for the seeds of innovation, but also for fertile ground, knowing that each time work takes place it may make the context more or less favorable to the consideration of some, but not other, concerns. The social innovator will take his decisions about where to attempt to catalyze a new socio-material assembly against the frame of a strategic imagining, of how that might fit into broader patterns of activity that might improve the potential for future work to take place. She may seek to connect different actions together within an overarching project, one that crystallizes the gains, or observe new potentials arising in one place that could be connected with another to form a new assembly.

Finally, social innovation as we have portrayed it is moot as to the value of markets in any absolute sense. This is not a question it needs to occupy itself with, any more than it does with the graphics on a PlayPump tower in a specific site in Zambia. Markets are a form of social practice. If people, with the best understanding of what their participation in a market means, choose to form or participate in a market, this may (or may not) be part of social innovation. The market will never be the whole of social innovation, nor the magical ingredient that causes it to blossom. However, neither can markets be excluded as a form, at least if participants see this as a way forward. This is as true for any other pre-conceived "solution" that presents itself as uniquely pre-qualified to dissolve a problem as it is for the miracle of markets. To pretend otherwise is to remove from those who seek change the right to specify what it looks like.

But aren't we, in fact, walking into the same trap, by placing co-design at the center of social innovation? Are we not suggesting that co-design, when applied in the sense we intend it and the only sense in which it can be effective, is the panacea for all social problems? I would argue this is not the case, as it mistakes co-design, the struggle and the process by which people are given voice to discover ways to deal with their own concerns, with co-design, the clever technique by which those with special knowledge are able to guide people who would otherwise not be able to make progress to an as yet undiscovered destination. The emphasis in the latter case is on the technique, and the (frequently highly paid) expert who administers it, not on the work itself. This is dangerous terrain for social innovation in general, and co-design in particular. The image of "professionalization" of social innovation makes of something that is perfectly normal something that requires special powers to be revealed. The focus swings to the piper, not the children. Co-design, enacted in this way, designates someone as having special capability to work with people who wish to achieve something, who then gives their work back to them, and appropriates credit for it, sometimes for a handsome fee. Furthermore, because the magic is brought into the situation, and leaves with the magician, the relationships between the people who are expected to enact the "solution" may well remain unchanged, leading to a high risk of failure and to the reinforcement of the idea that the problem is intractable (or the "client's" fault). If the "clients" involved are severely disadvantaged, as might be the case in the design of some social welfare or health services, this carries special significance. One of the challenges for our view of social innovation, then, is to reinvent our views of who does social innovation and how they relate to it. Social innovation needs neither ready-made miracle solutions nor venerated keepers of a methodological flame.

The Community of Practice

A key implication of the work done here is that the connections between social innovators are vital. They enable the introduction of new perspectives and ideas into the work of social innovation, not as replications or models to follow, but as provocations to the process. They also enable social innovators to see themselves collectively, consider what values and identity they wish to express and develop a sense of forward direction. We choose to see this as an emerging community of practice, engaging both expert designers and a group of people who are "non-expert", but "nevertheless skilled and experienced in design" (Manzini 2015, loc 1188). Members of the community concern themselves with enabling change in the way people live; change that the people themselves consider to be for the better. Although they are not the cause of social innovation, because change is actually brought about by all the people involved in the work, they are developing ways of provoking, supporting and enabling change and sharing their experience in ways that encourage further action in other places. These people might call themselves social innovators or designers; they might call themselves social entrepreneurs or activists. They might themselves form part of organizations that are focused on social innovation, or they may be part of public or private sector organizations that are not primarily interested in social innovation, but that are willing to support them. The important thing is that they connect with social issues in ways that allow them to enable people to better the conditions of their everyday lives. Let us for the moment, and only for the sake of simplicity, call them design catalysts.[1]

Although they are very diverse, this group of people share a few key values. Most importantly, they seek to achieve change by enabling people, not by controlling or silencing them. While this may sometimes reveal differences of opinion, perspective or interest, and may not lead to the fastest or simplest path to an outcome, the design catalyst sees such disagreement as both inevitable and potentially productive. In resolving it, people need to find sufficient common ground to proceed, in full awareness of how any trade-offs have been arrived at. Design catalysts also challenge the people they work with to ensure that the actions they take are sustainable, in terms of their impact on others and on the environment, and bring others who might be impacted by proposed actions into the conversation where appropriate, so that they too may contribute.

The process they engage in is iterative and not mapped out in advance. Although what it specifically deals with will vary in every case, its general purpose is to enable people to intentionally improve or design their lives. Beyond this general intent, the question of purpose is open to debate and is regularly revisited by those involved. Because we are in a world that is increasingly connected, this design process does not take place in isolation. It is able to call forth and contribute ideas, people and resources across distance and time, and so is inherently open and collaborative. Under these conditions, *"all design processes tend to become co-design processes"* (Manzini 2015, loc 1188, emphasis in original), and represent people intentionally changing the way they live. Let us call this process "social innovation", a process that connects communities and engages them in a collective imagining of their futures in context and in bringing those futures about.

Some of the people engaged in social innovation have special expertise. The design catalysts in particular might have formal design training; or they might have a business or entrepreneurship background; or experience in community development or community activism. In keeping with their central values, though, they will not see or apply their expertise so as to dictate "the right way forward". They will recognize that their expertise needs to be brought to life in the context in which they are applying it, and in the service of the people they are working with. They will also recognize and respect the knowledge of these people, regardless of whether it is everyday knowledge about their own lives or if it is a recognized specialty. Everyone involved is expected to contribute to building a common way forward. The major role of the design catalysts will not be to apply any particular methodology or tool, though they may use a wide variety of these. Instead, they will ensure that the group is aware of what trade-offs are being made as they move forward, and that every member has a way to intervene in the process. They will also facilitate access to experience and to people who may be able to help enable those involved in the process, and be willing to make such connections, in order to come up with better actions and assist the community to function better for its members.

Social innovation, in this sense, has always been a feature of human life, although probably performed without being seen or named as a particular process or activity. However, over recent years, it has become increasingly self-referential, aware of its own potential and of the possibility for it to be developed as intentional practice (Nicholls 2010). This has occurred at the same time as sweeping technological changes have enabled communication between people in ways, at speeds and at distances never before possible, and also allowed the preservation and retrieval of portrayals of people's experience over time, the distillation of people's stories, on a scale and in forms never before available. Both the capacity of human society to collectively examine itself and to imagine different futures for itself have been transformed. This is challenging traditional notions of social structures such as class, race and gender, as well as making it possible to experiment with new ways of living together that may or may not improve our lives, and that may or may not prove to be stable. Such changes cause uncertainty, challenge the basis of our identities and are sometimes hotly contested. We must now see ourselves, in all our diversity, as one (and only a small) actor in a system the scale and complexity of which we can only become more aware, but never master. We can accuse ourselves, as a species, of failing to act to ensure the future of our planet; we can imagine that we can influence the lives of others who are suffering, and so share guilt if we fail to do so. We can also, as never before, see how what we do actually impacts on what occurs. We can construct grand challenges; and because we can, we are morally obliged to attempt to meet them.

This vertiginous sense of possibility and responsibility offers enormous potential; it is also far from unassailable. Our individual and community identities are being challenged. Our sense of the differences between us is being amplified, at the same time as we are brought into closer and closer contact on an everyday basis; the roots of our condition can be revealed, and it is possible to blame others for their role in bringing it about. We should not ignore the fact that the technologies that have enabled our sense of possibility also enable those who would destroy it to mobilize; neither should we forget that other technologies allow us to destroy on a scale that has never before even been conceivable. Resistance is called forth in much the same measure as possibility: the battle of openness and initiative against absolutism and tribalism is far from over. But social innovation points not towards a battle of the ideologies, the political and social technologies of the past; it calls on each of us to imagine new ways to live that move us forward. Its answers are before us, not behind us.

The community of social innovation practice seems to be most visible in the various interlocking social innovation networks that have arisen at local, national, regional and global levels. Little systematic study has been done of these, but there is clear evidence that they see themselves facilitating the work of what we call design catalysts by connecting them, even though there are very significant differences in the way they work. For example, the SIX network states that its ". . . vison is that people all over the world can become better innovators by more easily connecting to their peers, sharing methods and exchanging solutions globally" (SIX 2016a), and sees itself as "more a community than a network". It specifically recognizes its role as not only acting to share experience "connecting innovators, designing experiences, curating knowledge and insights, and disseminating practical examples of social innovation", but also building capacity amongst non-members, which it does by running training programs and workshops with "universities, governments, foundations and other institutions interested in building skills, methods and social innovation capacity".

How might the knowledge and experience of members of these networks best be preserved and shared? This seems likely to consist of something more than "knowledge", as a codified or systematized body of understanding that exists separate from the contexts in which it has been or may yet be applied. Of course, such knowledge is not without value, particularly when it encompasses technological or bio-medical knowledge that might be employed by society. However, even in these cases, the application of knowledge is still a fundamentally relational problem. The central issues in eradicating polio are not technical, but rather social, organizational and political; how to organize to individually immunize every child in an area at risk; how to negotiate for vaccination to proceed in communities that may be suspicious of motive or torn by conflict; how to manage a vaccination program where populations are displaced or transient once an effective vaccine is identified; it is these (and a myriad other) local and practical questions that will determine its success.

Hence, in addition to codified knowledge, we need to find ways to share practice. While we are very good at distilling knowledge and carrying it far from the communities and applications where it was produced, we are much less effective at recognizing, let alone preserving or disseminating, knowledge about practice in a way that preserves its contextual and relational character. This form of knowledge might be seen as Aristotelian "phronesis" or practical wisdom: "the kind of prudential judgement by which equivocal circumstances are negotiated with both individual and collective good in mind" (Nonaka *et al.* 2014, 368). Because each social innovation process takes place in a unique context; because it proceeds by a series of imaginings and provocative proposals, through abduction rather than deduction; because it involves a fine balancing of interests and perspectives that are not purely rational in nature, successfully fulfilling the role of design catalyst involves much more than the application of a tool-kit of rule-based skills. It involves intuitively recognizing both a type of situation and the approaches most likely to move it forward, what Dreyfus and Dreyfus call "expertise" (2005), built on familiarity with a multitude of special cases that sensitize the design catalyst to what is happening without him ever having seen the situation before. It is not about rationality, and defies systematization, instead favoring "deliberation": "To reason is to remove oneself dispositionally from the situation encountered, and, increasingly, to invoke established rules as known standards, or yardsticks to guide comprehension. In contrast, deliberation arises from an intimate 'indwelling' or of being in amidst and embedded in a complex of social relations, a persistent and pressing entwinement in situations from which a form of direct and complete perception is made available, without any need for reason or justification from above. It uses a perceptual rather than conceptual repertoire (Dreyfus and Dreyfus 2005)" (Nonaka *et al.* 2014, 368).

Acquiring expertise, then, is about exposure to multiple different experiences of the sort that might be useful in recognizing future situations. Although rules, maxims, techniques and models may be useful in earlier stages of learning, expertise can only be achieved by engaging with and critically examining experience and outcomes (Dreyfus and Dreyfus 2005). This is necessarily a process of interaction: "competence" in a community of practice is socially defined, and it is in the interplay between socially defined competence and personal experience that learning takes place (Wenger 2000, 226). Hence, the community of practice that we see emerging is both the originator and the disseminator of experience and the arbiter of competence. According to Wenger, such communities develop a sense of "joint enterprise", of "mutuality" through their interactions; and a "shared repertoire of communal resources", access and contribution to which determines competency (229). At its current stage of development, the community of social innovation practice seems to have only a diffuse sense of shared purpose, and one which is linked more to universal human aspirations for a better life than to a set of craft-like capabilities that would enable achieving those loftier goals. However, the constant examination of experience and conversations around purpose and approach is already rich and diverse, and occurring across multiple networks and organizations that have global reach and local presence. This process is building a sense of mutuality, and appears to aspire to developing a shared repertoire of communal resources.

We have already noted the value of "boundary objects" to provide focal points around which different groups can gather and coordinate work. Star and Griesemer (1989), examining the way "translations" (in the ANT sense) occurred in a zoology museum, identified (non-exhaustively) four types of boundary objects: "repositories", such as libraries; "ideal types", abstracted concepts or models; "coincident boundaries", where objects such as maps allow different audiences to position objects of interest to them in a common space; and "standardized forms", which enable communication (411). The networks that constitute social innovation community would seem well placed to develop several of these, but in particular to facilitate repositories where stories become readily accessible in ways that facilitate asynchronous access on demand. Narratives retain much meaning and contextual richness that might support the development of expertise; and indeed, they appear to be being used in precisely this way in many books and conferences at which subsets of the social innovation community gather.

Technology has greatly expanded opportunities to do this in recent years, making it possible to store and disseminate large amounts of data, and allowing data to be kept in forms that are less "processed" and more flexibly searched. Some of the potential of such approaches at a local community level is seen in stories such as that of StoryBank in India (Frohlich *et al.* 2009, Manzini 2015, loc 2776–2793). Sophisticated approaches to searching and retrieving materials have also been explored. The Storymaker project (Taptiklis 2005), which specifically aimed to develop means of "construction and reuse of recorded narrative experience within professional groups" is an example. Initially conceived as a way to support nurses to engage in systematic reflection on their daily practice, it aimed to assist by "preserving the richness of spoken narrative, and then in sharing this experience between individuals who were not in the same physical or temporal space" (6). It was also used in social work, engineering and change management. Because "practitioners do not necessarily 'know'" what they know, collecting the stories involved a structured method of prompting performed by trained "elicitors", from which narrative fragments could be isolated. These were then tagged with short descriptors and organized into themes and ideas through comparison. This resulted in a "narrative body", from which "fragments may be retrieved and experienced by hearers individual or in combination", and that could be distributed across a variety of digital media. Taptiklis relates the effect to the concept of an "antenarrative", advanced by Boje (2001) as a means of distinguishing "story" from narrative: "Antenarrative is the fragmented, non-linear, incoherent, collective, unplotted and pre-narrative speculation, a bet. . . . story is 'ante' to narrative . . . [it] is an account of incidents or events, but narrative comes after and adds 'plot' and 'coherence' to the story line" (7). Boje insists on the importance of antenarrative as an antidote to the "impos[ition] of counterfeit coherence and order on otherwise fragmented and multi-layered experiences of desire" (8). Because of this nature, antenarratives are not only open, but specifically demand interrogation and reinterpretation: they are not "polished gems of knowledge" but "bets", speculative contributions or experiential prompts, calling to be brought to life in the context in which they are heard.

Whether this approach is ideal or not, it points to the possibility of establishing ways to access and interact with stories of practice that do not filter out ambiguity and uncertainty, or impose an interpretive frame that determines how the story is to be understood. It seems to respond to what Björgvinsson was seeking in his "extended participatory design project" in an intensive care unit in Sweden, when he stressed that "focus on practice necessarily requires in situ explorations to see if the proposed design explorations invoke relevant prototypical practices in the midst of work" (2008, 85). Other approaches exist to this sort of technologically enabled repository of stories, such as that developed by David Snowden, a leading contributor to thinking on complexity and narrative, whose SenseMaker® software and methodology collects data directly from respondents who "self-signify" the recordings to enable searching and pattern recognition. It is well beyond the scope of this book to evaluate these various different options, or the many others that no doubt exist. Rather, the intention here is to highlight the possibility of developing repositories of practitioner stories that would enable other practitioners widely separated in time or space to participate in a sort of asynchronous deliberation, an exploration of possibilities that would enable the connection of experience in one place with possibility in another. Such a repository, particularly to the extent that it collected narrative fragments, would incorporate moments of failure, false starts and errors, as well as moments later deemed to be successful that may not have been recognized as such at the time. Technology has advanced considerably since the Storymaker project, and there are certainly further advances to be made that might make this possibility all the more practicable.

Whatever shape or form the further development of a community of social innovation practice may take, there appears to be a strong role for the networks to which design catalysts belong to enable this form of exchange of experience around boundary objects, both by developing expertise and by

connecting sites of social innovation in ways that might spark further innovation on different sites. We are depicting a community where expertise,
methodologies and experience flow freely, where connections are specifically established to share and open the work of others up to inspection. This
is based on an understanding that "knowledge" is of little value beyond
the context in which it is produced; it must be reinvented, reinterpreted,
reapplied if it is to come to life in its new context. It is reminiscent of the
"commons", a "shared resource that is subject to social dilemmas" (Hess
and Ostrom 2007a, 3). Ostrom's early work on governing the commons
dealt specifically with physical resources, and yielded eight design principles
by which collective governance of the commons was enabled and the "tragedy of the commons" (amongst other possible effects) could be avoided.
The focus on physical resources was later explicitly extended to cover non-
physical resources such as knowledge (Hess and Ostrom 2007b). Given the
informational and developmental character of the network we are considering, which is therefore focused more or less explicitly on the development
of a shared body of knowledge in its broadest sense, this work would seem
to be applicable for our purposes. The particular concern in this case is
the possibility that members of the network might focus on the development of their own knowledge in deliberate isolation from others, bringing about a tragedy of the "anti-commons . . . the potential underuse of
scarce scientific resources caused by excessive intellectual property rights
and overpatenting . . ." (Hess and Ostrom 2007a, 11). This sort of effect
is driven by the so-called "free-rider effect", where some members might
benefit from the knowledge without themselves contributing. The gener-
alization of Ostrom's design principles to the productive configuration of
groups (Wilson, Ostrom, and Cox 2013), when taken as design principles,
rather than as "implementations" or elaborations of principles in specific
contexts (s26), seem to provide a basis for envisaging the sort of community
that might guide and support social innovation. They suggest that particular
attention should be paid to four questions:

1. How to develop a sense of identity for the networks that is both open
   and adaptable, but clear enough to establish when membership is appropriate and not. This might relate to a continuous negotiation, re-
   assessment and redefinition of the purpose that holds the networks
   together, as a means of establishing awareness of both what constitutes the knowledge being developed and the groups engaged with the
   process.
2. How members of the networks relate to the knowledge that is shared
   across the networks and how the knowledge developed by each of them
   is to be shared, without obscuring the connection of the knowledge to
   both the member and to the local context where it has meaning.
3. How to build a clear sense of common values that is shared across the
   networks, including the expectation that each member should contribute

for the benefit of all, with the understanding that a failure to do so would lead to exclusion, and the capacity for such concerns to be raised with members by or on behalf of the networks.

4. How to build the understanding of all members that they are free to set their own modes of operation and collaboration, but form part of a connected entanglement of specific projects, which may themselves be connected to more distant projects. All the various socio-material assemblies, while maintaining their distinctness and independence, themselves participate in broader levels of distillation, development and dissemination of knowledge.

Such an approach may risk challenging the various, often deeply held, legal and cultural conceptions of intellectual property that exist around the world. To the extent that beliefs about how social innovation occurs still hinge on developing "solutions" or "models" that are then placed in production and rolled out to the waiting world to "create value", these concerns also impinge on the question of how to remunerate the work of social innovation. If the assumption is that "a social innovation" can belong to a party different from the ones enacting it, sharing expertise represents a breach of property rights that is unlikely to go unchallenged. Alternative approaches exist. One such recent example has been the decision by TACSI to "open source" a program called "Weavers" (TACSI 2016). Weavers was developed and trialed in South Australia as an approach to enable "peer to peer support for carers by experienced carers" (Weavers 2016). Because the carer role cuts across the health, mental health, ageing and disability sectors, the program has potentially very broad reach and impact, and the necessarily limited capacity of a single organization to "implement" it would represent a significant brake on how far and fast that potential could be realized. Instead, TACSI is making available all the details of the Weavers model without charge (including its very interesting "StoryBank"), explicitly emulating practices from the open-sourced software world (Gruen and Vanstone 2016). TACSI does, however, offer to provide service to organizations that wish to use the approach themselves, assisting them to adapt the model for a fee. In this way, TACSI foresees maximizing application of the work (so greatly increasing its impact on society), and also capturing a share of the value generated over that much broader base. This attaches the remuneration of the work to its interpretation *in situ*, while allowing the "codified" knowledge to be freely available to those who might benefit from it.

At a more general level, the openness of the community of practice ("bridging capital" in terms of our earlier discussion) would seem to be a vital factor in enabling the discovery of new approaches to practice. We are not wanting to establish a "gated community" here, where increasingly remote specialists work to codify advanced knowledge behind walls of any sort (or in ivory towers). Practical wisdom is only valuable in its application, and the design catalyst is only one part of any eventual social innovation. Because of this, it would also seem appropriate to consider how to facilitate access to the community for "non-expert" contributors, in Manzini's terms those who might be, or wish to become, "competent designers", without becoming design catalysts themselves, and who may never seek to exercise their competence beyond a specific site or issue. Through its workshops and training offerings, this seems to be a visible feature of SIX's activity. However, encouraging diversity in access to the community represents a potential challenge because of the likelihood that there will be significant cultural differences and different value systems between potential members. The community of practice is likely to connect not only design catalysts, but also potential funders, often large philanthropic foundations; major corporates fulfilling their Corporate Social Responsibility obligations; or government agencies deciding how to distribute public money as effectively as possible and needing to demonstrate that they have done so responsibly. Many of the organizations actually undertaking social innovation, by contrast, are likely to have very different focuses and backgrounds, similar to Manzini's "*collaborative organizations . . .* social groups emerging in highly connected environments. Their members choose to collaborate with the aim of achieving specific results, and, in doing so, they also create social, economic, and environmental benefits. They are characterized by *freedom of choice* (their members can freely decide whether, when, and how to join or leave the group) and *openness* (they present a positive attitude toward 'others': other people, other ideas, other organizations)" (2015, loc 1919, emphasis in original).

While all organizations exist to regulate the tension between control and collaboration at some level, this sort of organization appears to tend very much to the latter in its balancing, in contrast to the formalized, disciplined and structured organizations they will usually have to deal with for funding. It therefore appears inevitable that a measure of tolerance, understanding and compromise will be needed by both types of organization if they are to cooperate or form relationships. Many "business" practices are actually technologies of control that attempt to ensure that rates of return (either financial or moral) are maximized, or at least that minimum levels are achieved, or that a "solution" is applied exactly as it was designed or procured. Whilst this discipline may play a vital role in attracting and reassuring potential suppliers of resources, such controls also ultimately impact on the people who are engaging with their clients. Hence, they are a key influence on the practice of social innovation. How does the funder orient the design catalyst to measure success? How do they allow the design catalyst to reconcile that purpose with the purpose of other participants in the social innovation process? How much do they need to be seen as being responsible for success, in order to meet the needs of their various stakeholders, and how does this shape the way they need to measure progress? The answers to these questions will have a crucial influence on the sort of social innovation that is possible, and on the quality of the relationship that is formed between funder and design cata-lyst. The paradox is that traditional organizations, together with their controls, play a vital part in enabling collaborative organizations to bring about social innovation but, by their very nature, may have the opposite effect.

Unger proposes the term "experimentalist collaboration" as something that exists already in the "... best businesses and business schools", but that is "reaching outward to the organization of politics and of culture" (2007, 171). He identifies five attributes of this new way of working: a

> ... softening of the contrast between supervisory and implementing roles. Tasks are redefined as they are executed, in the light of newly discovered opportunities and constraints[;] ... [a] relative fluidity in the definition of the implementing roles themselves. There is no rigid technical definition of labor[;] ... ability to move the focus of new effort, as far as practical constraints may allow, to the frontier of opera-tions that are not readily repeatable because we have not yet learned how to bring them under a formula[;] ... [a] willingness to combine and to superimpose, in the same domains, cooperation and competi-tion. Under a regime of cooperative competition, for example, people compete in some respects while pooling resources, ideas, or efforts in others[; and] ... a predisposition for groups engaged in experimentalist cooperation to reinterpret their group interests and identities as they go along—and to expect to reinterpret them—rather than to take them as given. (Le Dantec and DiSalvo 2013).
>
> (172)

It seems that such ways of working might need to be enabled if the vari-ous parties within the social innovation system are to collaborate effectively. The networks that bring together social innovators might also play a role here, to the extent that they act as a point of connection for design catalysts and facilitate the exchange of experiences around ways of collaborating. In this, they might be seen as potential sites of translation between funders and innovators, making emerging forms of collaboration visible as a resource for the community. Another form of boundary object that might enable such translations could be the values that the networks promote. These can be more or less explicitly stated, but will require interpretation in the con-text of any particular relationship. For example, SIX states that members

1. Value social impact (rather than ideas)
2. Celebrate solutions (more than heroes)
3. Engage honestly (more than just inform)
4. Inspire through action (not just words)
5. Connect as peers (not in a hierarchy)
6. Committed [sic] to openness (and welcome the unexpected).

(SIX 2016b)

Negotiating a relationship between a funder and a design catalyst or platform organization around these values might require developing an understanding of the different meanings of "social impact" to each party; the natures of solutions being sought (and agreement on how the credit for success is to be shared); the nature of communications between the parties (in particular, what sort of expectations exist not only for formal reporting, but also for informal reporting and handling of unexpected developments that might affect the relationship); and how experience is to be recorded and shared with other members of the network. Ensuring that these discussions are had, and that members of the community understand what common ground exists between members, as well as in a particular funder/design catalyst relationship, would also make a significant contribution to fulfilling the conditions described by Ostrom and her colleagues for the effective management of a knowledge commons.

Clearly, the understanding of social innovation being developed here, resting as it does on the engagement of people in the communities that will enact the change, favors the development of locally based design catalysts, or at least ones that are able to develop relationships with the communities with which they work. Geographic spread and cultural diversity of the membership base are therefore indicators that social innovation networks should monitor closely. We saw in chapter 1 that Ashoka, which could probably be seen as a platform organization or network in its own right, has changed its emphasis from seeking the rare individual social entrepreneur to a concept of "everyone a changemaker". While it still maintains its system of Fellows, who might be seen as corresponding in many ways to the design catalysts we are considering, it explicitly now recognizes that social innovation engages entire communities. It is also consciously monitoring its geographical implantation, and recognizes the need to ensure diversity. In the US, it says

> [w]e realized through a recent internal analysis that the majority of our amazing US Fellows live and work in only four cities: Boston, New York City, Washington D.C. and the San Francisco Bay Area. And we quickly saw that this geographic breakdown does not begin to reflect the power and breadth of changemaking in the United States.
> So in 2016, we committed ourselves to an 'All America: We See Changemakers Everywhere' vision. We decided to change our own story, and to help change the next chapter of social entrepreneurship in the United States, by better incorporating the rich ethnic, racial, gender and geographical diversity that America offers into the social change landscape.
> (Ashoka 2016)

We have sketched out a view of a community of social innovation practice, centered around design catalysts, supporting them and connecting them with each other and with the various enablers of their work, in an evolving dialogue about their practice, their challenges, opportunities and values. We have intentionally not suggested that this community should become more organized or consolidated. Instead, we have noted that there is an intertwined web of networks that are fulfilling many of the roles we have suggested, in different ways and with different foci. Because one of the attributes that enables the community of practice to function to its greatest potential is its openness, and the corresponding lack of barriers to sharing expertise, insight and experience, we believe that there is enormous inherent value in the diversity of these networks, the way that they overlap, and the fact that members are able to move from one to another across geographies and modes of practice. It is precisely the variegated nature of the networks, the wealth of weak ties that they allow and the different perspectives that they offer, that makes them adaptable and fosters new ideas.

The focus of this book so far has been almost exclusively on how social innovation occurs, through a process of co-design that is unique in every instance. We have said very little about what occurs when "project time" is finished, or design after design commences, except to stress that even then we are still dealing with a proto-solution that may evolve and is subject to further work. We have chosen to pay so little attention to this phase of social innovation for very much the same reasons as those advanced by Unger: "A way to accelerate the production of the new is to turn the way people work together into a social embodiment of the imagination: their dealings with one another mimic the moves of experimental thought. To this end, the first requirement is that we save energy and time for whatever cannot yet be repeated. Whatever we can repeat we express in a formula and then embody in a machine. Thus, we shift the focus of energy and attention away from the already repeatable, toward the not yet repeatable" (2007, 42). Repetition seems to correspond to Iversen's and Dindler's (2014) "maintaining", and we have already suggested that this may be difficult to achieve in reality. But how do we achieve it at all? This seems above all else to be an organizational achievement. We establish disciplined structures, procedures and processes that we agree to perform. We institute controls that either make it impossible for us to behave differently (perhaps protocols, like forms or approval systems) or that warn us when there is a deviation. Organizational arrangements hold the market for soap in rural India in place, even though they are distributed amongst small retailers, micro-financiers and Unilever. They ensure the market is brought into being again and again by the repeated acts of suppliers and purchasers. A single organization may be set up to embody a proto-solution—social enterprises, by definition, represent a "sustainable business model" that enables the agreed flow of interactions and resources to repeat itself indefinitely into the future.

It would seem, then, that the appropriate disciplines to understand design after design are probably management and organization studies, and there is no doubt much of interest in that space and much that is already known. However, a particularly interesting variant on this process occurs when a solution is enacted as an organization that forms part of a broader platform organization. Groupe SOS, mentioned in chapter 1, would seem to be a good example of this, providing an organizational template, management expertise and resources that allow them to incorporate a wide variety of social programs into an overarching structure. This could be seen as a platform social enterprise: an agglomerator of social enterprises that aims to improve their efficiency and provide governance and resources that make them sustainable. Another example is BRAC, which claims to be "the world's largest development organisation, dedicated to empowering people living in poverty. We operate across 11 countries, touching the lives of 1 in every 55 people" (BRAC n.d.-b). Headquartered in Dhaka, Bangladesh, BRAC was founded in 1972, and now runs sixteen groups of programs across five broad themes, including: Wellbeing and resilience; Water, Sanitation and Hygiene; Expanding Horizons (Education, Migration, Skills Development); Governance, management and capacity building; Economic development and social protection; and Empowerment (including gender justice and equity and human rights and legal services). In 2015, it spent USD 904 million including capital expenditure (BRAC 2015). It takes a systemic view of poverty and focuses on direct and indirect linkages that make it persistent, providing support services, but also "operat[ing] social enterprises that are strategically connected to our development programmes, and form crucial value chain linkages which increase the productivity of our members' assets and labour, and reduce risks of their enterprises. These enterprises, ranging from agriculture to handicrafts, also help to make us increasingly self-reliant" (BRAC n.d.-a). They also maintain significant training and research programs. They regularly work with governments, both of the countries they operate in and also as part of the aid programs of other countries, including Australia and the UK. BRAC appears to be an exemplar of a platform organization that not only incubates *things*, experiments and allows innovation to take place, but is also able to formalize proto-solutions as organizations. This approach allows BRAC to maintain a portfolio of projects, some new, some mature, and to adjust and adapt as changes occur. By consolidating such a broad range of programs and ensuring that they are taking place within a framework that ensures overall accountability and governance, they are able to work as partners with a wide variety of funders globally and meet their requirements for measurement. BRAC demonstrates the potential power of the platform organization, acting to connect social innovation activities and accumulating social capital as the potential to undertake further innovation, as well as in the form of relationships to the remote community level and connections to powerful funding institutions.

This chapter, then, proposes that providing a site where social innovators gather to connect with each other and with supporters is more than a convenience; that the networks where this happens may play a potentially vital role in developing a focus on the practice of social innovation itself, not just on the ways it might fit into a particular economic or institutional projects. This could potentially be seen as a type of "new age" governance of the social innovation project. It could also play a role in enabling the full development of a community of practice around social innovation and building a knowledge commons that would support the development of expertise in the field, at the same time extending it beyond the professional designer by building the broader level of design competency. The policies and other infrastructures the networks develop could also act as boundary objects that assist both social innovators and the organizations that support them (government, private or third sector) to translate and reconcile the requirements and the language of the very different cultures that are required for each to operate and collaborate with the other. We have also proposed that "maintenance" for a social innovation proto-solution is likely to be achieved through making particular organizational arrangements, and pointed to the possibility that platform organizations act as sites within which the capability to stimulate social innovation may reside, but where it can also be developed into an organizational form and maintained into the future. Of course, enabling social innovation still demands the same commitment to co-design and openness to purpose as it does everywhere else. To the extent that a framework project, social enterprise or platform organization attempts to assert control over the *thing*, innovation will not occur. Likewise, if these actors become "proprietary design networks", there will be no opening outwards and no connections to the broader community of social design practice. Ideally, all of them will remain committed to openness and contributing to the emerging community of practice.

Note

1 It is tempting to use the term "social designer" for this purpose, rather than the slightly awkward "design catalyst". I have chosen not to go this way, however, for two reasons. First, the term social designer seems to connote a role that is much more influential than is intended here, with overtones of an untrammeled Prometheus, rather than a cautious or agnostic one. Secondly, Manzini expresses the view that "social design" applies more narrowly to particularly problematic situations that need urgent external intervention, and distinguishes it from "design for social innovation", which refers to "social forms as such . . . to the way that society is built". The intention here is certainly the broader application, although I would argue that this fully subsumes "social design", and that many of social innovation's most important contributions may indeed be "social design" in these terms. This broader usage is also seen in Armstrong *et al.* (2014), for instance.

References

Armstrong, Leah, Jocelyn Bailey, Guy Julier, and Lucy Kimbell. 2014. *Social Design Futures*. Brighton: University of Brighton.
Ashoka. 2016. "About AshokaUS," accessed 11/11/16. https://www.ashoka.org/en/country/united-states.

Björgvinsson, Erling Bjarki. 2008. "Open-Ended Participatory Design as Prototypical Practice." *CoDesign* 4 (2):85–99. doi: 10.1080/15710880802095400.

Boje, David M. 2001. *Narrative Methods for Organizational and Communication Research*. London: SAGE.

BRAC. 2015. Annual Report 2015. Retrieved from http://www.brac.net/images/reports/BRAC-Bangladesh-Report-2015.pdf

BRAC. n.d.-a. "Our Approach," accessed 17/11/16. http://www.brac.net/our-approach.

BRAC. n.d.-b. "Who We Are," accessed 17/11/16. http://www.brac.net/#who_we_are.

Dreyfus, Hubert L., and Stuart E. Dreyfus. 2005. "Peripheral Vision: Expertise in Real World Contexts." *Organization Studies* 26 (5):779–792. doi: 10.1177/0170840605053102.

Frohlich, David M., Dorothy Rachovides, Kiriaki Riga, Ramnath Bhat, Maxine Frank, Eran Edirisinghe, Dhammike Wickramanayaka, Matt Jones, and Will Harwood. 2009. "StoryBank: Mobile Digital Storytelling in a Development Context." Proceedings of the SIGCHI Conference on Human Factors in Computing Systems, Boston, MA.

Gruen, Nicholas, and Chris Vanstone. 2016. "Open Source Human Services Weaves a New Way Forward." *The Mandarin*, accessed 7/9/16. http://www.themandarin.com.au/69842-weaving-professional-practical-knowledge-together-tacsi-launches-open-source-human-services-australia/.

Hess, Charlotte, and Elinor Ostrom. 2007a. "Introduction: An Overview of the Knowledge Commons." In *Understanding Knowledge as a Commons: From Theory to Practice*, edited by Charlotte Hess and Elinor Ostrom, 3–26. Cambridge, MA: MIT Press.

Hess, Charlotte, and Elinor Ostrom, eds. 2007b. *Understanding Knowledge as a Commons: From Theory to Practice*. Cambridge, MA: MIT Press.

Iversen, Ole Sejer, and Christian Dindler. 2014. "Sustaining Participatory Design Initiatives." *CoDesign* 10 (3–4):153–170. doi: 10.1080/15710882.2014.963124.

Le Dantec, Christopher A. Le, and Carl DiSalvo. 2013. "Infrastructuring and the Formation of Publics in Participatory Design." *Social Studies of Science* 43 (2):241–264. doi: 10.1177/0306312712471581.

Manzini, Ezio. 2015. *Design, When Everybody Designs an Introduction to Design for Social Innovation*. Translated by Rachel Coad. Cambridge, MA: MIT Press.

Nicholls, Alex. 2010. "The Legitimacy of Social Entrepreneurship: Reflexive Isomorphism in a Pre-Paradigmatic Field." *Entrepreneurship Theory and Practice* 34 (4):611–633. doi: 10.1111/j.1540–6520.2010.00397.x.

Nonaka, I., Robert Chia, Robin Holt, and V. Peltokorpi. 2014. "Wisdom, Management and Organization." *Management Learning* 45 (4):365–376. doi: 10.1177/1350507614554152.

SIX. 2016a. "About SIX," accessed 20/7/16. http://www.socialinnovationexchange.org/about#about.

SIX. 2016b. "About SIX: Mission and Values," accessed 10/11/16. http://www.socialinnovationexchange.org/about#missionvalues.

Star, Susan Leigh, and James R. Griesemer. 1989. "Institutional Ecology, 'Translations' and Boundary Objects: Amateurs and Professionals in Berkeley's Museum of Vertebrate Zoology, 1907–39." *Social Studies of Science* 19 (3):387–420. doi: 10.1177/030631289019003001.

TACSI. 2016. "Weavers," accessed 30/10/16. http://tacsi.org.au/project/weavers/.

Taptiklis, Theodore. 2005. "After Managerialism." *Emergence: Complexity & Organization* 7 (3/4):2–14.

Unger, Roberto Mangabeira. 2007. *The Self Awakened: Pragmatism Unbound.* Cambridge, MA: Harvard University Press.

Weavers. 2016. "Weavers: Support Along the Caring Journey," accessed 30/10/16. https://weavers.tacsi.org.au/.

Wenger, Etienne. 2000. "Communities of Practice and Social Learning Systems." *Organization* 7 (2):225–246.

Wilson, D. S., E. Ostrom, and M. E. Cox. 2013. "Generalizing the Core Design Principles for the Efficacy of Groups." *Journal of Economic Behavior & Organization* 90:S21–S32. doi: 10.1016/j.jebo.2012.12.010.

8 A Social Innovation Community?

This book has not aimed to revolutionize or redefine the field of social innovation, which would be both pretentious and unnecessary. For all the need to maintain a healthy skepticism towards many of the claims for social innovation, the energy and purpose that is being harnessed by practitioners, and the learning that is being created, is humbling, and being carried out by people with much more claim to phronesis than this author. Nevertheless, we hear Mulgan's (2012) call for advances in theory, and his observation that up to now social innovation has largely been about developing practice. Mulgan also points out that social theories are inextricable from their purposes; that they are likely to be hard to separate from their contexts; and that their claims to truth are, by their nature, never absolute. This position aligns with the pragmatist viewpoint that "even scientific theories can ultimately be judged on nothing else but their bearing on the pragmatic challenges of our everyday life" (Martela 2015, 547), reflecting the ethical standards discussed in chapter 6. The theories applied to the field of social innovation in this book have all been chosen because of the way they may be used together to generate insight and ideas, and their at least partially consistent views of the world. This contrasts with positivist investigations, which rest on there being externally valid "social" objects and structures that might allow reliably predictive theory to be developed, in the form of Mohr's (1982) variance theory. If such objective fixity can ever be achieved in a world created by human interactions, it is a long way from being so in the field of social innovation. Rather than seeking to "discover" such theory and pass social innovation over to Unger's "machine", it seems more productive to look for theor(ies) that might challenge or provoke practitioners who seek to produce novelty; "middle range" theories, rather than Grand Theory, providing a set of conceptual tools that allow us to make working hypotheses about how to understand a particular type of social context. Our purpose has not been to plug any gaping hole, or correct any deficiency in the research work that is currently being undertaken on social innovation. In the first place, the stated belief of this work, that eclecticism is a significant asset for the field rather than an impediment, stands in the way of making exclusionary proposals of any type. Secondly, this work has drawn on, and is founded solely on, work that has been produced across many countries and disciplines, necessarily skimming across the surface of much that would extend this offering significantly, and no doubt correct some misapprehensions or errors along the way. Instead, it has proceeded much as we suggest design catalysts might: by making connections between disparate bodies of work and conceptual repertoires, it has proposed a perspective on social innovation that might generate new ideas amongst both practitioners and researchers. Its intent is generative, rather than summative; its failings may be as useful as its successes.

Such an approach to research is open to critique at several levels, particularly if the standards by which research are to be judged are positivist and aim to provide theory with predictive validity independent of context. The objectivity with which such approaches like to invest their empirical investigations is replaced by a challenge to reinvent the elements that populate and constitute empirical reality in each new context, recognizing that they only exist in relation with each other. The "guidance" given to practitioners is at once inconclusive and points them back to their own perceptions, resources and inventiveness. Equally, from critical perspectives, the approach is likely to be seen to fail to engage with "big issues" like institutionalized power imbalances and ideological struggle, as well as getting too close to being "utilitarian" or even "instrumental". Such criticism is freely accepted, and it is acknowledged that no defense can be offered that would validate this approach in the terms of either tradition. However, what has been proposed also challenges both critiques to turn their attention to the concerns of the people actually engaged in working together to generate social innovation. Not only is this author skeptical of the possibility of coming up with theory that will tell such people what to do in any given situation, he is also deeply concerned by the implication such theory would carry with it that people can be effectively manipulated by following theoretical prescriptions, and the way such an approach would remove the obligation of the "innovator" to pay attention to the reality of the specific context and individuals within it, in favor of identifying what is relevant based on some exogenous model. Likewise, and without denying the importance of a political perspective on social innovation in the broad and social innovations in the particular, the author feels that the desire of individuals engaged in creating ways forward on time scales where they may see some benefit in their lifetimes needs to be respected, however imperfect and incomplete that progress might be relative to an ideal standard. Of course, what is "useful" depends on the perspective of the evaluator; it is a value judgment that is inevitably contextualized, political and ethical. We have already seen the different priorities and purposes that are assumed by each of the three narratives of social innovation from which this work departed. To these, we can now add the perspective of researchers who reflect the views of their different communities of what constitutes valid research, and policy makers, who need research to address questions that are relevant to their concerns. Although all these notions of what worthwhile research should look like, and what questions need to be answered, are not completely incommensurable, they will often be at cross-purposes. This might lead some to seek research that is better aligned to a specific need, or to suggest more specialized fora to respond to different audiences and purposes. However, it seems unavoidable that everyone in the social innovation world will need to continue to engage with each other and with research despite wide differences in values, ideologies, purposes and beliefs about how to get things done. It will be no surprise, given the positions developed in this work, that this author sees this messy and partly contradictory reality as a desirable state of affairs, rather than something that needs remedying. We can survive our differences of perspective, and even vehemently disagree with some aspects of many proposals, without needing to discard them in their entirety. We might even go further because of them. The problem is not one of validity, but of utility—how can each contribution be mobilized in support of social innovation that is valued by its beneficiaries? The dialogue between researcher and researcher, and researcher and practitioner, can be productively agonistic.

We propose to draw out some implications of this view of how research can be received and put to work by considering a recent example of a social innovation framework that has become both controversial and highly influential. With that analysis in mind, and employing our proposed catholic and inclusive approach to research, we will then make some tentative and non-exhaustive proposals for further research that we believe this work suggests.

Collective Impact

"Collective Impact" approaches to social innovation have recently become very popular with governments and some funders. They have grown out of a paper published in the Stanford Social Innovation review by Kania and Kramer (2011). At their core, Collective Impact approaches propose a way of achieving cross-sector collaboration between potentially very large numbers of organizations, each attempting to achieve a result in a particular domain, such as education in a particular region or addressing a local environmental issue. Although each organization continues to operate independently, they coordinate their actions by reference to a shared system of measurement and in response to what they see emerging as the collaboration proceeds. This allows them to focus on the particular aspects of the problem they wish to deal with, while at the same time contributing to making a joint impact at the systemic level, so generating progress in a way that could not be achieved by a series of unconnected initiatives. Collective Impact approaches are distinguished from "isolated impact" approaches, which are "oriented toward finding and funding a solution embodied within a single organization, combined with the hope that the most effective organizations will grow or replicate to extend their impact more widely. Funders search for more effective interventions as if there were a cure for failing schools that only needs to be discovered, in the way that medical cures are discovered in laboratories" (38).

A key aspect of the model is the existence of a "backbone support organization" which has its own staff and separate structure. It concentrates on coordinating the participating organizations, ensuring that they connect regularly and facilitating those contacts, monitoring overall progress and bringing emerging issues to everyone's attention, and maintaining the data collection and measurement and communication systems—in short enabling the collaboration and providing it with feedback on where it is going. Kania and Kramer assert that, in addition to the backbone support organization and shared measurement system, participants in a Collective Impact initiative must have a common agenda, engage in mutually reinforcing activities (but ones at which each organization excels) and communicate continuously.

In the 2011 paper, Kania and Kramer base their proposal on four cases, three in the US and one in the cocoa industry in Cote d'Ivoire. One of these cases had reached a stage of maturity at the time of writing of the paper at which it was starting to form a "community of practice" with like-minded-organizations across the country, sharing experience and stimulating development on new sites. By 2013, when a follow-up paper was published (Kania and Kramer 2013), Kania and Kramer were able to refer to Collective Impact initiatives "around the world", and noted the involvement of major funding foundations, including the Gates Foundation, in several of them. Also in 2013, FSG, the consulting group with which both Kania and Kramer are connected, together with the Aspen Institute Forum for Community Solutions, and other partners, established the Collective Impact Forum (Collective Impact Forum 2014, FSG 2016) as a "resource for people and organizations using the collective impact approach". The Collective Impact Forum currently claims that 15,000 practitioners utilize its resources and connect through it, and that eighteen funders and partners are contributing to it.

The Collective Impact concept carries many of the features of the sorts of approach suggested in this work. In particular, the concept appears very similar to the "framework project" proposed by Manzini and Rizzo (2011), although Collective Impact is more specific and prescriptive about the organizational arrangements that should apply. The "backbone support organization" of Collective Impact is not in any fundamental way incompatible with the idea of either framework projects or platform organizations, and the beliefs about how Collective Impact approaches create change by connecting multiple independent initiatives are also consistent with the approaches we have proposed. Kania and Kramer associate the operation of Collective Impact approaches with some of the key elements of complexity thinking, placing a particular emphasis on emergence in both the unfolding of the innovation process and the outcomes that are achieved, and frame it all as "collective learning": "Under conditions of complexity, predetermined solutions can neither be reliably ascertained nor implemented. Instead, the rules of interaction that govern collective impact lead to changes in individual and organizational behavior that create an ongoing progression of alignment, discovery, learning, and emergence. In many instances, this progression greatly accelerates social change without requiring breakthrough innovations or vastly increased funding" (2013, 2). Furthermore, we are firmly reminded that Collective Impact initiatives are long-term in nature and cannot start with a "particular solution in mind" (2011, 41).

However, there are also several differences between our proposals and Collective Impact, some of which can be characterized as vital, while others draw attention to challenges in the way the model is presented and "applied" in practice. At the more fundamental level, Collective Impact seems to severely de-emphasize the need to engage the beneficiaries of the innovations they seek to bring about. Although Hanleybrown, Kania and Kramer (2012) mention "community involvement" as an element in all three "phases" of Collective Impact, it remains an activity that is inherently external facing, "outreach", rather than the site of the actual innovation. In Kania and Kramer (2011), the term "community" is only used to refer to the community of organizations participating in an initiative; no mention is made of the community in which the innovations are produced. This reflects the phenomenon we have already commented on, where social innovation is confused with the organizational arrangements, funding structures and top-down planning and control mechanisms within which, if we are fortunate, it might occur. Our proposition would be that social innovation might or might not be connected with a framework project or a platform organization, but that it remains an activity of those affected by it, not of the organization(s) that may enable it.

Collective Impact is also conceived of as a fundamentally top-down process, in contradistinction to the approach we have developed in this work. We are told that three foundational conditions must be met before a Collective Impact initiative can get under way: "an *influential champion, adequate financial resources,* and a sense of *urgency for change*" (Hanleybrown, Kania, and Kramer 2012, 3). Although Hanleybrown, Kania and Kramer tell us that the first of these is by far the most important, because it is the only way to "bring CEO-level cross-sector leaders together and keep their active engagement over time" (Hanleybrown, Kania, and Kramer 2012, 3), we are struck by the implication that the "urgency for change" is at the organizational level, rather than at the level of those they seek to benefit. Continuous communication is between CEOs; and the "common agenda" is set by "a steering committee or executive committee, which consists of cross-sector CEO level individuals from key organizations engaged with the issue" (7), although in ideal conditions it "also includes representatives of the individuals touched by the issue" (Hanleybrown, Kania, and Kramer 2012, 3). This committee is then responsible for ". . . oversee[ing] the progress of the entire initiative". Although it is clear that this is intended to be an emergent process, with no pre-conceived destination in mind, it is also clear where decisions will be taken about what emerges; other "levels" are there to deliver the vision developed at the top.

In this context, it is interesting to note that there is also no apparent recognition that the process of developing and delivering social innovation through Collective Impact creates a resource, or social capital, that might be used for further innovation, or that the experience of working in such a way presents a significant opportunity to develop the experience of practitioners that would be available for the future. The horizon remains bound by an agreed objective, around which a "highly structured cross-sector coalition" (Kania and Kramer 2013, 1) is assembled. Not only is it visualized as a top-down process to deliver a desired result, its vision does not extend beyond that purpose or the coordination of the work of the member organizations. This is also evident in the lack of discussion of what we have called "cross-scale interactions", and particularly the idea of "scaling up" in the sense proposed by Westley *et. al.* (2014, 239), referring to seeking to change the institutional context, the system that may be the root cause of the social problem. This might involve advocacy and engagement with policy and politics, which appears to be considered out of scope for the model being proposed.

In all of these aspects, and some to be discussed, Collective Impact exhibits a good fit with the Philanthrocapitalistic narrative, and demonstrates that these narratives can indeed produce normative expectations of what social innovation looks like and how it is practiced that are likely to shape action. By challenging the narrative, some of these *lacunae* can be filled, although the more fundamental issues might require more significant building work. In addition, there are some aspects of Collective Impact where their compatibility with our proposition can only be assessed by considering how it is actually applied. When Collective Impact refers to a common agenda, particularly in the context of its self-attribution of being "highly structured", it might be seen to suggest a tightly crafted set of constraints, to which all participating organizations must subscribe, a formulation which we suggest would potentially severely limit the possibility of real innovation occurring. However, there is good evidence that this is not the way in which the common agenda is being proposed: "In fact, developing a common agenda is not about creating solutions at all, but about achieving a common understanding of the problem, agreeing to joint goals to address the problem, and arriving at common indicators to which the collective set of involved actors will hold themselves accountable in making progress" (Kania and Kramer 2013, 6). To the extent that the value of this process is recognized in its own right, and that it is seen to be an adaptive, on-going reinterpretation and updating of purpose, this is quite compatible with the directions we would see as most effective. Likewise, the "shared measurement" criterion proposed in Collective Impact, to the extent that it demonstrates close linkage with the common agenda and is adjusted to take into account the evolution of both that agenda and contextual factors, comes very close to the proposition advanced in chapter 5, where measurement and evaluation act as a sensing mechanism that enables social innovators to be conscious of the results of their actions and to direct themselves accordingly. Collective Impact apparently works from a different understanding of a theory of change than that developed here, seeing it as a "tightly worked out" basis for funding allocation ". . . ideally supported by an evaluation that attributes to the program the impact achieved" (1), rather than as a flexible point of reference that allows sense to be made of reality and assumptions to be surfaced as development and implementation progress. However, it also specifically endorses the use of Developmental Evaluation as ". . . particularly well suited to dealing with complexity and emergence" (4), suggesting that these are differences of interpretation and terminology rather than anything more deep-seated. Similar concerns would apply to the way the role of the "backbone support organization" is worked out in practice. If it were to become a "command and control" mechanism ensuring "alignment", rather than a facilitative, alert and enquiring entity supporting the efforts of participating organizations and ensuring they had the best understanding possible of how the collective project was progressing, then a serious divergence would appear with our proposal. Coordination should be of discovery, not an enforced compliance. The specifics of implementation are what will matter on all these counts. Although there are some fundamental disagreements, much is also shared: ". . . we must live with the paradox of combining *intentionality* (that comes with the development of a common agenda) and *emergence* (that unfolds through collective seeing, learning, and doing)" (7, emphasis in original).

Our evaluation of Collective Impact is, then, one that detects both close alignment and fundamental difference. From the point of view of a pragmatic social innovator, we would probably see the attention and support that has been generated by the approach and ask how could we apply it in ways that were as consistent as possible with our own principles. This might involve, for instance, reconfiguring "cascading levels of linked collaboration" to fully acknowledge the autonomy of the local level *things* that our collaboration aims to activate and connect; to ensure that the "highly structured" aspect of the collaboration refers to the effectiveness of our platform organization in monitoring our overall progress, picking up unexpected and perhaps important signals that not everything is as we expected and connecting everyone involved with that information so that they can take action. It might also add to the scope of the coordination an on-going deliberation on what institutional, political and policy goals might be held in common, and how they could best be advanced. Such clarifications would all be plausible, and would still allow the Collective Impact approach to serve as a translation meeting the needs of both funders/government and the social innovation process itself. This would appear to be the way most practitioners are likely to approach the models proposed by research; with a healthy willingness to take what works, adapt what can be adapted and leave aside what can't in the interests of moving action forward., knowing full well that most disputes around such points are likely to take longer to resolve than any opportunity to address the problem at hand stays open.

The situation for Collective Impact is, however, somewhat complicated by the way it has framed its narrative. It describes itself as "upending conventional wisdom about the manner in which we achieve social progress"; "not merely a new process that supports the same social sector solutions but an entirely different model of social progress" (1). In positioning itself in this way, it completely disregards the vast experience that already exists in constructing community collaboration, and assigns all current practitioners to the "obsolete" file without so much as a reference to support their relegation (unless, of course, they choose to follow the prescription). It tells us that the tendency to "isolated impact" is a feature of the not-for-profit and public sectors, as if it has nothing to do with the (mis)application of "business methods" that have been imposed on actors in the name of modernization and accountability. We see again here the watermarks of the Philanthrocapitalistic narrative; the certainty that "this changes everything"; the disregard for any existing knowledge in the field, whether from researchers or practitioners; and the focus on putting together coalitions of powerful new philanthropic foundations to validate its claims to special influence. Of course, none of these positionings are sustainable when held up to the light for even a brief moment. As has been seen in this work, most of the theoretical supports that would lead us in the direction proposed here and, to the extent that it is consistent, by Collective Impact, go back to the 1970s or earlier; the failure to connect the relationship of social innovation processes to broader political and institutional contexts makes Collective Impact fundamentally conservative rather than in any sense radical; and its complete disregard for any prior work fails to connect the approach to a weight of experience and evidence that could greatly strengthen and nuance its case if it had been brought to bear. It seems quite likely, for instance, that the longstanding work of Ostrom and others on conditions for enabling collective action and managing the commons would provide a much firmer and more adaptable base to guide the construction of collaborative coalitions, framework projects or platform organizations than the specific, but largely unsupported conditions advanced by Collective Impact.

In addition to this critique, which has more to do with the framing and argumentation of Collective Impact than its substance, it could be argued that Collective Impact, at least as originally proposed, was based on very little empirical evidence, particularly considering the uncritical applause it appears to have received from governments and other promoters. Such concerns go to the question of what we believe good research should look like, as well as to the deliberate blanking out of the past that has taken place in marketing Collective Impact. To what extent does a proposal such as Collective Impact need to conform to the requirements of academic research if it is to be taken seriously? This author believes there must be a place for such proposals, whose value lies less in their objectivity, reliability or validity than it does on their ability to motivate action. That Collective Impact was developed by a consulting firm that has been closely associated with its burgeoning growth across the globe; that it refused to pay respect to or connect with past experience or knowledge; that what it actually means in practice is very much dependent on the specifics of each application; all of these are significant weaknesses from the stand-point of high quality research. Nevertheless, it has connected with the concerns of significant stakeholders and opened up opportunities and released resources that might otherwise not have been available for social innovation activities, at least some of which may be successful. It has its faults and limitations, but can also quite readily be contextualized and adapted by both researchers and practitioners. Rather like social innovation process itself, perhaps we should be seeing research contributions as somewhat more provisional than we sometimes do at present, with an emphasis on starting discussions, encouraging exploration and balancing the need for rigor with the need to generate a vibrant and productive dialogue. Proposals of this provocative, even somewhat speculative, nature may have a much bigger place than is currently admitted in the research community (even as topics of interest in their own right)—indeed, it might be that the research community could treat them as a base for development and apply the full battery of research tools to that task, strengthening them rather than ignoring or discarding them.

The Social Innovation Community: Researchers and Practitioners Together?

To carry this further, perhaps it would help if we ceased to draw the distinction between practice and research quite so distinctly, while remaining very conscious of the demands each of the two worlds make on their own. After all, many social innovation and participatory design researchers are also practitioners. What would happen if we imagined the diverse world of funders, researchers, design specialists, policy makers and design catalysts (and many more) as a *thing* in its own right, assembled around "social innovation" as a matter of concern? Such a perspective would draw us towards discussing the purposes of social innovation, identifying potential ways forward and testing these proto-solutions to learn together what they might imply. It would encourage us to express ideas in terms of theories of change, not as tightly defined prescriptions, but as points of reference that assist us to measure progress and notice the unexpected. It might even suggest to us the possibility of treating research and practice as two aspects of the same co-design process, drawing researchers and practitioners together to develop and deliver an agenda that expressed itself in action.

This proposition is, of course, already partly visible in the social innovation world. However, it is notable in reviewing the literature that much research is currently focused on matters of interest to funders (government or philanthropic) or policy makers, particularly in the UK and Europe. It is, of course, only natural that this should be so, and such research plays a vital role in enabling social innovation. Nevertheless, there does seem to be significant potential to further develop the dialogue around the need of the process of social innovation in its own right, tailored to the interests and needs of design catalysts and the networks that connect them. Recognizing that much "practitioner" literature at present essentially takes the form of case studies or advocacy for a particular organization or technique (such as Collective Impact), what might be the potential if the research community were to engage with this audience, giving depth and rigor to our call for "reflexivity" for the social innovation community, acting as a "critical, but sympathetic" (Brandsen, Evers, *et al.* 2016) colleague in an emerging joint enterprise?

Further developing such an approach presents several challenges, as much of presentation as substance. The artifact around which the research community generally gathers is the journal article. It connects multiple systems by which the academic world is regulated and makes particular demands of genre, format and structure that are not always compatible with a fast-paced, to-and-fro examination of possibilities. Moreover, researchers juggle multiple identities, and in particular have to play roles within the disciplinary and academic communities to which they belong. Those roles make specific demands of researchers in terms of the types of questions they need to explore, the methods they use and the way they write conclusions, all of which are, of course, perfectly legitimate (or at least unavoidable). Most particularly, academia demands the performance of certain ritual activities such as journal publication, which may not support engagement in multi-disciplinary, applied interactions that extend beyond identified projects or organizations. These pressures, constraints and rewards all lean towards presenting relatively free-standing, highly developed, and well-polished cases and analyses, removing much of the ambiguity and contextual richness that would allow design catalysts to connect them to the perpetually unique contexts in which they work, and to also provoke new ways of understanding and looking. Phronesis is unlikely to be developed, gathered, preserved or presented in the same way as the codified wisdom we usually consider scientific. We have suggested that here may be some promise, in meeting this challenge, in exploring the sorts of narrative repository proposed in chapter 7. However, it seems likely that such forms will not integrate easily into a world that is driven by the academic journal, or a world that is focused on presenting polished claims to having developed "killer" practical models or unique capabilities. One of the great strengths of ANT is its ability to generate narratives that challenge "official" stories and call attention to the impact of connections that might otherwise remain hidden. For this reason, it seems to provide a very attractive methodological basis from which to depart, even as there needs to be significant attention paid to the point of view of the narrator.

Of course, much is already done in this area by organizations like SIX, NESTA and the Young Foundation (although not in the ANT tradition), and there are extremely valuable studies on methods, evaluations of successful approaches and case studies coming from academic institutions all over the world, but these do not generally answer the challenge of presentation we have noted here. The issues are magnified by the inevitably cross-disciplinary nature of research into co-design and social innovation. This is, of course, an important source of novelty in its own right: we have suggested that the very act of describing from different perspectives may create insight, and so see theoretical eclecticism, as well as an open approach to practical methods, as inherently desirable. However, the range of disciplines that are and may yet become engaged in researching social innovation is very broad, and they do not always share consistent philosophical or ideological foundations. This creates a significant need to build bridges and resolve contradictions between disciplinary partners, which may in turn have repercussions on the disciplines themselves. It is easy, for example, to impose a Philanthrocapitalistic frame on our understanding of social innovation if we come to it from the perspective of some management disciplines. This might lead to confusing social innovation with social enterprise, or imposing a managerialist view of how to "produce" social innovation that this work would consider untenable. On the other hand, connecting social innovation and co-design with innovation studies more generally, or to the more practice-oriented and constructivist streams of organization studies, would appear to produce significant resonances from both sides, as long as conceptual frameworks are empirically grounded rather than imposed from above.

There is also a potentially contentious issue around assumptions about which actors are engaged in social innovation. We noted in chapter 1 that there is a strong tendency to see social innovation as new, and being practiced by new actors. If we accept the understanding of social innovation that has been developed here, though, it is probably taking place in many different places, even if it is not being recognized as such. To focus only on "recognized" social innovators, such as members of SIX, Ashoka Fellows or "social enterprises", would seem to risk excluding a range of potentially extremely active innovators who might consider themselves community organizations rather than social innovators, including some of very large scale (for example, we mentioned Rotary International in chapter 1, which seems to meet all of the criteria for a platform organization). We need to ensure that we bring an extensive rather than exclusive orientation to identifying which actors are involved in social innovation, if we are to develop a truly empirically grounded understanding of it. Social innovation should not become a gated community.

This sort of exploratory, even experimental, approach was behind the co-creation of a recent report, "Co-creating a Social Innovation Research Agenda for Europe", and would appear to have had significant benefits, with the authors commenting that they "would like to encourage research funding organizations and public institutions as well as universities to provide the room to conduct more open-ended experiments like this one. Only if this space is provided with reasonable funding and resources can unexpected connections be made and thus unique new directions and findings come up" (Brandsen, Ecchia, *et al.* 2016, 2). In addition to providing a comprehensive and exciting agenda for social innovation research, Brandsen, Ecchia, *et al.* note that the co-creation process produced ". . . a collateral benefit for SI research [in] the confirmation that an incipient community of SI researchers exists but it needs to be carefully nurtured. Different types of actors have different responsibilities in order to reach the potential of articulating a lively galaxy of communities stemming from various disciplinary and geographic traditions" (20). Bringing the same spirit to the researcher-practitioner space might well have just as beneficial effects.

What might be some of the fields of activity for such a collaborative connection? Based on the proposals made in this book, we will now explore some non-exhaustive, and necessarily speculative, possibilities as a sort of complementary agenda.

Micro/Individual Level

Jenson and Harrisson called for research to focus chiefly on the meso- and micro-levels of social innovation (2013, 7), and Brandsen, Ecchia, *et al.* note that "[t]here is not much focus on individuals in SI, except in EFESEIIS and SOLIDUS [two on-going European projects]" (2016, 8). Following the framework proposed in this work, we would suggest seeing the individual in the context of the *thing*, where the focus might be seen as being as much about research into co-design as into social innovation, and in particular the way the *thing* unfolds. This would also respond to the call for research into "[p]articipatory and empowerment dimensions in SI as 'new' paradigms of social intervention, building patterns or typologies. Although the participatory and empowerment dimensions are highlighted as central to SI in several definitions, the approach to how participation and empowering processes emerge and develop, can be fostered or hindered in the framework of SI remain to be studied" (21). The way the design catalyst relates to the *thing*, and proceeds to map its actor-network and the controversies that arise and are accommodated within it, would also be fertile ground for empirical exploration. The principles of making such maps are similar to those proposed by Venturini (2012, 800), already noted in chapter 4, but there is significant potential to further develop the theoretical tools based on ANT and contribute to a deeper understanding of the nature of *thinging* and of the paths by which innovation proceeds or stalls. An exploration of the ways that social capital is generated, accumulated and made available for new purposes at the individual level would also be of particular interest. "Unfortunately, *research on the individual social capital of social innovators is practically inexistent*" (Habisch and Loza Adaui 2013, 68, emphasis in original).

Research at this level is likely to be especially challenging methodologically, particularly if the perspective desired is that of the participant in the midst of the action, rather than the external observer. We have suggested that one key focus for learning would be the development of "sensitizing concepts", orientations or ways of paying attention that the design catalyst takes into the *thing*, which might assist participants both to achieve agreements that are in some way "better" than they would otherwise have been and to develop relationships between each other that provide a better base to adapt to, or deal with, new matters of concern. They might include things like:

- An encouragement to look not at the structures and spaces of constraint, but at the empty, wild spaces where action is possible, an enticement to explore with a mischievous intent, to misinterpret, twist or divert what is holding the present in place. This might be done in a spirit of rebellion or resistance, or it might be apparently innocent, as a playful enlisting of others to experiment and discover themselves and their world anew (Schrage 2000). Akama draws attention to the potential of being sensitive not only to what is in the network of relationships between people, objects and interactions, but what is not but which might be becoming, and indeed suggests that "being in-between is central for co-designing to emphasise becoming with, not product" (2015, 263). Participants need to find a way to see what they are already familiar with in new ways, and at the same time take sufficient distance from controversies between them to allow them to go forward.
- A focus, not only on the issue participants are attempting to address and the ways they may be able to achieve agreement in response to it, but also on the way that issue orients them towards each other. What are the different connections that are activated for each of the participants by framing the issue in different ways? How do these create alliances and conflicts between participants, bring them together or divide them, remembering to ensure that non-human actors are considered as well as human? Equally importantly, how does the orientation to action that is inherent in different ways of framing the issue affect each participant? What interests does it activate for each of them? What constraints does it reveal, and which does it dissolve? Where are the "black boxes", the unquestioned understandings of how groups are constituted, things have arisen or problems occurred—and what is inside them?
- An encouragement for participants to challenge the boundaries of project and purpose, as well as the formats and protocols that channel their dialogue in unobserved ways, ask why they are being imposed and whose purposes those constraints serve and, if considered worthwhile, to renegotiate or remove the rigidities.

- A resistance to closure, an assumption that whatever is advanced is not unquestioningly taken as a final answer, but as a basis for another round of consideration, for a review of what new possibilities and issues are revealed. This might also be seen as peering to the side of the issue and the solution.
- A sensitivity to the potential that might be created by new relationships between participants, or by the way they orient themselves with regard to objects, spaces or technologies. What "infrastructuring" is taking place? How might it be harnessed by participants to develop new insights or proto-solutions—or matters of concern?
- An awareness of the different temporal orientations being adopted, perhaps unthinkingly, by participants:

    - Foreshadowing: how is the future being portrayed? Where are different participants positioning themselves with regard to it?
    - Back-shadowing: what "evidence" is being brought to bear? What is the narrative logic being used? What is excluded or left unquestioned by that logic?
    - Side-shadowing: What might have been different "if only"? What possibilities would that open up?

- Examination of proto-solutions, not only from the perspective of how they might work out and what effect they may have on relationships between participants, but also from an instrumental point of view on their impact on the process; their ability to stimulate further development (either as a base or as a rejected option), or to cause work to stop on other options and achieve a movement forward to the next phase. Making these effects visible is part of opening up the process to inspection.
- A consciousness of which type of abduction is occurring as people examine proto-solutions and explore ways to evolve them further. Are participants tending to choose between directions or generating new ones? Is it desirable to try to amplify or challenge those tendencies?
- A consciousness of working at two levels at once: the dialogue itself, and "as a cultural operator, collaborating in the creation of the shared images and stories that underlie a new idea of well-being" (Manzini 2015, loc 4278).

For all that these might be useful as general directions for further discussion, they are nevertheless highly preliminary, theoretically derived and expressed in the abstract, without any of the richness that is likely to contribute to the development of expertise. They are exemplary of the presentation challenge we have mentioned. There is therefore much work to be done to further develop this list.

Finally, it is notable that there is little research available into the effects of the form of social innovation work we have proposed on the design catalyst himself. The role is ambiguous, and potentially conflictual; stakes are often high, in terms of the implications of either "failure" or "success", and there are few guardrails to protect the design catalyst as she performs her unscripted and demanding contortions. It is also likely to be very difficult to decide what has failed and what has succeeded until well after much of the "project time" work is over. The design catalyst must remain open as to the interpretation of what is said and not become bound to any particular position. Instead he allows interpretation to develop as the debate develops, adjusting his understandings as new perspectives come to light, not attempting to simplify prematurely, but respectfully feeding back what he hears for checking and to ensure that participants' voices are heard, taking into due account the significance of the view expressed, and to provoke further discussion, all the time considering the ethical dimension of his interventions. Zaid Hassan, in his description of his participation in an initiative focusing on child malnutrition in India, the Bhavishya Lab, reveals some of the disorientation and self-doubt that is probably inevitable in this sort of work, and the importance of not declaring failure (or, probably, success) too early. He concludes that "[r]egardless of the many mistakes we made and all the things we would now do differently, the fact is that the Bhavishya Alliance went on for six more years and spun out many, many different innovative programs and initiatives. Our mistakes sometimes make it hard to acknowledge the good work that so many people did, the courage and the love that poured into trying to make the whole experience work. The smell of burning rubber, however, is still strong even six years later" (2014, 55). What are the effects of doing social innovation on the innovators themselves? What preparations, supports and coping strategies appear to work best?

Meso-Level

At the meso-level, we have proposed the concept of the "platform organization", and note that little investigation seems to have been done on this type of organization, from the point of view of how they operate and the different ways in which they integrate or relate to design catalysts or *things*. It would, for instance, be interesting to explore with practitioners the different ways that "labs" operate and how they relate to eventual innovations. The purpose here would not be to evaluate what is more or less "effective", but to reveal the different sorts of organizational configurations and dynamics that emerge. The concept of a "framework project" would also benefit from more attention, as it seems to offer significant potential for stimulating social innovation and connecting sites in productive ways. Of course, studies of major platform organizations like BRAC, ideally comparative, would be extremely valuable, particularly if they were able to shed some light on the ways that innovation is enabled or stifled within a controlled organization. This connects with voluminous streams of literature in innovation studies and organization studies, but the social innovation perspective is still unusual and insights might be generated in both directions.

We have also suggested that there may be a role for platform organizations, and framework projects, in providing a structural solution to the problem of how to mediate the tension between the requirements of social innovation, as an open-ended engagement that may evolve into an organized "repetition", and those of funders and other stakeholders who require control, accountability and predictability to satisfy their stakeholders. By creating a "portfolio" of initiatives, and perhaps developing stable longer term relationships with either communities that might engage in social innovation or with key enablers of social innovation, they may also provide a vehicle for spreading risks and avoiding overdependency on single funders or providers of other resources. Manzini (2015) points out the implication of Granovetter's (1973) work on "strong" and "weak" ties, and in particular the importance of weak ties in making social systems more open and accessible, by reducing the commitment required to make a contribution (Manzini 2015, loc 2306)—in some cases, there may be benefits in structuring for several smaller partners rather than one large one.

The interface between the various types of organizational actors involved in the social innovation process would also be a fruitful area for learning. What are the various forms these may take, and what are the sorts of contexts and outcomes that are associated with them? How do various approaches to measurement regimes imposed by any one type of stakeholder affect the outcomes of social innovation, and what strategies are used to attempt to manage their impact? What funding arrangements are most and least effective at preserving the autonomy of the social innovation process, and how is this effect produced? The forms of funding arrangements are constantly evolving. For instance, concepts like payment for success are increasingly popular, particularly amongst government agencies that have to demonstrate accountability for the expenditure of public funds. In these, the funder establishes certain objectives and only pays on their achievement. Does this effectively shelter the social innovation process from direct intervention by the funder? What is the effect when these types of arrangements are supported by instruments such as Social Impact Bonds, which can be used to finance the gap between initial outlays of such schemes and outcomes that may only occur long afterwards? There is an active research agenda in these areas that meets the needs of funders, but complementary research that investigates the ways that different arrangements shape and interact with the process of social innovation is very limited.

The drive to measurement is ubiquitous in the field of social innovation, to the extent that it sometimes looks like an unquestioned value. This work could not (and would not dare) suggest that this might sometimes err on the side of slavish devotion, rather than a well-thought out commitment to achieving the best possible results. However, it does clearly establish a need to distinguish between what sorts of measurement and data are useful for what purposes, match them to the appropriate activity and be conscious of the way measurement may impact on the innovation process itself.

We have observed that there is a strong preponderance of measurement approaches aimed at meeting the needs of funders, and suggested that there is a need to more consciously elaborate approaches that might be useful for those actually doing the work, which guide and support the development of innovation as a formative tool, rather than evaluate it in a summative way. We have advanced the possibility of using theory-based approaches such as realist evaluation and developmental evaluation for this purpose, as well as made a case that, right from the commencement of the social innovation process, there should be an explicit articulation of emerging theories of change, both as the heart of an eventual measurement process, and as a tool that contributes actively to the development of insight and to progress. We have observed that platform organizations may offer a means to make the necessary translations between measures needed for different purposes, a proposal that could be expanded and explored in more depth. There would appear to be significant potential to develop a more fine-grained and empirical approach to understanding how different "measurement" and project management approaches impact on the work of the *thing*, and how translations might be made between it and the various actors that enable its work.

We have observed that social innovation processes may frequently require finding spaces where the exercise of power is either suspended or subverted in some way. Benn and Martin relate the case of the establishment of the first Water Users Association in China, in the Zhanghe Irrigation District, Hubei Province (2010), which brought about significant improvements in water management in the area, and has since been extended as a model to many other irrigation areas in China. This involved "the transfer of management powers away from several levels of government and devolution of those powers to the lowest level" (401), and was seen to be ". . . dependent upon a network that brings international academics and practitioners in water management and irrigation together with the students and academics of the Wuhan-based scientific community and with the personnel associated with the field experimental stations. Importantly, the seniority of the Wuhan academics has lent legitimacy to the network in the view of top levels of government—basically it has lent support to the formation of a radical new form of sustainable water management and governance in China" (Benn and Martin 2010). Drawing on Beck, Benn and Martin relate this to "subpolitics": "new sites of action that emerge often ahead of government action and outside representative politics and indicate a weakening of the bureaucracy of state-dominated politics" (408). This concept might apply equally well to the relationship between a *thing* and any powerful external actors it may need to be aware of, whether they are state, private or third sector. In this case, interestingly, the credibility of some key participants became a lever to negotiate freedom to maneuver. However, it would be valuable to examine the phenomenon of sub-politics (or micro-resistance) in more depth and develop a better understanding of how it relates to social innovation and co-design.

Macro-Level

This phenomenon is also of interest at the macro-level, with the often-asserted breakdown in sectoral boundaries that social innovation is producing, as new ways of mobilizing are deployed, whether they be hybrid organizations or crowd-funded causes. As Unger puts it, "The innovators have a seat in civil society outside both the state and the market. The powers of society are never reduced to the activities of market exchange or of governmental politics alone" (2015, 249). The way that participants in social innovation are able to exert influence to ensure that they have sufficient freedom to act, whether it be freedom from controls, commitments or the license to imagine new ways to relate to power, is likely to be a common enabling factor of their work, and therefore an important area of enquiry for design catalyst and researcher alike. Conversely, a failure to find such a space may doom even the best resource and most urgent quests to generate solutions, in the way Hassan suggests the necessity to work through a sovereign government disabled attempts to achieve progress on complex social challenges in Yemen (2014, 30–31). The observation that social innovation can occur in spaces in which government is not free to act is also a potential opportunity, so far underexplored by the social innovation literature. Many major government policies and programs have unpredictable, systemic effects that extend well beyond government's ability to foresee or control. In particular, they may bring about changes in social relationships that are beyond the scope of government to engage with. An example might be low-cost housing: governments may be able to influence the supply of housing, but find it extremely difficult to ensure that occupants are integrated into communities where that housing is situated, even though it is likely that integration (or lack of it) will have by far the largest effect on the success of the program, as perceived by both beneficiaries and other community members. Social innovation provides means and possibilities to operate in this space in ways that government cannot, bringing policies to life and adapting the way they impact on specific communities that have needs or preferences that government has not been able to take into account. The introduction of the new National Disability Insurance Scheme (NDIS) in Australia is creating major restructuring across an entire system of funding, caring and ancillary services, but will also lead to fundamental changes in the way beneficiaries, service providers and funders relate to each other that go far beyond the ability of any party to predict or control. The longer-term consequences of these changed arrangements will be emergent and may have both positive and negative aspects. TACSI has identified this as an area of focus and is working with several actors in the process to "ensure the potential is realized" (2016). Needless to say, it is also quite possible to see a similar role for social innovation as a practice to assist in integrating major technological changes, such as the sweeping effects likely to arise from workplace automation; or as a practice in post-conflict environments, where direct government intervention may be difficult or where there is a vacuum of authority. It seems quite plausible to imagine social innovation processes established side by side with such institutional change, facilitating the emergence of the new relationships and contributing to getting the best results possible out of the new systems.

Research about the networks that make up the social innovation community of practice is also rarely seen. This book has proposed that these networks may have a much bigger role than is widely recognized, but little has been written on how they operate and how they actually connect to the practice of social innovation and to each other. This is a potentially vast field, and one that is constantly evolving. In addition to empirically describing the various networks, much of interest could be done in exploring what different frames, ideologies and agendas they might be pursuing, and what outcomes these orientations are associated with. In both cases, it would be useful to take a longitudinal perspective, examining how initiatives connect and develop over time, as emerging responses to complex issues, rather than neatly bounded units of work that are retro-fitted into a strategic vision.

Another developing role for the research community is the definition of data frameworks to monitor and guide social innovation at the macro-level, and also at the level of specific domains of innovation, such as health or education. The framework proposed by Schmitz *et al.* (2013, see also Bund *et al.* 2015) is a robust approach to this, for the purposes of informing policy makers in a European context. However, whether it meets the needs or maximizes the potential for such data from a practitioner point of view is unclear and, in any case, the approach would need to be adapted for use in other geographies. It is likely that, to be as useful as possible from a practitioner point of view, such information would need to be sufficiently detailed to both set the context for building initiatives and to allow some feel to be gained for what impact sustained social innovation activity might be having at sub-national, regional and global levels. To be of the greatest value, this data would be longitudinal, rather than a series of disconnected snapshots, and would encompass economic and other "hard" data, as well as measures of key "soft" aspects, such as alienation/empowerment and views of the future. At present, there is a risk that the agenda for social innovation is being set by interested parties such as government, in response to their policy concerns and frameworks: but these are not always the most reliable means of gauging what work would be most valuable over the longer term. The social innovation networks would be useful interlocutors in directing this work over time, and this would potentially support their advocacy role.

Finally, there seems to be an opportunity to develop a more historically oriented view of the way social innovation has developed and is developing into the future. We have referred to some useful historical perspectives in this book (for example, Moulaert and Ailenei 2005, Westley 2013), but the struggle to claim social innovation for various purposes and direct it in specific ways suggests that this could usefully be framed as an on-going and much more comprehensive and rigorous stream of work, one that might go some way to remedy the exclusion from the narratives of longer-standing platforms for social innovation and reveal the connections between different interest groups, ideologies and cultural and geographical traditions and social innovation. This would serve a different purpose from the on-going collection of specific cases, which at the moment act as anecdotal indicators of the broader stories, but are usually more concerned with either adducing lessons for practice or promoting social innovation as a harbinger of a better world. The scale of social innovation activity, and the prominence it is starting to take in many domains and political projects, deserves a broader, more dispassionate view, which might also serve to reveal a more qualitative and enriched perspective of the impact it is having.

References

Akama, Yoko. 2015. "Being Awake to Ma: Designing in between-ness as a Way of Becoming With." *CoDesign* 11 (3–4):262–274. doi: 10.1080/15710882.2015.1081243.

Benn, Suzanne, and Andrew Martin. 2010. "Learning and Change for Sustainability Reconsidered: A Role for Boundary Objects." *Academy of Management Learning & Education* 9 (3):397–412.

Brandsen, T., G. Ecchia, J. Eschweiler, L. Hulgård, and R. Nogales. 2016. *Co-Creating a Social Innovation Research Agenda for Europe*. Social Innovation Europe/EMES Network. Retrieved from http://emes.net/content/uploads/post/2956/SIE-CoSIRA-report_July2016.pdf.

Brandsen, T., A. Evers, S. Cattacin, and A. Zimmer. 2016. "Social Innovation: A Sympathetic and Critical Interpretation." In *Social Innovations in the Urban Context*, edited by T. Brandsen, S. Cattacin, A. Evers, and A. Zimmer, 3–18. Cham: Springer International Publishing.

Bund, E., U. Gerhard, M. Hoelscher, and G. Mildenberger. 2015. "A Methodological Framework for Measuring Social Innovation." *Historical Social Research-Historische Sozialforschung* 40 (3):48–78.

Collective Impact Forum. 2014. "About Us," accessed 1/12/2016. http://collectiveimpactforum.org/about-us.

FSG. 2016. "Collective Impact Forum," accessed 1/12/16. http://www.fsg.org/collective-impact-forum.

Granovetter, Mark S. 1973. "The Strength of Weak Ties." *American Journal of Sociology* 78 (6):1360–1380. doi: 10.2307/2776392.

Habisch, André, and Cristian R. Loza Adaui. 2013. "A Social Capital Approach towards Social Innovation." In *Social Innovation: Solutions for a Sustainable Future*, edited by Thomas Osburg and René Schmidpeter, 65–76. Berlin: Springer.

Hanleybrown, Fay, John Kania, and Mark Kramer. 2012. "Channeling Change: Making Collective Impact Work." *Stanford Social Innovation Review*, accessed 1/12/16. https://ssir.org/articles/entry/channeling_change_making_collective_impact_work.

Hassan, Zaid. 2014. *The Social Labs Revolution: A New Approach to Solving our Most Complex Challenges*. San Francisco, CA: Berrett-Koehler.

Jenson, Jane, and Denis Harrisson. 2013. *Social Innovation Research in the European Union. Approaches, Findings and Future Directions. Policy Review*. Luxembourg: European Union.

Kania, John, and Mark Kramer. 2011. "Collective Impact." *Stanford Social Innovation Review*, Winter 2011, 36–41.

Kania, John, and Mark Kramer. 2013. "Embracing Emergence: How Collective Impact Addresses Complexity," accessed 18/2/13. http://www.ssireview.org/blog/entry/embracing_emergence_how_collective_impact_addresses_complexity.

Manzini, Ezio. 2015. *Design, When Everybody Designs: An Introduction to Design for Social Innovation*. Translated by Rachel Coad. Cambridge, MA: MIT Press.

Manzini, Ezio, and Francesca Rizzo. 2011. "Small Projects/Large Changes: Participatory Design as an Open Participated Process." *CoDesign* 7 (3):199–215. doi: 10.1080/15710882.2011.630472.

Martela, Frank. 2015. "Fallible Inquiry with Ethical Ends-in-View: A Pragmatist Philosophy of Science for Organizational Research." *Organization Studies* 36 (4):537–563. doi: 10.1177/0170840614559257.

Mohr, Lawrence B. 1982. *Explaining Organizational Behavior*. 1st ed. San Francisco, CA: Jossey-Bass.

Moulaert, Frank, and Oana Ailenei. 2005. "Social Economy, Third Sector and Solidarity Relations: A Conceptual Synthesis from History to Present." *Urban Studies* 42 (11):2037–2053. doi: 10.1080/00420980500279794.

Mulgan, Geoff. 2012. "Social Innovation Theories: Can Theory Catch Up with Practice?" In *Challenge Social Innovation: Potentials for Business, Social Entrepreneurship, Welfare and Civil Society*, edited by Hans-Werner Franz, Josef Hochgerner, and Jürgen Howaldt, 19–42. Berlin: Springer.

Schmitz, Björn, Gorgi Krlev, Georg Mildenberger, Bund Eva, and David Hubrich. 2013. *Paving the Way to Measurement—A Blueprint for Social Innovation Metrics*. A short guide to the research for policy makers. A deliverable of the project: "The theoretical, empirical and policy foundations for building social innovation in Europe" (TEPSIE), European Commission—7th Framework Programme. Brussels: European Commission, DG Research.

Schrage, Michael. 2000. *Serious Play: How the World's Best Companies Simulate to Innovate/Michael Schrage*. Boston, MA: Harvard Business School Press.

TACSI. 2016. "Focus Area: Disability," accessed 11/11/2016. http://tacsi.org.au/focus-areas/disability/.

Unger, Roberto Mangabeira. 2015. "Conclusion: The Task of the Social Innovation Movement." In *New Frontiers in Social Innovation Research*, edited by Alex Nicholls, Julie Simon, and Madeleine Gabriel, 233–251. Basingstoke: Palgrave Macmillan.

Venturini, Tommaso. 2012. "Building on Faults: How to Represent Controversies with Digital Methods." *Public Understanding of Science* 21 (7):796–812. doi: 10.1177/0963662510387558.

Westley, F. 2013. "History of Social Innovation." Keynote speech NESTA Social Frontiers Conference 14/11/13, NESTA, London.

Westley, F., N. Antadze, D. J. Riddell, K. Robinson, and S. Geobey. 2014. "Five Configurations for Scaling Up Social Innovation: Case Examples of Nonprofit Organizations from Canada." *Journal of Applied Behavioral Science* 50 (3):234–260. doi: 10.1177/0021886314532945.

Index

For Product Safety Concerns and Information please contact our EU
representative GPSR@taylorandfrancis.com
Taylor & Francis Verlag GmbH, Kaufingerstraße 24, 80331 München, Germany